THE ENTERPRISE ARCHITECTURE MATTERS BLOG CHAPTER II

THE DIGITAL TRANSFORMATION AND THE CLOUD ENTERPRISE

ADRIAN GRIGORIU

Table of Contents

INTRODUCTION TO THIS

This is the second part of the collection of blogs on Enterprise Architecture (EA) I posted since the very beginning of 2007. The blogs were hosted by eBizq, an expert forum in Business Process Management (BPM) and Service Oriented Architecture (SOA) and ITToolBox, an online site that enables exchange of knowledge in IT.

The posts are inserted as is and as they were at the time of publication since they exhibit the freshness or crudeness of the time while they record the progress made in the maturity of profession and my own. They are informal. Some formatting and editing was applied to render the book more readable. Nevertheless, formatting is kept simple so that the book can be converted to most formats, on most devices or paper without problems or particular care. Links refer you to the original postings.

The posts were grouped in categories of interest to the reader and where necessary, were set in chronological order. Sometime you'll find duplication and overlapping because it was relevant, it is perhaps useful for immediate comprehension or it might simply happened at the time.

My inspiration was often drawn from the many issues raised in EA fora such as LinkedIn or from the blogs of reputed EA personalities and firms. At times, I needed to sum up the state of art or objectively assess or even criticise current EA methods or the positions of various bodies with regard to EA. I also responded to my fellow bloggers' challenges or I commented on the opinions of the day.

The book includes too my articles and presentations on enterprise developments and EA which I produced in years past. It also makes references to the GODS-FFLV, my own EA framework.

You'll find that EA is still open to debate and that not even a definition, scope or framework were agreed upon. In the end, this is a collection of views. The book is not devised to be rigorous in an academic sense. You'll find more information on my own web site and in my Kindle and Amazon books.

I hope you'll enjoy and even find useful the hundreds of pages of thoughts on EA, its design, governance, role and benefits.

THE ENTERPRISE PROBLEM AND THE EA SOLUTION

Conquering the Enterprise Complexity and Chaos

https://it.toolbox.com/blogs/adriangrigoriu/conquering-the-enterprise-complexity-and-chaos-082519

Sept. 03, 2019

Complexity comes from Latin denoting 'entwined,' 'twisted together' while linguistically. '**Complexity** *defines something as 'complex' if it is made of (usually several) closely connected parts,'* according to the Oxford dictionary.

Chaos comes from Greek, meaning chasm or void. **Chaos** is defined as *'complete disorder and confusion'*, according to the Oxford dictionary, Chaos + no order, no structure or at least we cannot discern.

A complex system has a larger number of nodes in interaction. The more complex the system is, the harder it is to understand, model, control and change.

A chaotic system, on the other hand, has no clear structure. It consists of many singular functions, interacting ad hoc, rather randomly, standard-less and procedure-less. Similar inputs may result at times in different outcomes that are hard to predict in terms of duration and effort.

Complexity does not equal chaos, even if the growing complexity may increasingly look like chaos, while chaos does not infer complexity.

But, simply put, complexity is still characterized by structure while chaos denotes high randomness. That is, little or no structure, order, and according to chaos theory, no predictability.

Systems, even if complex, work. Chaos does not because it is unpredictable.

Both concepts are relative, exhibiting degrees varying from less to more. 'More' means more of a kind. That is, more similar structures in the case of complexity and more diversity in the case of chaos. With 'more' complexity, a system is increasingly more difficult to control and change.

As we became better at what we do, what we considered complexity in the past looks like normal today and what we even found order in the cosmic chaos. Hence, the concepts are relative. Not so much to time, but to our degree of understanding of the world around. Besides, depending on education, what is complex or chaotic to some, it is not to others.

And, to most, complexity and chaos are pretty much indistinguishable.

Complexity and Chaos in the Enterprise

Since firms add new systems, which as a rule add complexity and chaos, the number of functions and links is also growing rapidly today. The amount of information is growing. The knowledge in various domains is increasing quickly. That is as it should be, but the enterprise should still function.

While unchecked, complexity bogs down the enterprise, chaos is created in an existing enterprise through the proliferation of many different, but unique functions, interconnected ad-hoc to the existing, without pre- planning.

The term chaos is used less than complexity in relation to the enterprise because a chaotic enterprise would not survive long.

A chaotic enterprise can hardly operate, but by chance and with variable outputs.

But, if the enterprise growth is unmanaged it alters its capability to deliver and respond to market change. Enterprises ought to manage this new functionality since otherwise it may turn against them in terms of operation stability, reliability, integration, response time, cost etc.

The core issue is that complex and chaotic enterprises are difficult to control, change and evolve, stalling, as such, the enterprise from keeping up with the business needs, markets, competition and rapid technology progress. That is why both complexity and chaos have to be under control.

Untamed, complexity creates for the human enterprise a problem that grows. Unmanaged complexity amplifies problems and slows down opportunity realization.

Worse, complexity and chaos coexist and perhaps fuel each other through, for instance, complex solutions for unstructured, chaotic enterprises.

Complexity, evidenced by an abundance of functions and relationships, and chaos, illustrated by the excess of dissimilar singular functions and developments, are impeding the reliability, rapidity and nimbleness of the enterprise. That is, complexity and chaos reduce the flexibility and agility of the enterprise.

Managing complexity diminishes problems and their solving cost and amplifies opportunities. At similar complexity, competing firms are differentiated by their capabilities to manage complexity.

Since simple is the opposite of complex and order is the other end of chaos, an enterprise today has to be simple and ordered.

The more simple and ordered the enterprise is, the more flexible and agile it is.

To achieve simplicity and order, both complexity and chaos have to be minimized and managed.

Complexity and Chaos Impede the Flexibility and Agility of an Enterprise

To succeed, the enterprise has to adapt, in real time, to business needs and market changes and overtake the competition. To that purpose, the enterprise has to be flexible, agile. Flexibility and agility are the abilities of the enterprise to re-configure itself easily and quickly.

Agility means fast response to change which presumes an optimization of processes, developments, decisions. In the Business Dictionary an Agile Enterprise is: 'Fast moving, flexible and robust firm capable of rapid response to unexpected challenges, events, and opportunities.'

Hence, they say that an Agile Enterprise should be also flexible. Agility demands flexibility which is the ability of the enterprise to be reconfigured as required sufficiently fast.

But, complexity and chaos concur to bog down flexibility and agility. Hence, they must be dealt with.

Mitigating Complexity and Chaos in the Enterprise

The 'unnecessary' complexity and chaos in an enterprise have to be first reduced and afterwards managed. To start with, adopting and employing Architecture Principles would not only reduce complexity and chaos, but will improve flexibility and agility of the enterprise. The most known principles for flexibility are decoupling, encapsulation, modularity API's. For Agility as a fast response principles such as predicting, caching and overall simplifying help.

To reduce complexity, that comes with the expectations of our contemporary ways, to a simple necessary you have to structure the enterprise to minimize the number of functions and relationships. To manage it, the complexity has to be packaged so that enterprise stakeholders deal only with the complexity they are concerned with. The principle is well known from history of conquest: 'divide and conquer' .

To reduce chaos, one, obviously, has to reduce the amount of unnecessary diversity by minimizing uniqueness, singularity and individual developments. Order is restored as such in chaos.

Enterprise Architecture Conquers Complexity and Chaos (i)

https://it.toolbox.com/blogs/adriangrigoriu/enterprise-architecture-conquers-the-complexity-and-chaos-of-the-enterprise-by-revealing-and-controlling-its-structure-090719

Sept. 28, 2019

Complexity grows in the world we built today. The key to conquering complexity is understanding, which comes with knowledge. That makes complexity relative and dependent on those who look at it. In practice, a system is complex for some, but simple or simpler for others. It depends on who and education.

We employ specialists, experts, and people with experience. A team of them may cover the whole system. Each expert speaks for its own part though. So, complexity is mitigated as such by committees and meetings. But, the teams are often too large and members still talk in different expertise in different languages.

But, even for specialists the complexity is hard to beat when there is no proper description of the system. It is also the case today that we have lots of specialists, but still no big picture. And, the deeper the specialization the shallower is the big picture for an expert.

How can you manage complexity if you don't even know what you have today, hence you have no idea what you can achieve? Besides, a target enterprise that fails to consider the current operation and technologies that deliver your products to customers would make your management cringe, to put it nicely.

Hence, what we need is a good description of a system. Graphical at that, because a picture is worth a thousand words. And, one that satisfies most, if not all, stakeholders and experts. For an Enterprise, this is the Enterprise Model or Enterprise Architecture (EA). But, EA is so much seen as IT today that it is hard to mention without raising objections. How would you understand otherwise how your enterprise works if you have no schematics depicting it?

A high level logical picture of the enterprise would help all stakeholders see the same enterprise picture and components. Once agreed, experts establish responsibilities and depict, to the necessary level of detail, their parts of the enterprise.

How do you project the future states of your enterprise if you do not know how the current enterprise looks? How do you plot your way from point A to point B if you do not know where point A, the departure point is? How are you going to transform the enterprise to its digital future if you don't even know what you presently have? How can you plan the enterprise transformation if you do not know the current processes and capabilities, systems and technologies to act on their strengths and weaknesses? Ignoring them means to abandon the current processes, platforms and investments. The enterprise evolves incrementally rather than in revolutionary cycles. But, even revolutions re-use existing structures.

Enterprise Architecture would describe that big picture for you in which the parts, depicted by experts according to guidelines, fit in. Architecture helps us, as such, manage complexity since it groups functionality, it encapsulates it in blocks, which can be independently managed like computer chips and it documents the enterprise and reduces chaos by reducing singular developments and platforms.

The architect standardizes to reduce diversity and, as such, chaos and creates the high level target picture so that complexity would grow in a controlled manner rather than feeding on itself to result in even more complexity in diversity.

If the business suggests a new application, of which the enterprise already has a few of the kind, the architect has to analyse it in the EA context so that the proposal does not introduce duplication, then suggests solutions for re-use. In fact, the architect has to automate that decision for others to do, by creating EA principles and standards that are agreed by and enforced by all stakeholders upfront.

The architect establishes the principles of organization, development, technology recommendations, and sets controls in development processes, effectively enforcing an EA governance framework, so that the architecture and its principles are employed. But, the architect does not stall the growth in complexity since this is inevitable, it just renders complexity manageable.

Enterprise Architects have to guide the enterprise evolution to manage its complexity. To do that, they employ the EA blueprint, principles, service orientation, and roadmaps etc. In the first place, the Enterprise Architecture discovers and documents the enterprise to enable the understanding of its structure, functions and relationships.

To conquer its complexity, EA reveals and controls the structure of the enterprise. Then, EA facilitates the enterprise simplification through re-design based on architectural standards and rationalizes/orders the enterprise development along architecture principles that hold in check the growth of diversity and tangled connectivity.

Complexity is managed by such architecture principles such as modularisation, encapsulation, decoupling and SOA, principles that group functionality and standardize interactions through interfaces that hide the implementation complexity and technology.

Chaos is reduced by eliminating singular applications and technologies and enforcing re-use. The evolution of the enterprise would be controlled by such principles as reuse, de-duplication, technology standards and selection guidelines that reduce chaos by minimizing the unnecessary diversity.

Taking in consideration the big EA picture, the enterprise evolution can be properly planned leaving no function or relation out or allow for functions to be duplicated.

The EA enables, as such, a transformation of the enterprise that takes into account complexity management. But, while complexity is inherent in today's enterprise, chaos is what mars the enterprise because it grows by allowing for too many degrees of freedom and singularity that impede proper governance and change. And, the chaos grows indeed in the absence of the big picture, EA, since new developments may duplicate the old in very different ways, repeatedly.

It is true though that today, the current EA knowledge resides in people's minds. Often a strategic transformation starts, unfortunately, from this state of affairs. Mind you, the EA architects of today do IT. In fact, they are just hijacking the concept to the detriment of the future of the EA discipline.

THE ENTERPRISE STATE AND ITS IT PERFORMANCE

UK Regulator to link Banker bonuses to Operational/IT Performance

https://it.toolbox.com/blogs/adriangrigoriu/uk-regulator-to-link-banker-bonuses-to-operational-(it)-performance-030319

March 03, 2019

In the *UK financial services regulator to link top banker bonuses to IT performance* the FCA head tells Commons Treasury committee:

'We expect banks' policies on variable remuneration to reflect operational resilience. They have to – if they don't, we will act...'

In the UK:

'The *IT problems at TSB last year* was an example of the difficulty traditional banks and financial services firms face with upgrading IT to keep up with customer demand. In April 2018, TSB moved millions of customer accounts from the systems of Lloyds Bank, which had hosted them since TSB was separated from Lloyds, to a new core banking platform from its current owner, Spanish bank Sabadell. As a result of problems, customers were *locked out of their accounts and experienced money disappearing* from accounts. Some were even able to see other customers' accounts'.

Bottom line, people lost money, privacy could not pay for their necessities...

FCA deeply concerned as no end in sight for IT failures in banking

'The FCA has reported a massive increase in the number of banking IT failures in the UK and admitted there is no end in sight... IT failures at UK financial services firms increased by a massive 138% in the past year with failed IT changes being the leading cause, according to research from the Financial Conduct Authority (FCA)...The most common root cause of these incidents was IT change... FCA still suspects that under-reporting is a problem...'

'The Financial Conduct Authority (FCA) will reduce the bonuses of bank leaders if IT failures at their banks cause outages for customers'.

So they said. but what does it mean? Bank operations do rely on IT, extensively so. So FCA points out in fact that from now on the CEOs are hold responsible for IT malfunctions and transformations that negatively impact customers.

The dire situation

Banks fail their customers by failing in their business transformations while reputed and expensive IT contracting firms fail the banks. It all comes back to IT. With the Digital a hot issue the situation is dire. Worryingly,

'this is the first year where the total number of debit card transactions has outstripped cash transactions'.

'...in September, Barclays, Royal Bank of Scotland (RBS) and NatWest customers experienced problems accessing mobile and internet banking over a two-day period. Barclays customers were unable to use the bank's mobile banking app, and customers of RBS and NatWest – which are both part of the RBS Group – were unable to use mobile and internet banking services'.

In Cognizant 20-20 insights | June 2013 '*Understanding Failed Core Banking Project*' it is stated:

'Most core banking IT system renewals suffer significant overruns of cost and time estimates... Experience shows that there is a high failure rate of core banking system implementations. We estimate that 25% of core banking system transformations fail without any results while 50% do not achieve the transformation objectives – costs and implementation times double or triple. Only 25% of the transformations can be called successful...'.

'In February 2011, Irish Bank AIB sued Oracle over a failed €84 million implementation of its Flexcube banking software. In July 2011, the Union Bank of California cancelled the implementation of Infosys' Finacle Solution – almost two years after the program was initiated'.

'*How five brands learned from digital transformation failure*' talks about:

'The Co-operative Bank's £300-million IT fiasco. The bank made the decision to embark on a in 2006 and began to consider how to rebuild systems from the ground up. New regulatory requirements in 2010 pushed for a single view of customers, necessitating a major digital transformation... but the programme was abandoned in 2013'. Yet, the failure is not restricted to banks'.

'The BBC launched its Digital Media Initiative (DMI) in 2008. This ambitious project was set to fundamentally change how the BBC both manages data and provides content to audiences, at the same time as reducing costs'.

Since the situation repeated itself even when manned by the biggest names in IT, the net result was that companies fear now any IT transformation.

Because now the CEOs might be hold responsible (well to the degree to which their bonuses can be arrested) for the Digital Transformations, the CEOs will fear the must do Digital Transformation. The problem is though that they still don't know why transformations fail even when they employ the most reputed and have no tool to grasp control of the transformations.

Commissions, committees, experts... have analysed every failure. What they could not fail to notice is the cost and time estimates overruns, failed objectives and the toll on customers. See a few articles proposing remedies *'12 reasons why digital transformations fail'* or *'Why Digital Transformations Fail: Closing The $900 Billion Hole In Enterprise Strategy',* beginning with the lack of proper specifications, resistance to change, lack of focus, sponsorship, teamwork... to lack of systems of record of work done. People fluctuation is another cause they say but that only starts after the project begins to fail.

What is not said aloud though is that the root cause is the poor governance of the transformation and as such incompetence.

When embarking in such a transformation political appointments would ensure sure only failure. A proper Project Leader is key to success. Because the transformation is not only about planning but about understanding and determining the business components, their interconnections, the fittest digital technology for each considering all parts in integration and about partitioning the transformation in workstreams accordingly.

The Project Manager, tasked with planning and monitoring the work pieces, while important should be an assistant to the Project Leader (PL) rather than leading the project as it happens today. Planning alone without understanding the partitioning of the work per components, the dependencies... can lead to major disconnections and failure as such.

Many companies and agencies do transformations piecemeal today avoiding the big bang approach. This is okay for as long as architecture and a plan based on it are drawn beforehand. The lack of blueprint and such a plan will render the transformation brittle because without the big picture, it is very likely that the pieces would not fit well in the whole and the gaps will make the final operation faulty. You may end up with a more disjoint enterprise that you had before.

The Costs of 'Bad' IT

https://it.toolbox.com/blogs/adriangrigoriu/the-costs-of-bad-it-121715

March 01, 2019

The true cost of IT failures:

'The *e-borders scheme* was meant to collect and analyse data on everyone travelling to and from the UK before they arrive at ports and airports. But the National Audit Office says checks remain 'highly manual and inefficient', and IT systems outdated. Among the report's key findings:

- £830m was spent on the project between April 2006 and March 2015, with another £275m likely to be needed by March 2019

- The project is not set to be finished until 2019 - eight years late

- While it has been upgraded... suffers an average of two 'high priority incidents a week' and 'efficiency is impaired by a failure to replace old IT systems'.

Shadow immigration minister David Hanson said the project had been 'quietly dropped'.

The problem is that bad IT does not deliver or perform its business function. In this case, it does not provide the accurate picture of what is happening at the borders, no matter how arduous the government, parliament, political parties, think tanks or other organizations need that for understanding the situation and making policy. We do not do IT for the sake of IT. The business operation depends on good IT.

Keith Vaz, chairman of the Home Affairs Select Committee at the time, described the report as a 'devastating indictment' of the e-borders project.

'With the terrorism threat level currently at severe, a failure to properly cover millions of people entering the country without having passenger information in advance gives a green light to people who wish to come to the UK for illegal or dangerous activity,' he said.

The project failure impedes the government ability to manage security and customs at the borders. And, given the importance and scale of consequences, it may have an impact on society.

Moreover, it may also have a commercial impact on business, tourism and travel industry with people giving up travel due to long delays and formalities encountered at the border.

This is the cost of bad IT today.

Good IT is essential for any border operation, because passenger's data should be processed in real time for everyone's convenience.

And that is valid for many any critical industries such as Health, for instance.

But we all fail at times. The purpose of this is to learn from experience so that to avoid a repeat of this, to look into the root causes of bad IT and ways of improvement the state of art.

A look into the 12 IT best practices you should or should not use

https://it.toolbox.com/blogs/adriangrigoriu/a-look-into-the-12-it-best-practices-you-should-or-should-not-use-081217

Aug. 12, 2017

In *12 'best practices' IT should avoid at all costs*, Bob Lewis, CIO columnist, says that *'industry best practices are sure to sink your chances of IT success'*...

'What makes IT organizations fail? Often, it's the adoption of what's described as 'industry best practices'.

Let's go along and comment. As a note, the numbered statements below represent the best practices which Bob Lewis recommends avoiding at all cost.

1. "Tell everyone they're your customer "

'Legitimizing the idea of internal customers puts IT in a subservient position, where everyone in IT has to make their colleagues happy'.

IT is a support function for the business. Without business there would be no IT. Then, no matter what you call your stakeholders, the relationship between Business and IT remains that of Customer (Business)- Supplier (IT). No supplier in such a relationship is by default, subservient. In fact, the other way around may be true today, that is, the business in a relationship of subservience (dependency at least) to IT, that is, at the hands of IT. Anyway, there is no 'subservience' or shame in serving the business with the appropriate deference we'd like to be served as customers. After all, the business pays the IT salary.

Today, most enterprises put the customer on the frontispiece today.

But since IT had traditionally no competition in the enterprise, it claims the right to be aloof and superior today. The unintended result may be though the increasing adoption of Shadow IT and the Cloud.

2. "Establish SLAs and treat them like contracts"

Defining the services IT delivers, the associated SLAs and the contracts and the penalties for non delivery, is the way to formalise the relationships with business customers.

This way, the business would be able no more to change ceaselessly the IT requirements. IT would deliver the service to the SLA sanctioned by a mutually agreed contract and not to the potentially ever changing business requirements. That confers the IT autonomy and, as such, motivation. Any late business change would indeed be performed only through contract negotiations. The IT would obey the letter of the contract and SLA rather than responding subserviently to random late requests from the business.

The contract between Business and IT is mutually beneficial since it clarifies tasks, terms, costs and apportions responsibilities. The SLA replaces a relationship based on word of mouth, promises and best efforts with contractual clauses.

In practice though, the protracted implementation may disappoint.

The 12 IT practices CIO says you should not use: Stories, Charge-backs (ii)

https://it.toolbox.com/blogs/adriangrigoriu/the-12-it-practices-cio-says-you-should-not-use-stories-charge-backs-ii-082517

Aug. 25, 2017

In 12 'best practices' IT should avoid at all costs, Bob Lewis, CIO columnist, says ....

3. "Tell dumb-user stories"

Too many emphasise the power of stories in the enterprise today. Is that really a best practice though? I see not much use for IT stories in the enterprise. But I am not sure what 'dumb-user stories' are.

Yet, stories have no place in the enterprise today. No management would have the patience to listen to stories at the current pace of change today. Perhaps stories are good to motivate people to illustrate by example new paradigms, to render an arid topic approachable, to explain its worth.

But no IT professional would seek the technical detail they need in a stack of books or a collection of stories. Perhaps stories are the modern day tales, the fiction the technical professional only reads today.

Besides stories, to be effective, should be rather narrated by master story tellers. Blueprints or diagrams are what people should do today tough. A picture says a thousand words. That is because it shows structure, relationships, the whole in a single page and view, speeding up the understanding process. A story, sequential as it is, fails to illustrate nodes in relationships as a picture does. People have to imagine it rather than see it.

4. "Institute charge-backs"

Charge-backs only work with the service paradigm, with SLAs and contracts.

A catalogue of IT services is first established. Then, every IT operation is assigned a cost which is to be paid by the business to IT, in a client-supplier like relationship.

The business can see then what operations are performed, how often and how much they cost. It may evaluate as such, not only the cost of IT - which is one of the contention issues between the two parties -, but also, in premiere, the IT services the business spends money on.

Uncovering where the most money goes, the business may trim costs.

Without chargeback the IT would be paid in bulk, non-transparently, without understanding the cost structure. Business management would barely be aware how the money is spent inside IT.

Chargeback is indeed the way an outsourcing company charges an enterprise for performing support operations in the IT catalogue.

Establishing SLAs, contracts and charge-backs for IT services decouples the IT department from the Business which is the first step in outsourcing the IT and adopting the Cloud.

The 12 IT practices CIO says you should not use: ROI, Charter IT... (iii)

https://it.toolbox.com/blogs/adriangrigoriu/the-12-it-practices-cio-says-you-should-not-use-roi-charter-it-sponsors-cloud-iii-082617

Aug. 26, 2017

In 12 'best practices' IT should avoid at all costs, Bob Lewis, CIO columnist, says that *'industry best practices are sure to sink your chances of IT success'... 'What makes IT organizations fail? Often, it's the adoption of what's described as 'industry best practices'.*

Here they are, the practices you should not follow:

5. "Insist on ROI"

Without ROI no supervising or financial authority would approve your project. Volens, nolens, you have to do it. Besides, business must understand what's in it for them, the Return of their Investment.

It's not always easy to quantify intangible benefits, but it is possible when necessary. Customer satisfaction could be assessed in terms of more sales, less returns and less complaints, for instance.

6. "Charter IT projects"

And right, you can only sign up for the delivery of the IT application and service rather than guarantee the greater business outcome and benefits the business had in mind. Because they may not materialise.

Hence, your IT delivery should be checked against the IT requirements modelled from the Business specification rather than against the business intent. And IT project should be specified in terms of the IT requirements extracted and modelled from the Business requirements.

7. "Assign project sponsors"

Project sponsors are nothing more than the ultimate decision makers. They are or should be accountable for failure. Also, the someone one can escalate issues to be resolved to. Sponsors should handle the politics of a project too.

That in practice the sponsors are rather hard to involve it's another matter.

A good sponsor is a factor of success though. The expectations and attributions of the sponsor have to be clarified from start though.

8. "Establish a cloud computing strategy"

One thing becomes clearer and clearer today. The IT in the Cloud is a scalable, elastic, reliable, secure and even a cheaper overall solution to IT today.

No enterprise needs to own and maintain its own data centre, infrastructure, applications, licenses... with all the overhead and the never ending problems. Without IT issues the enterprise can focus on its business rather than on the technology that supports it. Anyway it's not the IT but the Business that adopts the Cloud because it hides the IT implementation.

The Cloud is more effective than outsourcing and in-house IT because it is delivered by best of breed firms that take advantage of the economy of scale of tested multi-tenant platforms. Another reason to adopt the Cloud today is the rather aloof attitude and the air of independence of the IT today.

The 12 IT practices CIO says you should not use: Agile, Offshore... (iv)

https://it.toolbox.com/blogs/adriangrigoriu/the-12-it-practices-cio-says-you-should-not-use-agile-offshore-interruptions-iv-090317

Sept. 03, 2017

In 12 'best practices' IT should avoid at all costs, Bob Lewis, CIO columnist, says...

9. "Go Agile. Go offshore. Do both at the same time"

I am not convinced of this one either. Agile seems to apply more to software development rather than IT systems development. The best practice today is Rent-Buy-Build, in this order, to avoid in-house software development because enterprises are not software houses. Besides there all these risks associated with small teams that are not aligned with the business profile. Soon your own team of experts would move on to promote own careers, leaving you open to all sorts of problems.

Agile is best for startups and applications in the social/web domain rather than for mission critical or financial applications that are hardly error tolerant. Agile is about a team that is enthusiastic, knows, trusts itself and quite often delivers to itself in the beginning. Anyway, any paying stakeholder would want to make sure that it has all possible controls in the development project and process before paying for milestone deliverables.

Right though, going offshore is cheaper but with issues, not least cultural.

Go Agile and Offshore may work though for standalone software development where the team is tested and is paid on clear staged deliverables.

10. "Interrupt interruptions with interruptions"

I am not sure why has this been included here. Perhaps only for a round count of 12. I am not even sure it is a best practice, more rather like a practice.

Multi-tasking is necessary today though, as discussed previously. Interruptions are a fact of life in the enterprise. If a key application fails, the expert in chief should rest prompto the ongoing task to help prop the application asap. A business may incur heavy losses if the IT says is busy doing their own things while the online sales web site is down. It is a rather an adverse business-IT relationship, when IT is refusing to interrupt BAU work when the business the IT has to support fails.

That is exactly why business bypasses IT to buy in the Cloud. Because IT is unresponsive. Such an IT keeps aloof as if they are not sharing the problems of the company, as if they are an independent company even though IT is paid en gross by the the company it belongs to.

The 12 IT practices CIO says you should not use: Juggle projects... (v)

https://it.toolbox.com/blogs/adriangrigoriu/the-12-it-practices-cio-says-you-should-not-use-juggle-projects-say-yes-or-no-v-090317

Sept. 03, 2017

In *12 'best practices' IT should avoid at all costs*, Bob Lewis, CIO columnist, says that *'industry best practices are sure to sink your chances of IT success'... 'What makes IT organizations fail? Often, it's the adoption of what's described as 'industry best practices'*.

Here they are, the practices you should not follow, discussed:

11." Juggle lots of projects"

IT can juggle projects as long as they are properly prioritised and resources are available. Multitasking is our way of life nowadays, volens nolens.

There is no point in turning down projects when they can be prioritised and set in a queue in agreement with the business. An alternative too is to employ external resources. For that, the enterprise architect must work together with the programme manager, business and application experts to evaluate properly dependencies and the sequence of execution, the prioritisation.

Yet, more projects, more risks. True.

12. "Say no or yes no matter the request"

Say yes or no, not yet... after evaluating the situation as at point 11. Include the project in a program so that it becomes clear that the projects compete for the same resources and have dependencies. Any new project may push another one down the queue until it falls out of the time horizon. Overall, It looks to me that the author has a rather IT centric point of view, that is, IT First. Still the IT exists in the enterprise today because of the business which is its client. That becomes clear when IT moves in the Cloud. While full SLAs and contracts are costly and rather difficult to approve, because while they bring long term benefits they increase the immediate cost and resource utilisation, a simplified form of them must exist so that the discussion between the business and IT takes place at defined interface and SLAs. Also, a simplified Payback would help quantify the IT work does, the costs of IT and its effectiveness.

Importantly, contracts, SLAs are the first step towards the Cloud and an API economy that would simplify business and render the IT lean.

In the end, it is my opinion, such anti best practices attitude from IT, may be perceived as resistance to change and push faster the business towards the adoption of the Shadow IT and the Cloud.

Also, people interviewed for the report described *"managers managing managers, managing managers"*. That is, a tall management tree.

But was there an associated governance structure? That is, who was making what decisions then? Failing to establish a clear governance may have caused a lot of grief along the way.

A known management principle states that decisions should be made by those in the know perhaps, those on the working floor.

The report signalled also poor communication and coordination between the departments. "Dysfunctional and unconstructive working relationships across these areas did not help matters".

But that really meant competition between departments which is a cultural issue too. To start with, because culture is inspired by management practices and example and strives when tolerated by management, the issue may come down to leadership again.

But to cut this short *"the fish rots from the head down"*. The question is that those who nominated the transformation management are as guilty as the leadership charged.

With regard to culture since you may not want to transform the culture during the transformation, plan to work against the existing odds. Establish common interest goals and common teams, communications channels, reporting procedures... from the beginning.

Lessons from an IT Transformation Failure (I)

https://it.toolbox.com/blogs/adriangrigoriu/lessons-from-an-it-transformation-failure-i-011615

Feb. 16, 2015

We've seen the predictions of the year end from the usual culprits, the analyst firms and the kind. But you would most likely discover that more often than not, there are few practices or lessons learnt from our successes and failures. So, we keep doing the same things same with the same results.

To work on that, I analyse this case from Harvard Business Review "*The IT Project That Brought a Bank to Its Knees*" that discusses the Co-Op bank digital transformation failure in the UK.

"Sir Christopher Kelly, a former British senior civil servant, recently produced a *damning report*, which reviewed the events that led to the £1.5 billion capital shortfall announced by the U.K.'s Co-operative Bank in June 2013... One section highlights the problems the bank encountered as it attempted to replace its core banking systems, a program that was cancelled in 2013 at a cost of almost £300 million".

The IT failure affected the credibility and, in fact, the very existence of the bank. Nevertheless, the IT or today the digital transformation of the enterprise is rather unavoidable because banking is an IT intensive industry.

Hence, what went wrong anyway and what can we do to do it right?

Sir Christopher writes: "It was beset by destabilizing changes to leadership, a lack of appropriate capability, poor coordination, over-complexity, underdeveloped plans in continual flux, and poor budgeting".

Translating in our terms, "*destabilizing changes to leadership*" means poor and changing leadership choices. Since a leader establishes the management in its own image, like God made man, improper management practices may proliferate down at all levels, while a change in leadership may affect the whole management structure of the transformation, with all the ensuing serious drawbacks.

Therefore, chose the right leader right from the beginning e.g. a leader than can comprehend, beside the business problem, the technology and stakeholders' requirements. This reads like common sense, but it is not

Lessons from an IT transformation failure (part ii)

https://it.toolbox.com/blogs/adriangrigoriu/lessons-from-an-it-transformation-failure-part-ii-011915

Jan. 19, 2015

The Kelly report also observed that there were "*plans in continual flux, and poor budgeting*", "*lack of capability*"... and "*poor coordination*". That looks like... inadequate program management. But is that so?

All failed programs I know were besieged by the same problem, that is, the initial poor evaluation of the problem, of its complexity and dependencies and as such of its solution. The subsequent program planning fails because it is based on this poor initial assessment.

If you don't know the dependencies, for instance, then you don't plan to work on them. Because you may find out later that you must take them into account. That may require new resources, a re-worked time schedule, more budget... The program slips and the costs increase.

After hitting a few such hurdles the program enters a downward spiral, with time schedules perennially sliding, resource overloading, tempestive decisions, process short cutting and ultimately panic, blame game, desertions and leadership changes which destabilise the programme.

Moreover, the situation is compounded by subsequent problems. Other programs may have to be postponed for lack of resources. The Business may be obstructed in delivering to objectives. Customers suffer because of the unavailability and instability of the business systems.

The delivery of the new planned functionality is delayed indefinitely and as such revenue is lost. Tensions soar high.

Lessons from an IT transformation failure (iii)

https://it.toolbox.com/blogs/adriangrigoriu/lessons-from-an-it-transformation-failure-iii-012715

Jan. 27, 2015

See also "*The IT Project That Brought a Bank to Its Knees*"

Still, the four questions asked by the HBR analysis of the report bring no new light to the issue.

"*Are we doing the right things?*

Are we doing them the right way?

Are we getting them done well?

Are we getting the benefits? "

To start with, they do look like a panacea, a cure all rather than addressing this specific transformation. Most people would just skim them as well known catchphrases. They sound "academic" too in that they are not really helping us draw any practical conclusion.

The four questions are "common sense" because there is hardly any endeavour that does not consider doing the right things right while observing the benefits. Yet, different are the practical reasons we fail to do the right things right which reasons should have been the object of this analysis.

The questions have been used in business academia since Peter Drucker, if not before.

"*Management is doing things right; leadership is doing the right things*. Or "*Efficiency is doing things right; effectiveness is doing the right things*".

In light of this, the answers to the first two questions (.1, .2) are evidently "no". The project failed because it was both a matter of leadership and management, as the report discovered, that is a matter of both effectiveness and efficiency.

But that is as much as we can say by answering the questions.

Question .3, "*Are things get done well?*" asks the same as question .2.

Question 4 "Are we getting the benefits?" makes little sense because can we even ask about benefits when the transformation fails to deliver at all?

There are a few legitimate questions left out though:

- Where the risks of failure properly evaluated and tracked?
- Was the program organised to minimise risks by employing Go/No-Go milestones where the program could be stopped early to limit harm?
- Were there any contingency plans from start?
- Had the management assumed full accountability from start?
- Have the managers, consultancies and suppliers been chosen by concourse to ensure the best man and resources for the job?

To me, it looks like, while in every day operation the lack of leadership and proper management are easy to conceal, during a large transformation they will most likely let the company down.

A crucial cause of failure though for any such transformation is the lack of Enterprise Architecture. EA provides that enterprise overall blueprint which offers a common understanding and vocabulary to all stakeholders so that they can talk about the same thing, see their parts in context identify and synchronise developments. The program can be designed around the components of the EA while most problems and solutions could be evaluated on the blueprint.

The EA offers the mapping between business processes and functions and the technical systems and people roles that implement them, so that the impact of change can be properly assessed.

The EA also supplies the method, principles of transformation and the technology selection guidelines that would ease decision making and provide consistency and coherency to the development.

Lessons from an IT transformation failure (iv), accountability

https://it.toolbox.com/blogs/adriangrigoriu/lessons-from-an-it-transformation-failure-iv-accountability-020315

Feb. 03, 2015

The report also found a lack of clarity about responsibilities, that is, poor governance.

But since, as in aviation, most accidents are the result of human error, by analogy, who were the pilots of the transformation, i.e. who was accountable for the transformation program?

Were there any penalties for failure for those accountable or was failure even contemplated?

Because at the root of any transformation failure is, in my view,

   a) a lack of a clear sanctioned and documented governance, i.e. what type of decisions, how and who makes them.

   b) the current culture of lack of accountability in the enterprise and its transformation programs

Because those responsible, i.e. in charge, must be accountable as well which is not often the case.

Also, once governance is embedded in processes, chances of "honest" mistakes and failure to diminish considerably.

Today, making decisions by committee seems to be the rule nevertheless. Conveniently, no one is accountable as such. To me, this appears to be against the very grain of the capitalist system which stresses the individual. You cannot fly a plane by committee either.

While consulting all parties and recording arguments is a must, only one role should make the decision for which it is accountable as pre-set in governance. To avoid a command and control culture, a governance board should recommend and review the decisions.

Without accountability, the decision makers have no true stake in the well being of the endeavour, that is, they have little to lose, no matter how inadequate their decisions are which may be biased towards personal interests.

Because the truth of the matter is that, while top managers are paid many times the mean salary of a company, executives are rarely held accountable and sanctioned proportionally with their failure. At worst, in such cases, they are retrenched with generous packages, as set in contracts, only to move elsewhere.

In the absence of legal standards, many scandals in the banking world appear to have been solved by fining the banks, that is, in the end, fining you, the shareholder and customer, while the management kept getting golden handshakes.

Moreover, the absence of penalty for failure, encourages the wrong crowd to bid for leadership. But, had these managers been asked to assume full accountability up-front and sign up against the potential consequences, many would have declined the leadership role for an endeavour they could have neither properly understood nor been able to properly drive. Even politics would turn honest should personal accountability of the kind "what you say is why you must do" be enforced or   otherwise...
But, where are great rewards but no accountability, even the hopeless would give it a try because there is little to lose but only to gain.

The cost of bad IT (i)

https://it.toolbox.com/blogs/adriangrigoriu/the-cost-of-bad-it-i-122915

Dec. 29, 2015

"The cost of bad IT, the e-borders project failure at £830 million and rising" as BBC reported.

The report of NAO, **National Audit Office of 3 December 2015** *"finds several reasons for the failure to deliver".*

"The Department has lacked a consistent strategy or realistic plan for delivery. According to the NAO, the delivery plans for e-borders were too ambitious to be achievable in the timeframe"...

Now, why has the plan been found unrealistic, too ambitious in fact?

There may be a few explanations in fact a combination of them all.

The timeframe and costs have been overly optimistically appraised. In other words, complexity, workload and in the end the schedule were underestimated.

This is where the experience of a technology planning team comes in. Without experience, the team may fail to recognise components, dependencies, issues and risks, resources, skills and time to delivery.

In other words, political appointees without professional experience may cost dearly.

Perhaps, the planners had to squeeze the execution schedule at the political pressure from above. It happens all the time. But when squeezing schedules, risks increase by accumulation exponentially, turning minor issues which resolution keeps sliding into major problems. This affects eventually the business as usual operation of the enterprise.

Or perhaps, the planners have not been given a true picture of the reality on the ground, components and relationships. That is, they lacked the initial big picture and perhaps the target one, that is they had no Enterprise Architecture.

That hinders a wide range of activities, from an incomplete discovery of the landscape allowing for missing components and dependencies, to common understanding and communications with outcomes such as "I thought you are doing that" or "who is doing that?"...

An EA blueprint though enables the identification of the processes and systems which are part of the transformation and the impacts on rest of the landscape. The EA blueprint is the reference for the transformation project.

There has been an inability to make decisions due to gaps in capability and resourcing.

EA enables the work breakdown per components and proper planning of the corresponding workstreams and the evaluation of complexity of the tasks and, as such, the determination of the capabilities and the resourcing of the skills necessary.

Furthermore, EA facilitates consistent decision making based on architecture principles, standards, technology guidelines, roadmaps...

See also The ten commandments of a successful digital transformation

The cost of bad IT begins with a poor situation appraisal

https://it.toolbox.com/blogs/adriangrigoriu/the-cost-of-bad-it-begins-with-a-poor-situation-appraisal-123115

Dec. 31, 2015

"The cost of bad IT, the e-borders project failure at £830 million and rising" as BBC reports.

"Failing to appraise the situation properly is perhaps the main cause of failure for IT projects. Yet, we always knew that "fail to prepare means prepare to fail".

Without a proper Enterprise Architecture, the appraisal of enterprise landscape is done ad hoc because there is no clear end to end picture of the processes and systems neither at the beginning nor at the end of the transformation. The gaps left can hurt the outcome of your transformation. In this case, the program failed to implement the links and data interchanges between new and legacy systems as below:

"... Between 2011-12 and 2014-15, the Department spent £89 million improving systems that e-borders should have replaced and information about travellers is still being processed on two systems that do not share data or analysis effectively...

Planning as such, must be preceded by the discovery of all current systems in scope, their state of obsolescence and their interconnections. Hence the blueprinting of the current Enterprise to the level of detail necessary to experts and planners is a must.

Without EA, the programme may keep discovering new components and issues which, unfortunately, have to be solved on the run provoking delays, new costs, unnecessary stress and in the end, workforce fluctuation, situation that can only aggravate as time goes. That is what happened in fact.

"... there have been eight programme directors on e-borders and successor programmes between 2003 and 2015."

But all this amounts to disruption and further delays. New issues appear in the mean time beginning with the availability of staff, interference with holidays time and as such personal life. Delays generate other delays. Skilled resources, tools and systems are no more available in the new scheduled slots. Licences expire and systems turns obsolete. Business operation is affected. Costs grow... Dissatisfaction with the transformation soars. And worse, this is an avalanche process starting deceptively small but ending up with total business disruption.

Once a project encounters major issues, it must be paused, analysed and rescheduled. Because going on with the old schedule or new schedules every other week can only hurt the project and even worse, the people.

Ultimate cost of bad IT is the fear of change that paralyses industries

https://it.toolbox.com/blogs/adriangrigoriu/the-ultimate-cost-of-bad-it-is-the-fear-of-change-that-paralyses-industries-010516

Jan. 05, 2016

Such IT project failures we learn nothing from, have a debilitating effect on future projects. Organizations are paralysed by the fear of change. Hence, things continue to be bad for fear they can get worse. Because bad is better than worse.

And any major IT failure means a major government service, key business services - bank, utility... - failures. It's worse when public money is spent because people care even less.

But here are a few proposed good practices for major projects:

   - A proper planning has to start from the enterprise description, the EA, that helps identify the business entities, technology systems and people roles

- The Enterprise Architecture must be in place before the transformation begins so that the program can devise projects around capabilities.

- The planning has to have the feedback and sanction of the enterprise architects and the stakeholders on the ground so that nothing is left out or insufficiently defined.

- Planners would have to juggle planning, resourcing and timeframes until the plan is fit for purpose in that resources exist and get committed prior to the start of the programme.

- The risks associated have to be pinpointed in the programme plan and tracked for eventuation. A risk may even be a system or information store left out at planning. Contingency buffers should be left for any event.

- Responsibility and accountability have to be apportioned for each important role in the programme.

It is revealing though that, today nobody at the top is really accountable for failure. Where is the chain of accountability breaking down?

Accountability is key to success though, because it motivates people to take precautions and employ only the competent for the purpose rather than political appointees.

With the increasing amount of anything in the world, from population, inequality, immigration, poverty, health issues, food scarcities, wars, ... the consequences of failures of major IT projects, that are supposed to inform and manage the society, could be dire.

Usually, once failed, such projects reverse to that uncoordinated piecemeal approach that delivers only pieces of the information. Hence the governments and organisations fail to assess problems and solutions to forecast, prepare for, prevent issues and legislate properly.

The banking industry challenge today

https://it.toolbox.com/blogs/adriangrigoriu/the-banking-industry-challenge-today-040615

April 26, 2015

The Banking industry, besides its current challenges such as technology obsolescence, the advent of new payment business models, competing online platforms, regulatory changes for money washing and preventing financing of terrorism, cyber fraud... has to have a strategy to cope with the sweeping changes which may come with the Bitcoin and other such competing mechanisms which primary objective is to eliminate the hefty banking levies.

The industry has to think now of the digital banking of the future to cope with new entrants like Google and Apple.

Nevermind that the banking processes are obsolete while the information lacks consistency and integration between services.

Today the increasingly reliable open source technology must be considered because it can lower the banking costs significantly. The Cloud must be also included now before replacing the old platforms.

The bank must become agile to cope with rapid change since change has become the norm today. The longer the delay, the bigger the risks.

The industry must also remember that Apple demoted in a few short months the big players in the mobile phone industry.

Since such large transformation programs have a history and high probability of failure, real enterprise architecture programs must be initiated now to replace the tinkering the banks do today.

Yet the industry looks paralysed by the fear of big transformations. Such transformations do fail but the solution is not to wait or perform it change by change.

Enterprise wide programs should be able to effect the coordinated transformation to deliver a stable transition and end states that deal with all the matters in synch in a consistent manner.

A real EA program should first document the current state, project the future bank architecture and establish a transformation plan so that the architecture debt, digital transformation and business vision are realised in the same transformation with developments synchronized and prioritised to prevent duplication, information fragmentation...

The relevance of analyst companies' surveys

https://it.toolbox.com/blogs/adriangrigoriu/the-relevance-of-surveys-121015

Dec. 10, 2015

Most practitioners expect the analyst and consultancies to lead the way. Yet, too often though surveys ask the practitioners' target audience for input only to end up mirroring their issues and views, that is, summarising and recommending the practitioners' own thoughts instead of leading them with innovative thinking.

But, since a survey often underlines what we already know and plead for, we are pleased with its findings.

Besides surveys starting from incorrect definitions or assumptions may corrupt the results. For instance, the assumption that EA architects should engage in solution projects. We are lead to believe as such that this is the way the enterprise architects return value to the enterprise. This is not in the job description of an EA architect though.

Had we defined the outcome of EA as the structured diagrammatic representation of the enterprise which the architects have to model, the survey would not have come to the same conclusion.

The purpose of EA discipline is to describe the enterprise. And hence, this is the primal task of any EA practitioner. This is how the EAs show their relevance to the enterprise rather than working as solution architects.

Because the EA blueprint in turn enables the solution development, improved management and investment in the enterprise, malfunction fixing, complexity management, enhanced change control and not least enterprise planning and evolution.

But such a survey too often returns what the issuers expected to learn beforehand. That is because outcomes depend on the questions asked, which in turn, were formulated from the knowledge of an existing problem.

As a question leads to another, you may also end up with right answers for irrelevant questions.

Surveys hence, may be sometimes as irrelevant as polls are.

In this case, McKinsey's "EA management" tips make sense only because they are already common practice: keep things simple, make people accountable, measure, separate strategic from operational, collaborate with stakeholders, invest in leaders,... are the basic good practices of any management. But the recommendations do not help us much because we already know them all even if we chose to ignore them at times.

Yet, the attraction of the ten count lists at the end of the year recap articles is big.

Big Data Analytics Fail because...

https://it.toolbox.com/blogs/adriangrigoriu/big-data-analytics-fail-because-073118

July 31, 2018

Big Data (BD) analytics fail today to bring the touted benefits.

The paradox with the Big Data analytics is how to uncover anything which was not already programmed in the analytics intelligence. The outcome truly depends on expectations. This looks like a hard to break vicious circle.

Also people see what they want or are programmed to see in the first place.

In addition, (big data) analytics outcomes may need a lot of work to be presented in a form suitable for successful decision making (i.e. alternatives with business cases, pros and contras, size of effort and costs, profit projections, business proposals...). Do analysts really do that?

Even when successful, Big Data outcomes may require unexpected change, that often demands new behaviours in the enterprise. Yet new behaviours mean change in the company Culture and, as we all know, cultural change is hardest to achieve.

Hence, the fact that "analytics fail" at the cultural scale of change is no news. But, that's no different from any other larger enterprise change. One cannot effectively change a process without changing the human activity involved and its performance. Any big change requires cultural transformation as well.

So, our own organization and its culture may be a roadblock for analytics success in the first place.

The analytics results have to be presented to the right level of management, that should be high enough for the kind of decision that affects the whole enterprise and its culture.

Anyway, simple observation, market research and statistics may be relevant enough for most enterprises. There is no need as such for BD analytics.

Big Data analytics applies really only to the companies that have a huge amount of data, perhaps companies operating with customers internet wide. But, most companies have little data by comparison.

And anyhow, most of the time there is no great treasure hidden under the mountain of data. Would the outcomes be worth the costly effort?

But, under the pressure of the market, we do seem to assume today that is a trove of information buried in our systems which would change the fate of our enterprise. Without any hints for the better the BD may be not worth the time, effort and cost.

THE BUSINESS VALUE CHAINS, MODELS AND STRATEGY

A Business Model is not solely a sales paradigm

https://it.toolbox.com/blogs/adriangrigoriu/a-business-model-is-not-solely-a-sales-paradigm-021515

Feb.15, 2015

Andrea Ovans in HBR's What Is a Business Model? does a good job at exposing various definitions, approaches and examples of Business Models (BM) starting with Michael Lewis' view of "how you planned to make money" to Joan Magretta's "stories that explain how enterprises work".

A business model is all that and more. Most definitions though are too general to aid us in practice.

Often, a Business Model is taken as strategy. But a business model becomes a strategy only if you plan to implement a specific Business Model to compete differently.

Too often the operation to model a business model is called Business Modelling. It shouldn't because the "modelling" term has already been used in Business Process and Architecture design and has a different meaning.

A Business Model is not a Business Architecture. The two terms have, in fact, roots in different disciplines, like business management and respectively, enterprise architecture.

I also remarked that the business model is, in practice, taken often as a sales and distribution paradigm. See Mark Johnson's basic models such as bundling, fractionalisation, freemium... in the table at the end of the article.

 A Business Model is more than a sales approach. It is and describes the specific implementation of the end to end Value Chain that delivers a product, consisting not only in sales to a customers' segment but also in sourcing from specific suppliers, manufacturing location and distribution channels, after-sales models...

Variations in terms of market segment, channels, production facilities, use of resources, outsourcing, sales paradigm,... make a different business model.

For instance, your business model is to manufacture in Asia, design in Europe, sell on-line and employ an international courier for distribution.

The Business Model exposes the variations to the standard value chain that differentiate your approach from competitors.

To properly specify, change or implement a business model you need to start from Enterprise Architecture (EA) that illustrates the end to end delivery processes, the resources that implement them, the delivery channels... Then you have to calculate the costs of operation based on the above enterprise configuration and estimate revenue.

When the business model is analysed, justified... information about revenue and the cost of value chain operations is necessary to calculate the value proposition of the business model in order to make its business case.

The Business Model is ultimately a specific configuration of the enterprise delivery value chain.

Is the Value Chain concept still valid today? More than ever.

https://it.toolbox.com/blogs/adriangrigoriu/is-the-value-chain-concept-still-valid-today-more-than-ever-030415

March 04, 2015

Porter's value chain outlines the key activities of an enterprise.

The question arose though, does the rapid progress of the technology in the enterprise render the Value Chain insignificant? The question came to light at least because technologies like net services and Cloud Computing change now how the value chain activities are distributed and owned.

Nevertheless, the answer is "No" because the Value Chain still illustrates the key enterprise activities, its basic operation. It also constitutes the chassis of the enterprise modelling.

In fact, the Value Chain is even more important today when the enterprise turns virtual, by employing capabilities in the Cloud or delivered by third parties.

Essentially, Business process outsourcing (BPO) and cloud computing enable the enterprise to outsource value chain activities (such as manufacturing), business support processes (payroll...), business services (SaaS = Software/Application as a Service) and IT infrastructure (IaaS) to other companies which become as such part of the virtual enterprise value chain.

This enterprise concept might be called the Cloud Enterprise (see more at http://www.bptrends.com/public...) since the value chain activities and services are executed now by various firms in different locations, all interconnected over the net cloud to deliver the product.

The technology progress makes possible the automation of the enterprise interactions with partners enabling as such remote links in the Value Chain.

Most importantly, the service oriented architecture make possible the virtual enterprise since it creates the premise for the distributed enterprise services in the first place.

Porter's five forces (the forces of Competitors, Suppliers, Buyers, New entrants and Substitutes) apply equally well in this virtual or networked enterprise context even though the links of the Value Chain belong now to different physical enterprises.

The Business Model as a Value Chain

https://it.toolbox.com/blogs/adriangrigoriu/the-business-model-as-a-value-chain-051916

May 19, 2016

In the 1980s, Michael Porter proposed the Value Chain (VC) concept to illustrate the operation of a company.

A **Value Chain** is a set of activities that an organization carries out to deliver value to its customers and return a margin of profit to the company and stakeholders.

The profit is the VC margin, as in the picture.

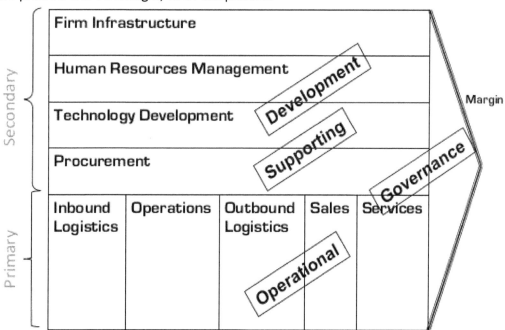

Revenue returned - Costs = Profit Margin

On the other hand, a Business Model (BM) shows the way a company, in delivering to its customers, makes profit and, in general, returns value to its stakeholders. Here is Osterwalder's and Pigneur's BM canvas.

The major elements that determine a Business Model were defined as the

The Business Model Canvas

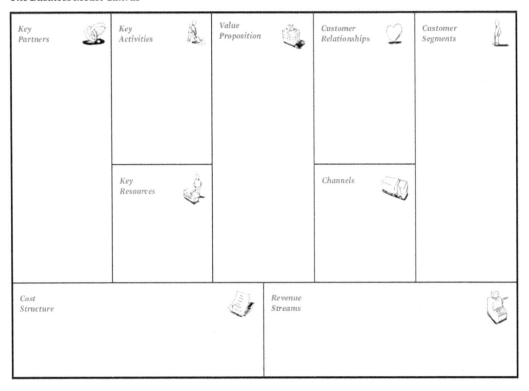

- target Customer Segments

- Channels employed to reach them

- specific type of Customer Relationships

- key Activities - the processes involved in manufacturing

- key Resources - the physical resources that execute the processes

- kind of Partnerships with 3rd parties that execute activities

- Revenue Streams - the revenue generated by the business model

- Costs - per activities and resources.

Ultimately, the Value Proposition financially quantifies the worth of the Business Model.

Enterprises may deliver the same kind of products, to different customer segments, through different channels, employing different processes and resources while outsourcing operations and parts to different partners and geographies.

Some choose to deliver luxury products while manufacturing takes place in-house. Some chose to sell online bottom priced products. Both companies make profit though, but in different ways.

Hence, the Business Model, is the specific enterprise configuration that makes it profitable, generally speaking.

The Business Model works back from the profit realised or desired to discover how profit is made. As such, the business model analyses the activities and costs of the Value Chain by looking at customer segments, delivery channels, manufacturing processes, physical resources and partnerships.

The Business Model as a Value Chain that returns a margin

https://it.toolbox.com/blogs/adriangrigoriu/the-business-model-as-a-value-chain-that-returns-a-margin-052416

May 24, 2016

While a Business Model (BM) identifies the way a company (activities, resources, channels, partnerships... as described in the BM canvas) returns value/profit while delivering the product, the Value Chain identifies the company sequence of activities (from sourcing to sales) that deliver the product while returning a "Margin" to the company.

While the Business Model evaluates the returns to the company in terms of Value Proposition, Porter's concept of "Margin" quantifies the profitability of the Value Chain.

While the BM primarily stresses the return of the approach to product delivery, the Value Chain identifies the key activities that add value in the process. Since ultimately value accumulates in the outcome, the product, both the BM and VC emphasise simplistically the "profit" made by the company.

There always is though a Value Chain which delivers a Business Model. As a corollary, any Business Model should be evaluated or built on the Value Chain that realises it. The Value Chain offers the key activities of the enterprise based on which the Business Model calculates its Value Proposition that is the Value Chain margin.

The Value Chain is the business concept that enables the Business Model assessment.

The Value Chain of a Business Model identifies the sequence of activities that deliver the product. Based on these, the associated resources and partnerships can be analysed to determine the Value Proposition of the Business Model.

Therefore, in addition to representing a Business Model as a number of boxes on a canvas, you can represent BM as the associated Value Chain that returns a Margin/Value Proposition to the business.

Here is a mapping between the generic Business Model and the Value Chain representation.

The Business Model Partners box would be mapped all along the Value Chain Inbound Logistics, Operations...

The BM key Activities would be the Porter's VC Primary activities while the BM Channels would be part of the VC Sales and Services.

The Value Chain becomes as such the basis for analysis and construction of a Business Model.

The Business Model may distinguish though the key elements of the Value Chain that differentiate the company operation from competition.

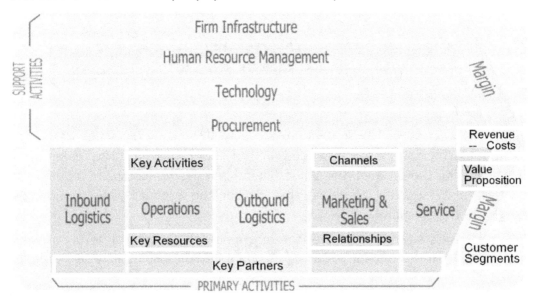

The Business Model as an Enterprise Architecture view

https://it.toolbox.com/blogs/adriangrigoriu/the-business-model-as-an-enterprise-architecture-view-052916

May 29, 2016

A Business Model expressed as a Value Chain (VC) shows the sequence of top processes that add to the VC Margin and accumulate cost at each stage of the chain.

Different Business Models for similar types of products may have different customers segments, channels, Value Chain activities, resources and partnerships. One may address, for instance, the high end market while the other the low end or the mass market.

Apple, for instance, seems to aim at the top end by investing in artistic design, innovation, reliability and, in general, perfection. That is A high effort, high cost, high prices business model. On the other hand, to minimise costs, it outsources manufacturing activities. And to achieve best in class, it outsources industrial design to partners. And that while it remains focused on what it does best, the electronic design.

Partnerships are key in the realisation of the Value Chain for a Business Model since, without outsourcing of manufacturing to partners, for example, the Business Model may turn negative.

Today, without the Internet, the Cloud and partnerships many Business Models would not be viable.

Customer relationships are also key to the Business Model. Loyalty programs that realise customer retaining strategies are effective because it costs less, marketing says, to retain a customer than gain a new one.

But to truly estimate costs, the value chain which implements the business model should be mapped on the architecture of the enterprise which documents in sufficient detail not only the activities but also the technology resources which costs have to be estimated. Without EA, the business model assessment is, more or less, guess work.

A business model, evaluated on an enterprise architecture, underlines the configuration of the enterprise comprising of processes and channels and the organizational and technology resources that implement them.

In the end, any Business Model may be represented as an Enterprise Architecture view.

Business Model Canvas mapped on Enterprise Model

Partnerships are included in the virtual Value Chain as Services. While their costs are known, their implementation and resources are hidden and not of concern.

Without Enterprise Architecture, it is hard to identify the activities, resources and channels that ultimately determine the viability of the Business model.

The EA supports the design of new Business Models.

The Enterprise vision and strategy

https://it.toolbox.com/blogs/adriangrigoriu/the-enterprise-vision-and-strategy-012414

Jan. 24, 2014

Top management sets a vision. That is, a big picture they see the enterprise evolving to. But so (should) do the departments for their own functions. For instance, technology may have a vision. Human Resources may have their own etc.

In doing EA one has to consider the business, the technology and the people tiers. Same applies to vision, one for each tier cascading from and feeding into the overall vision.

The enterprise vision is the integrated vision. An enterprise wide group would have to specify this balanced enterprise vision.

The executive vision alone may be too vague, ignore or even come in conflict with the departmental plans and goals.

Also, a reality check must be performed before elaborating the vision and the ensuing strategy. How could a vision come true if it is not rooted in reality?

 One has to analyse

- the environment to discover the trends (what is going to eventually happen) in markets, technology, regulatory... competition and

- the company itself, that is the inner strengths and weaknesses of the company... so that the enterprise be able to take advantage of and code them in the vision and strategy.

Here is a strategy framework that helps you do that.

EA exists independently of strategy because EA may be employed not only to transform the enterprise but to analyse and understand the current enterprise landscape, to aid maintenance, to enhance and fix operation/processes, to provide the context for solution projects etc.

Strategy as well, had existed without EA, for a long time now.

Hence we can say that strategy and EA are independent of each other. They are complementary though, they work better together.

The Vision must be realised by strategy though, employing, hopefully, EA in the process.

In TOGAF though the ADM suggests the architecture vision rather than the enterprise vision, talks little or at all about strategy and the vision phase comes before the evaluation of the current state and hence it's footless.

That makes hard to employ TOGAF in specifying or implementing the enterprise strategy.

The Business Model Versus Value Chain and Strategy

https://it.toolbox.com/blogs/adriangrigoriu/the-business-model-versus-value-chain-and-strategy-090319

Sept. 03, 2019

Business Model, Business Modelling and Strategy are often used interchangeably even though they have different meanings.

The Business Model is employed by a business to elaborate a preliminary business case for a new way to operate after analysing the competitive landscape or at launching a new product.

Business Modelling, often used solely for process diagramming, denotes in fact the activity to diagrammatically describe the enterprise business functions, processes, capabilities and information in relationship.

Strategies, are specified so that the enterprise chooses a development path in advance making the key choices in the endeavour to fulfil the goals and overall vision.

Business Model

from Business Model Canvas: nine business model building blocks, Osterwalder, Pigneur & al. 2010 (Wikipedia)

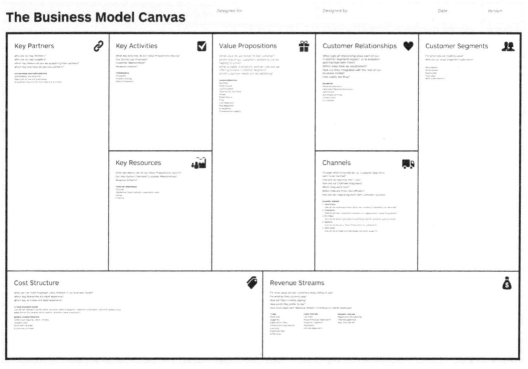

"Osterwalder's canvas has nine boxes; the name of each is given in bold...The Business Model Canvas can be printed out on a large surface so groups of people can jointly start sketching and discussing business model elements with post-it-notes or board markers. It is a hands-on tool that fosters understanding, discussion, creativity, and analysis".

Business Models Versus Business Modelling

A Business Model is not the outcome of Business Modelling, the Business Architecture is.

Any enterprise today already implements a few Business Models.

Business Models Versus Strategies

Strategy is the path chosen to implement the goals of the business. In some views, it includes the choice of goals themselves.

A Business Model describes the way the enterprise operates to deliver products in a customer segment so that it returns value to stakeholders.

Any enterprise today already implements a few Business Models which have little to do with company strategies.

Hence, strategy is a path to the future while a Business Model is a present configuration of the business resources to deliver a product to a market and make a profit.

Hence the Business Model and Strategy concepts have nothing in common.

Business Models are called strategies only when they become themselves an enterprise goal, implementing another Business Model to achieve profit.

Business Models Versus Value Chains

If you want to adopt a new Business Model in your enterprise, you first have to understand how a Business Model (BM) is realized by your enterprise.

A Business Model shows how a company goes about its business to be able to return added value/profit.

"*A value chain is a set of activities that a firm operating in a specific industry performs in order to deliver a valuable product (i.e., good and/or service) for the market. The concept comes through business management and was first described by Michael Porter in his 1985 best-seller, Competitive Advantage: Creating and Sustaining Superior Performance*".

Porter's Value Chain is a set of activities that an organization carries out to create value for its customers and return a margin of profit. Michael Porter created the concept in the 1980s. Also Porter defined the Margin as the difference between the value created and costs:

Value Created - Cost of Creating that Value = Margin

Representing properly a business model down on paper is a bit more difficult though. In fact, on paper, a business model, rather than showing a list or map of disconnected boxes on a "canvas" as it is often illustrated today, should be represented on the Value Chain (VC) to illustrate how the VC is configured to deliver the Business Model.

While the Business Model (BM) identifies primarily the way / configuration the company employs to return added value from the activities, resources, channels, partnerships..., the Value Chain identifies primarily the sequence of activities, from sourcing to marketing and sales, that deliver the product while returning a "Margin" to the company.

Hence we may conclude that **there would always be a Value Chain (VC) that implements a Business Model (BM).** As a corollary, any Business Model could be best evaluated on the Value Chain that realizes it.

The Value Chain that a Business Model is evaluated upon, identifies the key sequence of activities that deliver the product. Based on these activities, the associated physical resources and partnerships that deliver in the value chain can be assessed to determine the value proposition of the Business Model.

Therefore, in addition to representing a Business Model as a number of boxes on a canvas, you can represent it as the associated Value Chain that returns that Margin, (calculated by the Business Proposition).

As an observation though, profit appears to be the only value taken into consideration by a business model today. Still, there are other things that matter to a company today, such as the impact on the environment and in general corporate social responsibility and customer satisfaction. In addition, added value has to be returned to all key stakeholders of an enterprise.

The key activities (processes) and resources that realize a Business Model are included in the operations link of a Value Chain.

The channels and relationships of a Business Model are represented over the marketing and sales link of a Value Chain.

But, while the Business Model evaluates the return to the company in terms of Value Proposition, Porter's concept of "Margin" quantifies the profitability of the Value Chain. Which means pretty much the same.

To estimate the costs and revenue for the calculation of value proposition, the BM and its associated Value Chain should be mapped on the Enterprise Architecture.

The EA exhibits in detail the processes/activities and resources that deliver the product. The assessment of the business model processes and resources and estimation of total cost can be properly calculated only on the EA which describes the value delivery in sufficient detail.

But true, it is not often that we see an EA blueprint today. Anyway, a BM canvas with disjoint boxes would not allow the visualization of the processes, technology, people resources and partnerships that add value and accumulate cost at each step of the value chain, necessary to estimate the business model profitability.

A Business Model has to be analysed on the current Enterprise Architecture, in order to analyse the customer segments, channels, activities and the technology and human resources that deliver the product and return profit to the company. A target Business Model is the projected configuration of an EA so that it can deliver the target value proposition.

Applying different Business Models on the EA by varying factors as product types, market segment, distribution, make process outsourcing, type of resources and outsourcing the value chain links may return different or even negative margins (that is, no value proposition for the Business Model). Deciding on in house manufacturing for instance can, in comparison to outsourcing to an overseas partner, turn the Value Proposition negative.

The KPMG's view on Changing IT Operating Model or rather IT Value Chain

March 18, 2018

In Next Generation IT Operating Models — Part One: Broker Marc Snyder, managing director with KPMG in the U.S., states that *"trends are rendering the traditional "Design-Build-Run" operating model for IT to be less relevant. A next-generation IT operating model, originally discussed by KPMG in 2014, focuses on three new and essential roles for IT:* **"Broker, Integrate and Orchestrate""**.

KPMG further explains the roles:

"Broker

Understand business needs

Advise on innovation and technology enablement opportunities

Facilitate matching business needs and service options

Monitor and discover new and evolving service offerings

Evaluate available services and potential value

Integrate

Integrate data and services from internal and external sources

Manage integration architecture, tools and methods

Source services

Manage service integration and solution development

Orchestrate

Manage solution delivery (performance, cost and quality)

Ensure enterprise obligations met and assets protected

Monitor and manage service performance, cost and quality

Coordinate across service providers and resolve issues"

CIO elaborates:

*"**IT as Broker** ...IT serves as a broker by connecting their business colleagues with the vast and growing sets of technology options that may be available to them.*

IT as Integrator. IT works with service providers to configure, customize and integrate their service offerings into their organization's specific business environment.

IT as Orchestrator. IT makes sure that the acquired and integrated services continue to meet the functional and performance needs of the business".

To conclude, the new role of IT is BIO: Broker-Integration-Orchestration

The **Broker** role is about analysing and proposing technology solutions to the business.

The **Integration** is about integrating the sanctioned solutions in the enterprise operation.

The **Orchestration** is about overseeing the overall IT operation.

As an observation, the **Value Chain** concept seems to be the appropriate concept, rather than **Operating Model (OM)**, because, at least for the purpose of this, it is the Value Chain that consists of the sequence of key activities (such as Design-Build-...) that deliver the IT value.

The reality is not so one sided though, the IT Operating Model is still mixed with the two IT roles, **Design-Build-Run** and **Broker-Integrate-Orchestrate** co-existing.

In the Digital Age, the Role of IT is Supplemented by EA (I)

https://it.toolbox.com/blogs/adriangrigoriu/in-the-digital-age-the-role-of-it-is-taken-by-enterprise-architecture-ea-i-032018

March 20, 2018

The IT role of building, maintaining, running IT technology is disappearing because, with advent of outsourcing and the Cloud, the enterprise owns, hosts, maintains and operates less and less IT technology. anyway, in many cases, technology becomes too complex and expensive to own and operate in the enterprise.

Hence, with the Outsourcing and Cloud growth, the IT role has been increasingly delegated to 3rd parties.

From driving the entire IT (**Design-Build-Run**), the role of IT is being reduced today to that of

IT Brokering, Integration and Orchestration (BIO) says KPMG

(see Next Generation IT Operating Models — Part One: Broker).

Agreed. The change is happening gradually. Historically, the IT Build role has been replaced by Buy. Then, the IT Design and Realisation roles is gradually changing to Broker of technology and Integration of IT solutions.

Hence, today, the Operating Model of IT is increasingly **BIO: Broker, Integrate and Orchestrate IT**.

Yet, rather than calling it **IT Operating Model**, it is more appropriate to call it **IT Value Chain** because it consists of the sequence of activities that deliver the IT value to the enterprise.

But I argue that, the role of IT should be applying the Enterprise Architecture (EA).

As a consequence, rather than solely a new IT Operating Model, we should be also talking about an IT EA Value Chain where the IT works with the EA team.

Then the resulting IT EA Value Chain of today may consist of three roles:

IT EA role

.1. Model current IT to produce blueprint

.2. Design target IT states starting from strategy

.3. Assure the e2e enterprise operation

+ IT new BIO role

.3. Broker technology platforms and suppliers

.4. Integrate IT solutions

.5. Orchestrate IT operation

+ IT traditional role

.6. Design

.7. Build

.8. Run IT as usual

The IT EA Value Chain adds as such the Modelling and Design activities to the IT Broker-Integrate-Orchestrate and Design-Build-Run value chains.

The New Model-Integrate-Assure IT Role in the Enterprise (ii)

https://it.toolbox.com/blogs/adriangrigoriu/the-new-model-integrate-assure-it-ea-role-in-the-enterprise-ii-032018

March 20, 2018

The **Broker-Integrate-Orchestrate** new IT Operating Model is blind without EA because change is applied to a rather unknown landscape (no current architecture) and any transformation would integrate solutions without the benefit of the big picture.

Yet, given the EA state today, EA has little role to play. It is true as such that IT performs mainly the traditional Design-Build-Run (DBR) and the Broker-Integrate-Orchestrate (BIO) roles today. Nevertheless, with the growing penetration of Digital, EA must be employed to manage the increasing enterprise complexity and change.

If we assume that

a) Model includes the Broker and Design roles (that is, introducing technology is part of the target Enterprise Design) and

b) Orchestration is rather part of an end2end business Assurance role

Then the IT Operating Model is replaced by a simplified EA Value Chain consisting of the following activities:

- **M**odel enterprise states

- **I**ntegrate business/technology solutions

- **A**ssure e2e operation

that is The IT Value Chain = **MIA**

The IT Model-Integrate-Assure (MIA) value chain merges the EA Model-Design-Assure (MDA) and the IT Broker-Integrate-Orchestrate (BIO) value chains and roles.

That is, the EA and IT teams should operate together for the foreseeable future, to Model the enterprise current and end states, Integrate own, outsourced and Cloud solutions and Assure the e2e performance and operation of the enterprise.

To play the **MIA** role, the IT has to work with the EA team. The existing IT team alone cannot execute the new MIA Value Chain because of the business processes are executed by people as well and the technology is placed in the Cloud today.

Yet, the legacy Design-Build-Run IT role will still survive for a while.

The *Model-Integrate-Assure* IT Value Chain takes over from Design-Build-Run (iii)

https://it.toolbox.com/blogs/adriangrigoriu/the-ea-model-integrate-assure-model-would-replace-the-it-design-build-run-role-in-the-enterprise-today-iii-032118

March 21, 2018

According to some figures, the Cloud penetration is about 21% today. IaaS, SaaS, PaaS, FaaS... have enabled the outsourcing of hardware, data centre, applications and utility functions so that the enterprise, rather than owning and administering IT, can focus more on managing its business.

The transfer of IT technology to the Cloud has increasingly reduced the amount of in-house IT systems ownership, licensing, development, maintenance, run and support. The enterprise will be no more concerned with IT in 20 years or so. Hence, the IT as usual will be increasingly diminishing in the years to come.

As a result, the IT force too would move out of the enterprise, to the Cloud and outsourcing providers. IT would also evolve with the times, acquiring new skills about the Cloud, Artificial Intelligence, Virtual Reality, IoT...

The IT team in the enterprise will be increasingly co-operating with the EA team which will execute the **Model-Integrate-Assure** (MIA) value chain.

Today though, while we strive to move to a MIA (Model-Integrate-Assure) EA Value Chain, the reality is that we still operate in IT **Broker-Integrate-Orchestrate** mode or even the legacy **Design-Build-Run**.

That is partly because the current EA frameworks barely serve their purpose, to model the enterprise.

In any case, EA frameworks come short in delivering that EA modelling chassis we need to plug architecture parts back in the framework to give EA. Take for instance, Zachman, while it is largely a development process (from Concept to Implementation on the vertical dimension), it is not a modelling frame. Filling the matrix cells won't return the EA.

In that sense, many existing EA frameworks are fake, to use a term dear to the public today, delivering anything but EA. They are in fact delaying us in moving towards the enterprise MIA value chain so necessary in the Digital age.

In conclusion

To mitigate the enterprise complexity and amount of change today, the Enterprise Architecture increasingly plays a role of enterprise modelling, integration and operations assurance. While IT deals with technology, EA deals with the architecture of the business services supplied by the technology.

A key development is though that most of the existing IT force has to move out of the enterprise to the new IT hosts, the outsourcers, Cloud providers.... Since today we assemble the enterprise out of services provided by the Cloud, BPO (Business Process Outsourcers)... while orchestrating their operation as a whole to deliver the goods we operate the **MIA (Model-Integrate-Assure)** enterprise development value chain.

Enterprise strategy is more than management's business strategy

https://it.toolbox.com/blogs/adriangrigoriu/enterprise-strategy-is-more-than-business-strategy-062314

June 23, 2014

What we do in the enterprise on a daily basis is, more or less, patching the enterprise to survive. Unless we have an enterprise strategy.

Strategy is about a long term thinking that guides the evolution of the enterprise to channel developments in the desired direction.

It is a common practice indeed to cascade the strategy top down at all levels of the organisation chart. Unfortunately, that is not enough.

For one, to realise the enterprise strategy in practice, one has to map the strategy to all enterprise architecture components, that is, not only to the organisation chart but also to business capabilities, processes and technology.

The management strategy also fails because, in the attempt to specify the enterprise strategy, only the management strategy is considered while most other function specific strategies are too often ignored. In practice though, these function specific strategies would be still implemented by stealth because they are often unavoidable. But this generates though uncorrelated parallel programs that compete and divert the resources from the initial strategic direction implementation.

It is also most likely, that the top business strategy, by ignoring the lesser function strategies, is incomplete, insufficient and too abstract in the first place.

Strategy execution fails as such, not only to implement the business vision but also to coherently transform the enterprise.

In fact, it is the overall enterprise strategy that matters rather than the management business strategy alone. The enterprise strategy is the outcome of the harmonization of the management vision with the specific business functions strategies.

How do we assess strategy?

https://it.toolbox.com/blogs/adriangrigoriu/how-do-we-assess-strategy-032215

March 22, 2015

We often talk about strategy but, how do we know if strategy does what it should?

Strategy is understood, usually, as both what we are aiming for and how are we getting there.

What we are aiming for, i.e. the goals have to be assessed first for alignment not only to the firm's vision but what the competitors do and the trends, threats and opportunities that affect the environment. See this strategy development framework here.

While we can debate the vision of the company, it all ultimately depends on the leadership and its flair. Hence, there is not much to debate after all.

We can still make sure though that the "how to get there" is right. For that we have to make sure that

- trends, threats & opportunities and competitors are considered

- stakeholders' aims are taken into consideration

- goals achieve vision

- projects implement goals

- projects address all systems in scope and are conducted according to architecture principles,

that is, they do not create duplication or add unnecessary complexity in the process of transformation

the transformation program covers all projects and dependencies

Check Strategies for:

Suitability: Is the strategy serving the stakeholders? Is the strategy delivering the goals? Verify the appropriateness of a strategy, based on company's strategic goals (check against vision and goals).

Feasibility: Can you do it? Asses if the company has the resources and capabilities (core competencies, assets, strengths) to deliver the strategies.

Acceptability: Is the potential cost realistic? Decide if the strategy is achievable in terms of financial returns and delivery timescales.

Evaluate again the outcomes in the light of stakeholders' expectations (including community, regulatory, company itself...) and financial results in terms of business cases".

At implementation, make sure that you use Enterprise Architecture (EA) to ensure that strategies are properly cascaded to technology components and organisation chart and initiatives are synchronised and harmonised to reduce duplication, unnecessary complexity etc., according to EA principles and transformation guidelines.

Then monitor the strategy benefits realisation.

The Rings Strategy Development Framework

https://it.toolbox.com/blogs/adriangrigoriu/the-rings-strategy-development-framework-101619

Oct.16, 2019

About Strategy

Strategy is the path chosen to implement the goals of the business. In many views, it includes the choice of goals themselves.

Business Models (BM)are often called strategies though. Yet, BMs are not strategies but solely a choice of implementation of a Product to Market Strategy, that is a certain way to achieve profit by targeting specific markets with such processes executed by so resources which cost so much.

A BM describes the way the enterprise uses its resources to deliver its products to a customer segment so that it returns value and makes a profit.

There are rather a few standard generic academic business school choices valid for and considered by most enterprises.

"At a fundamental level, all *strategies for Porter boil down*, HBR says, to two very broad options: **Do what everyone else is doing (but spend less money doing it), or do something no one else can do.**

One could perhaps usefully divide the vast universe of subsequent strategy ideas into those that focus on:

 - Doing something new.

 - Building on what you already do.

- Reacting opportunistically to emerging possibilities."

Theory aside, what are the product and market strategies most often met at corporate level? More often than not, these few options are put forward with gravity and self-possession: "diversify", " divest", "develop new" and "expand" even though they are so common that we often use them in our daily life, for example for our investments. But, even though these strategies determine the enterprise future path, they are essentially just marketing strategies.

Even if they make it cheaper, it is so common in practice it would be added as a strategy, but I would rather qualify it with "make it differently" that is reflected in a change of the business model. For instance, for the same product, we can choose to outsource key operations, activities and IT.

The devil is in the detail though, that is, the real strategies are in how to diversify, in what to divest or what new services and in where to expand.

These product to market options cover predominantly the requirements for enterprise situations like growth, disruption, regulatory changes or response to competition trends. New delivery business models may be indeed required for each strategy above.

But, strategies are not restricted to product to market or even outsourcing. A high concern today is the digital technologies pace of progress that may affect the enterprise, like it or not. New business models from competitors such as Uber, which was enabled, after all, by a digital technology, has brought in many new competitors. The enterprise strategy has to consider not only the product to market strategy, but also the trends such as social (because social media is taking over), the increased wariness about the environment, the regulatory changes for information and the Internet, the substitutes (such as mobile phones is replacing cameras today).

Strategies are affected as such by a change in the enterprise goals, vision, industry aspects, markets, politics, economics, social, environmental and legal (PESTEL) forces and Porter's 5 forces (competition...). The updated strategies will be effective yet again then.

Strategies are not valid for ever though. They should be updated as regularly as deemed necessary. A strategy renewal process establishes new goalposts by evaluating in light of company vision the trends, opportunities and competition behaviour in the environment. It also assesses the current situation of the company in terms of strengths, weaknesses, requirements, and on-going strategies.

Refreshed strategies are formulated to take advantage of strengths to pursue opportunities, plugging in the weaknesses to prevent risks, materializing to adopt new technologies to pursue a competitive advantage and implement new business models for the enterprise.

Since the digital pace of progress may endanger your companies very existence, an emerging technology strategy must be thought out after analysing the new technologies landscape.

The Rings Strategy Development Framework

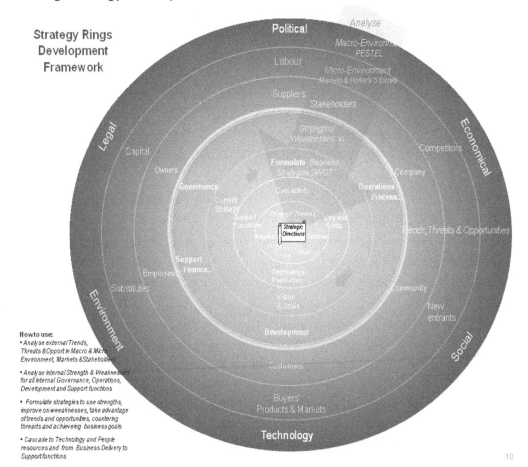

There is a need though for a more clear strategy analysis and specification frame in order to repeat the enterprise strategy process, as periodically as deemed necessary. Here is a proposed Strategy Development Framework, called the Strategy Rings. We begin from the outside ring looking in.

1) At the external ring we collect the changes and trends from the enterprise macro environment by analysing the political, economical, social, environmental and legal/regulatory factors. Had the regulation changed? Is the economy taking a downturn? And so on.

We analyse the environment and come up with a list of factors that may affect the enterprise, the products , the market, the workforce, the finance, the currency exchange rate and so on. We come with threats, opportunities and plain requirements coming for instance from the regulatory.

The digital technology trends would be analysed at this level.

2) We look at the micro environment for our industry by analysing such factors as Porter's Five Forces and the digital technologies progress, Capital and labour markets. The outcome is a set of threats and opportunities that must be considered

in elaborating the strategies.

3) This ring consists in stakeholders and their requirements: customers, owners, employees, suppliers, company, community, environment and last, but not least, the company. Requirements from each should be formulated and listed. That is, we will comply with the requirements of our key stakeholders. The company must be included as a stakeholder because the company itself is endangered if we fulfil solely the other stakeholders demands neglecting the company they all exploit.

4) This is the first ring within the company remit. It is meant to gather requirements coming bottom up from all company functions such as operations, development and support. What are the internal stakeholders needs to achieve to work optimally?

We come out in this ring with companies' strengths, weaknesses and known requirements.

Hence the outer rings 1,2,3,4 gather and analyse requirements from the external PESTEL and Five Forces environment, stakeholders and the company strengths and weaknesses.

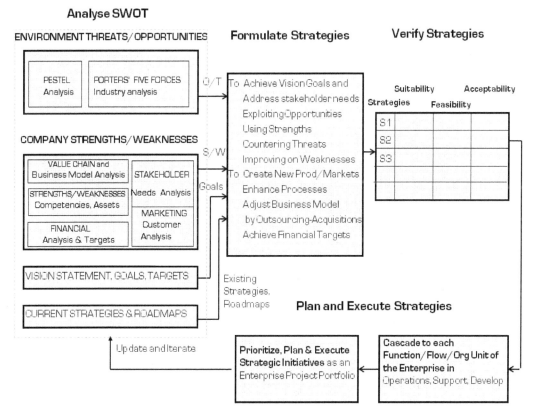

5) In this ring we formulate the Business Strategic Directions taking into account all requirements from the superior rings.

We analyse the Threats and Opportunities from for external rings (1, 2, 3) - that is from PESTEL Analysis, Porter's Five Forces and Stakeholders - against the company Strengths and Weaknesses (ring 4). We SWOT.

We formulate strategies to achieve the opportunities taking advantage of strengths and measures to improve on weaknesses to be able to take advantage of trends.

We establish now the vision and goals of the company taking into account the existing ones and the existing strategies and programs.

We list all possible strategies and we funnel them through the suitability, feasibility and acceptability.

6) We map each strategy elaborated in the previous ring back to all departments in the organization chart and enterprise functions and each of their processes, technology and people.

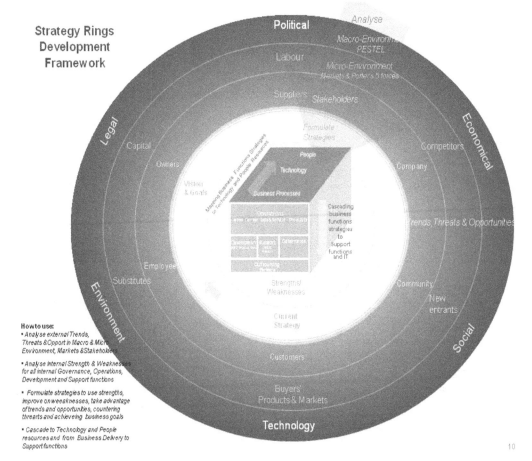

Each function determines what needs to be changed in terms of process, technology and organization and people roles and proposes projects to realize the impacts as part of the specific strategy direction realization program.

The outcomes put together lead to an overall Strategic Transformation Program that implements all strategy directions in alignment.

There is also the overall Strategy Rings framework mapped on the GODS-FFLV EA framework.

7) In the central Ring, The Strategic Directions are prioritized in road-maps. The Transformation plan is elaborated here.

The view with the enterprise cube in the middle replacing rings 4-7 describes the strategy mapping process on the enterprise organization and architecture.

The mapping is done each business function in operations, development and support and inside the function on process, technology and people roles. Strategies at units at the higher level in the organization, chart as for instance the Enterprise Operations Support have to implement and support the strategies of all units below.

You will find plenty of detail for the strategy analysis here, but it's upon you to employ them. After all it's all common sense.

See also some of the strategy analysis tools:

SWOT Analysis

https://www.mindtools.com/pages/article/newTMC_05.htm

The ADL Matrix Arthur D Little (ADL) Matrix

https://www.mindtools.com/pages/article/newSTR_88.htm

The Boston Matrix

https://www.mindtools.com/pages/article/newTED_97.htm

USP Analysis

https://www.mindtools.com/pages/article/newTMC_11.htm

VRIO Analysis

https://www.business-to-you.com/vrio-from-firm-resources-to-competitive-advantage/

Why is the sharing paradigm taking industries by storm?

https://it.toolbox.com/blogs/adriangrigoriu/why-is-the-sharing-paradigm-taking-industries-by-storm-110515

Nov. 05, 2015

"The Sharing Economy is a socio-economic ecosystem built around the reuse of little utilised private physical resources available at most locations through an application that manages their availability and lease.

Sharing is a rather new enterprise business model in which a virtual enterprise, consisting of a central dispatcher unit which asks the closest private resource present locally to provide the service.

The sharing business model is about a virtual enterprise which workforce consists of members of society participating in the enterprise value chain with their own assets and/or labour for a percent of the service fee.

Sharing though has existed for a long, long time in society. Hence we have to draw a line between the good old public property sharing and this model.

What is specific to the Sharing enterprise is the digital application **which interconnects the local Participant to Client Peer To Peer**. The participant is a member of the public which has been contracted by the firm.

Sharing companies include at this time Uber, Zipcar, Lyft, RelayRides, EasyCar Club, Parking Panda, Taskrabbit, Airbnb, HomeAway, NeighborGoods,... and perhaps Etsy, Poshmark...

But where is this Sharing of today coming from?

Sharing enables today the full utilisation of the little used otherwise private assets such as cars and houses for example.

What makes Sharing possible today is the digital technology though. Yet another impact of the Digital on the enterprise.

Uber and Airbnb are made possible by such technology capabilities today as the network ubiquity, two way web, mobile technology, secure electronic payments, instant messaging, location services, maps and directions and indeed by the processing power and friendly GUIs of the today mobile terminals.

Why is the Sharing economy important now?

Sharing results in product substitutes on the market, in Porter's Five Forces terms, that threaten the incumbents in well established industries like taxi, hotels, household chores...

 It is also the way to enter quick and with diminished risks a competitive market today by exploiting already the existing assets and available labour.

The win-win... of the Sharing enterprise (i)

https://it.toolbox.com/blogs/adriangrigoriu/the-win-win-of-the-sharing-enterprise-i-110615

Oct. 06, 2015

The Sharing success comes from the increased satisfaction of both the client and participant. Sharing is in fact advantageous to all parties since:

The enterprise

 - created quickly out of pre-existing assets and participant workforce without long term contracts and only a smaller upfront investment. The glue between the enterprise, clients and participants is a digital application.

 - flexibility and agility with the workforce and readily available on location

 - workforce and assets are already geographically distributed so that the firm may instantly get a wide coverage

 - the newly created enterprise is ready to take on the big firms

Participants (employees)

 - have sufficient autonomy to feel empowered, free and motivated

- go through a simple process to join; no heavy contracts, no long term commitments.

- do not have to create their own company to deliver the service

- their assets depreciate with use while returning profit rather than turning obsolete with time, unused

Customers are satisfied because

- service is amiable with the firm members are motivated by participation

- the both ways service feedback process ensures that only good service is tolerated

- competitive pricing

- service is available at all times...

Society/environment

- through re-use and sharing of abundant or scarce resources it increases the utilization factor of expensive assets and reduces their proliferation while reducing their impact on the environment

- it creates competition that may render the existing traditional services better and cheaper

Governments and state administration

- work and enterprise are taxed properly reducing the black labour market and increasing the revenues from taxation

- reduced unemployment

What Sharing brings new is flexible workforce and assets on demand (ii)

https://it.toolbox.com/blogs/adriangrigoriu/what-sharing-brings-new-is-the-flexible-workforce-and-assets-available-on-demand-ii-110715

Nov. 07, 2015

What participants in a Sharing enterprise do is join their resources and assets together to form a virtual enterprise. The production means do not belong to the enterprise but to the participants.

Participants do not work or share their assets for free though, they lease them for a fee. Sharing is still about profit and capitalism, there is no public property. Sharing offers a better utilisation of resources which is good for the environment in this consumerism era.

Participants want a fair deal, autonomy and flexibility, they want to avoid that central authority, the big brother that tells them what to do, that taxes and regulates them often only because it can.

A participant is a member of society that is employed and remunerated for a service rather than engaged in a permanent employment or typical contractual relationship.

The Sharing industry is the revolt of the man against the bureaucratic and greedy machine of the big enterprise.

Ironically, this revolution is based on Person to Person services/commerce and is enabled by the digital technology that provides the web, social media, global communications, remote access and transactions, smart terminals, secure payments, intelligent applications, maps, location services...

What Sharing brings new, beside the digital technology, is the flexible individual workforce and assets, available on demand and location.

The central enterprise entity that coordinates the whole does not have to provide assets or tools to participants because they use their own. This enables an agile, competitive enterprise easy to set up, manage and grow, that is, beneficial to everyone.

The central enterprise confers to this virtual organisation the operation framework, the governance and the brand. It ensures a certain quality of service which entices the public to employ its services.

If you think of a company as made of these four essential functions, Governance (coordination bodies), Operations (production activities and technology), Development (product and enterprise development activities) and enterprise Support, then for the Sharing business model the Governance is provided by the central enterprise core while the Operations is outsourced to many Participants which own the resources.

The enterprise Development and Support functions may be either performed by the central enterprise or, most likely, outsourced.

Sharing implements in fact a Cloud Enterprise with most functions, bar the coordination function, outsourced to 3rd parties in a services Cloud.

The pitfalls of Sharing

https://it.toolbox.com/blogs/adriangrigoriu/the-pitfalls-of-sharing-111015

Nov. 10, 2015

Not every industry is suitable for Sharing as yet but only the some delivering services to the public, specifically where the participants own the means of the trade and can work individually, such as such as hospitability, transportation, logistics, leasing...

Sharing works less good when:

- legal issues may be raised because of the regulation imposed on incumbents
- assets are so cheap that renting one is not worth the effort.

See variations of NeighborGoods, companies renting to locals garage tools. Many went bust though because, while the idea was welcome, the assets where cheaper to buy than rent.

Hence, Sharing does not really work for renting items that come cheaper to buy even if our "green" sense says differently.

CBS's Erik Sherman, in this article (https://www.cbsnews.com/news/5-ways-the-sharing-economy-disadvantages-workers/), posts on the drawbacks of Sharing for workers:

 - No Stability, no steady income

 - Small Income, not sizeable enough in particular when considering the costs of running the service and wear and tear of the asset

 - No Benefits, no Health Insurance, Pension, sick or annual leave...

 - No Control over own life due to unpredictable hours and income (one cannot obtain a long life mortgage?).

From this, it looks like that the kind of Sharing jobs may rather suit part time workers or those who wish to supplement their income.

If you add to that some disadvantages for clients such as the Uber uber charged prices for the New Year night you get a fuller picture.

Besides, in the long run, the advantage of the innovation may erode in time. The incumbents may adopt themselves latest technologies to respond to the threat. They may also demand that more regulation is enforced on the Sharing players, same as the regulation imposed on them. Many law suites took place exactly about that.

Nevertheless, in the end, the Sharing paradigm is here to stay in one form or another. Not every endeavour would succeed but those who do may become big players. Same happened with the Dotcom revolution. The few companies which survived got bigger.

Would the Participating term reflect better the Sharing business model (iii)

https://it.toolbox.com/blogs/adriangrigoriu/would-the-participating-term-reflect-better-the-sharing-business-model-iii-111315

Nov.13, 2015

Is the name Sharing relevant for this type of economy or proper enough to describe the plethora of diverse developments under its umbrella today? I am not trying to change the name of the Sharing enterprise though but to clarify its meaning.

The Sharing industry takes advantage of assets such as cars, tractors, rooms, power tools... sitting unutilised in garages everywhere. This may apply to skilled labour as an asset as well.

The Sharing enterprise brokers the owners' labour and assets to the citizens requesting the service at a location. This ensures a greater degree of utilisation of citizens' assets, protecting in the process the environment.

Many Sharing enterprises employ a Peer to Peer mechanism where the operation takes place between two people in which one is renting an asset or selling a service to the other.

But the privately owned assets are rented rather than shared for free.

We may call it as well Participating enterprise since people become part of the enterprise by contributing with own assets and labour. The core enterprise organises only the transaction.

A Participant, an enterprise certified and registered owner of an asset, selected by the sharing application based on location and availability, offers own labour and asset for rent to a client (which downloaded the app and registered the bank card) who demanded the service and pays for it over the application.

Hence the service providers are all participants in the Sharing enterprise. The Participant still shares though own assets with clients, utilising as such the assets to their full potential.

But no matter the naming, the Sharing/Peer to Peer/Participating enterprise is a type of Cloud Enterprise in which the operation is outsourced for execution to many participants in a Cloud.

In a Cloud Enterprise the Operation process, labour and technology are outsourced to a Cloud of certified participants

The Sharing enterprise reduces the granularity of participation in the enterprise Value Chain rendering the enterprise more flexible, agile, distributed and easy and cheap to create.

The Sharing/Peer to Peer/Participating enterprise paradigm aims to avoid the heavy weight central entity that tends to control everything. Its glue is, typically, a digital distributed application that offers messaging, location, billing...

While sharing has a future, many companies will be sifted out until the few solid ones remain.

THE ENTERPRISE CULTURE, VALUES, MERITOCRACY AND CONSTITUTION

The Values of the Enterprise

https://it.toolbox.com/blogs/adriangrigoriu/the-values-of-the-enterprise-051016

May 10, 2016

We have values, policies, standards... in the enterprise that guide its operation, behaviour and further development. They keep the enterprise effective and honest, or, at least, they should.

Values constitute a moral code, expressed as a set of maxims, that aims to render the enterprise a happy, honest and effective working place at all times. Often summarised in single expressive focus words such as Passion, Commitment, Honesty, Professionalism, Innovation...

Principles are often lessons learned and distilled as best practices which employees not only should keep in mind but apply in their work and decision making process. Principles are often employed in the Enterprise Architecture domain to guide its development.

Yet, how do you enforce today the "Values" of an enterprise? Or how do you make the principles work? Is there a framework for doing just that? How are they to be employed to make a difference?

Are they to be stuck on the lobby wall or on a portal banner? Must then everybody check the wall for adopting an attitude or taking a decision?

In reality, there is seldom a mechanism to realise Values. That means that the Values we often see bannered in the enterprise prescribe just an aspirational world with few means of realisation. Hence Values are sometimes seen as exercises in cynicism. While the Values glow up there, the practice down in the enterprise sucks because everybody, starting with the management, disregards them while gushing.

Is there a need then for a values regulatory body, a code of application (penalties) and a "values" police to penalise the non compliant?

The answer is, perhaps, yes, you need a framework for values realisation and an overseeing body to enforce them. These may not exist right now, at least not to my knowledge. Thus, Values do look nice stuck on the wall, as decoration for visitors while everybody conspicuously ignores them.

Applying company Values in practice

https://it.toolbox.com/blogs/adriangrigoriu/applying-company-values-in-practice-051216

May 12, 2016

To be applied in practice, the company values must be embedded in every day behaviour, in enterprise processes, in meeting protocols, at regular reviews... so that any development, body and action shall consider them.

Hence you automate the Values implementation rather than pray that sticking them on a wall does the trick.

To start with, the Values should be heart-felt and easily translated in practice. One implicit value is courtesy. Without it any debate would degenerate.

You may consider the company Values in any decision making process. For that, you may start by looking into governance questions such as Who makes decisions, What kind and How, that is on what basis.

The Who are the key employees, experts, managers, boards, committees...

The What accounts for the type of decisions taken by each Who.

The How indeed enrols the company Values, Principles, Rules, Policies, Standards, Guidelines, past cases...

Every employee, manager in the hierarchy,... decision board should have to consider the Values in the daily work and decision making. Overlaps in governance decision making remits should be avoided at all costs to prevent conflict between bodies.

And indeed, Values, starting with meritocracy (promotion on merit), should be reflected in the organisation design.

A special ethics body should be created to establish, clarify, interpret, improve, develop the Values, the associated artefacts and their governance and judge their application.

An appeal hierarchy should be also in place starting with direct managers' managers and ending up with the ethics board that will review decisions, make final decisions, record the decisions made and typical cases for further application, and in general, observe the application of the company Values. Unless you like them as a feature wall.

Since Values do not return profit, they are not always taken seriously in the enterprise. In fact, they are first to sacrifice, when "need" be. Still, a consistent application of Values would ensure a good working culture, mutual respect between employees, trust, dedication, loyal customers and, why not, brand recognition.

The Mission, Vision, Values and Constitution of the Enterprise

https://it.toolbox.com/blogs/adriangrigoriu/the-enterprise-values-and-policies-harmonisation-051416

May 14, 2016

The Company Values establish a standard to guide the behaviour of a company and its employees.

The Values, which state the expectations from the employee behaviour and company, are to steer everyone's behaviour, decision making and actions.

"A mission statement describes an organization's purpose and answers the questions "What **business** are we in?" and "**What is** our **business** for?" (Wikipedia).

In essence, it describes what the business does and why.

"A **vision** statement provides strategic direction and describes what the **company** aims to achieve in the future." (Wikipedia).

The enterprise strategy would establish the directions of action that would make the Vision happen.

Besides, companies establish policies and procedures that set the rules of conduct within an organization, outlining the responsibilities of both employees and employers. Take for instance the following policies: Equal Opportunity, Ethics, Employee Conduct, Information Disclosure, Data Protection, Confidentiality...

One may indeed add enterprise architecture and design principles and technology standards that guide the structured, as opposed to organic, development of the enterprise.

In addition, there are quite a few policies and procedures that go down in specifics that may constitute, perhaps, the Enterprise Regulation, such as:

Health and Safety Policy, Employee Dress and Manner, Anti-Corruption Procedure, Innovation, Attendance, Time Off and Absence, Substance Abuse, Personal Harassment, Disciplinary and Grievance Procedures, Personal Property, Email and Internet etiquette, Political–Religious Activity, Bonus policy, Smoking...

Hence, there is quite a collection of values, rules, policies, ... that guide the workings and behaviour of the enterprise which collection is often disjoint in that the policies are specified, governed and applied independently and in various ways if at all.

But if we can duplicate and group it in such structured categories of policies as

- Company behaviour with regard to external stakeholders

- Employee conduct

- Information management

- Regulatory Policy

- Communications Guidelines

- Company Development

- Decision Making...

- Technology selection principles

we can harmonize it, render them consistent and we may even discover gaps and fill them in.

All these above policies will form the Constitution of the Enterprise, the book that guides the enterprise operation.

The Culture and Constitution of the Enterprise

https://it.toolbox.com/blogs/adriangrigoriu/the-culture-and-constitution-of-the-enterprise-120519

Dec. 09, 2019

How do we make sure that our enterprise is happy and productive?

We motivate employees. We empower them and recognize their achievements. We establish as such a meritocracy.

We set up values for all to aim to.

We establish an overarching Law of Behaviour for the enterprise, its Constitution.

What Motivates Employees

To perform on a global level, a company needs more than ever to motivate their workforce and to smoothly cooperate to achieve the enterprise goals. But, to succeed, we have to make sure that the employee goals are part of or achieved in the process of realizing the greater common goals. When the employees goals are not achieved, the greater enterprise goal is in peril. Because employees get engaged only if they feel that their contributions are welcome, if their company listens to and empowers them to realize their own goals.

Employees have to see that the company has vision and direction and that their work contributes to that vision.

Enterprise Values

The employees would respect the company, not so much for its brand alone, but for its culture and realizations. For a great culture, the company and its leadership have to act in the spirit of their values.

To keep the enterprise honest and stakeholders happy, an enterprise has to establish values to guide the conduct of its employees.

The ensemble of values compose in effect a moral code of conduct that aims to guide and prevent employees from adopting attitudes that impede the collective work promote themselves and selfishness and, as such, hurt the enterprise effectiveness.

While values usually enunciate common human traits as "honesty", principles enunciated in a sentence, represent practices that should be kept in mind and applied in work relationships and decision making.

How do you make values work in practice though?

How does one make the "values" work in an enterprise? Are there any means to realize values in practice? Is there a framework for doing just that? Should the values be stuck on a banner or a wall in the lobby? Must everybody check the wall or banner for making a decision?

In reality, there is seldom such a values enforcement mechanism implemented. What this means is that the values we often see as a banner in the enterprise prescribe just an aspiration world. Yet, this may often be seen as an exercise in cynicism. We have all these values, but everybody disregards them in practice.

Do we need to enforce these values somehow? Is there a need for a values police and a code of conduct that prescribes penalties for the non compliant?

The answer is yes, you do need a framework and an internal regulation body that does not often exist now, at least not to my knowledge. Otherwise the values do remain stuck on a banner, a nice decoration that everybody ignores or mocks. Like a law everybody ignores since there is no enforcement. We need a values police to enforce the values, principles and regulations. This body would guard the enterprise values and ethics. In fact, the ethics of the enterprise should be derived from values.

A body should be created to issue, update and evolve the values, principles, policies and at the same time oversee their application and enforcement in processes, decision making bodies and so on.

For reviews of such enforcement decisions, a special appeal hierarchy should also be created starting with the line managers and governing boards. They should review decisions and observe their application.

But, to be applied in practice, the values must be embedded in the everyday processes of the enterprise. This way we automate value enforcement in everyday operation.

And indeed, the values and their governance should be reflected in the organization design. Every employee, manager, decision board should have the responsibility in the job description to take the values and principles and their derivatives into consideration in daily work.

The Constitution of the Enterprise

Not last, to make a difference, the sum of harmonized values, principles, best practices and policies should form the high code that guides the desired conduct in the enterprise.

To make the values happen, we should cascade them top down, from conceptual in banners to principles of conduct, job descriptions and policies. What we ultimately get is a coherent set of enterprise values and governance structure that realizes the values and, as such, the desired behaviour of the company and conduct of its employees.

The Enterprise Regulation Policies, consisting of the enterprise in-depth behaviour rules, should inherit and expand the enterprise constitution, same as a code of law expands and enacts a nation's constitution.

The harmonized values, policies, principles, standards and best practices may form then the high code of the enterprise that guides the effective, honest and ethical operation of the company.

We may call it the Constitution of the Enterprise.

A constitution, according to Dictionary.com, is *"the system of fundamental principles according to which a nation, state, **corporation**, or the like, is governed"*.

The Culture of an Enterprise

Ultimately, all values and principles, if successful, should be in time reflected in the organization culture, that is, in the behaviour of its employees. A proper culture would minimize the need and cost of formal mechanisms that have to enforce the company values. While the Constitution of the Enterprise dictates the culture, it is the culture that ultimately realizes the constitution of the enterprise. A positive culture reduces the effort of an ethics enforcement body.

"Organizational culture is a system of shared assumptions, values, and beliefs, which governs how people behave in organizations. These shared values have a strong influence on the people in the organization and dictate how they dress, act, and perform their jobs".

But, in practice, we cannot count on culture alone. The relevant rules, cascaded from the Constitution to an Enterprise regulation book, should be included or referred to in the employees contract so that they can be legally acted upon in case there are transgressions. It is easier and cheaper when citizens don't litter in the first place rather than fine each and every offender.

An enterprise culture grows ad hoc through examples, by seeing and doing. But, we can educate and constrain the culture by establishing a Constitution of the Enterprise and Its Regulation book and body.

Culture can render fruitless the Enterprise Transformation

https://it.toolbox.com/blogs/adriangrigoriu/culture-can-render-the-enterprise-architecture-efforts-fruitless-100516

Oct. 05, 2016

Culture can render fruitless an enterprise transformation. In fact, culture tends to maintain the status quo, to inhibit change. For example, in a blame culture, everybody avoids taking risks. But no transformation can be achieved without risks.

People often entrench, for example, in rejecting the new technologies or processes and continue apply old practices.

Culture is, by and large, the unwritten code of behaviour in a firm. Culture manifests in the behaviour of the company. It lives in people's minds and hearts. It makes people proud of the company and set personal interests secondary or it may determine people detest it. It shapes the attitude towards colleagues and work. Culture stems from the history of the company, its anecdotes and legends. Culture is evoked as traditions to newer generations.

The company must establishes values, principles, code of ethics... to regulate it. These must be meaningful, realistic, even measurable. Unlike the values of most companies today which are often vague, meaningless or worthless in practice.

An Code of Ethics based on values represents a code of rules. The code has to be communicated and policed, because, otherwise, it turns into "lip service". If obeyed, the code may enforce an open, positive culture. In not, it may render employees cynical and hard to mobilise.

Networking, nepotism, discrimination, politically correctness... begin to manifest until, like in society, the company loses its ways and competitive edge.. To revive it you have to reform the culture and, with it, its top management, practices, values, code of ethics...

God had created people in its own image, it is said. But in a similar manner, a top Executive determines the culture of the organisation through personal example, choice of direct reports and respect for its culture in general.

Empty words won't do! People, intuitively, have an n-th sense, the ability to feel the truth from gestures, expression, phrasing and intonation.

Company culture and meritocracy (i)

https://hr.toolbox.com/blogs/adriangrigoriu/company-culture-and-meritocracy-i-101116

Oct. 11, 2016

A good company culture rests in a few principles (in no order):

 - clear governance that eliminates overlaps or gaps

 - authority comes with accountability

 - empowerment, delegation

 - promotion on merit - fair promotion and distribution of benefits (unlike the CEO to employee salary ratio today of more than 50!)

- transparency in operation and decision making

- freedom of speech

- code of ethics and values that are observed...

Ideally, a culture should be meritocratic because it channels individual energies towards the company goals while the employees are promoted on the merit of achieving them.

Meritocracy establishes as such a balance between the enterprise and employees' interests. It encourages team work to everyone's proportional benefit. Nobody is afraid any longer that contributions would be appropriated as it often happens. People are more happy and productive as such. The "work hard and play hard" principle applies.

The alternative is a culture where minor personal interests and feuds come first against those of the company. In time, the company sinks under the weight of the many individual interests that work against each other and against the common good of the enterprise.

Innocent practices like "networking" work against meritocracy because the company fails to achieve by failing to employ the best for the job. Positions are not advertised but to the members of the grapevine.

Networking not only works against meritocracy but comes with "spin" to project the appearance of correctness. And networking grows on itself.

The disease starts at the top and spreads downwards, by example. People do what they see the management do rather than what they are preached to.

If formal ethics correction mechanisms are not set in place, culture deteriorates. People begin to take advantage of the trustful, the weak and the unaware.

Culture deviations and correction mechanisms (ii)

https://it.toolbox.com/blogs/adriangrigoriu/culture-deviations-and-correction-mechanisms-ii-101316

Oct. 12, 2016

Culture is influenced by the enterprise organisation and vice-versa. A flatter hierarchy motivates people because they have the autonomy to act, to prove themselves and to assume responsibility and accountability.

A confused governance though generates problems that degrade the company culture. Typically, managers clash over jurisdictions because the boundaries for decision making are not clear.

I once created a simple table with the IT management roles and their key decisions they are entitled to make. Called a meeting with the culprits and ask them to work on it employing a RACI framework.

In the end, the tension disappeared and agreement was achieved. The few remaining issues were ironed by the higher management. In time, such a table must evolve and be kept updated. Yet every role in the enterprise should describe in more or less words the powers, decisions... one is entitled to take within a group.

Hence a good governance design smoothes out conflict and enables collaboration.

The division between business and IT can often be attributed to a poor governance at the level above. The division exists because there are two different organizations with different objectives, plans and roadmaps and as such, un-harmonised missions and products. Thus, the two organisations do not concur to deliver together to the same goals. It is that simple.

The organisation has to be properly adapted first so that the related business and IT groups can align mission and vision.

A positive culture begins with transparency, openness, empowerment and meritocracy. Internal corporate mechanisms are necessary though to enforce and maintain the desired cultural traits such as spontaneous collaboration, freedom of speech... Truth must be told with impunity.

A special group could be created to observe behaviour, ethics, receive notifications of breaches and act on them.

Ideally all employees behave. But like in society there are always exceptions. This is why enforcement of a code of ethics is a must. Before that there must a shared motivation and education.

Culture deviations and remedial mechanisms (iii)

https://it.toolbox.com/blogs/adriangrigoriu/culture-deviations-and-remedial-mechanisms-iii-101516

Oct. 15, 2016

Culture, usually, grows organically, without much planning, in a similar manner to the Enterprise today.

But when deliberately changed, the culture must be built on company values and ethics. That is, it must incorporate them in the daily behaviour.

Yet, leaders play a key role in shaping and maintaining a culture. They must lead by good example to start with. A single top level bad example undealt with can derail the culture.

For instance, leaders often speak in the name of the abstract good while failing to act in stakeholders' interest. Like politicians who, to raise their moral profile and prospects, talk about humanitarian goals while they often act to the detriment of the people they were elected by to protect. And that while calling derogatorily populists those who speak and act in the name of the people.

But when rules do not equally apply to management, culture sinks. When it is hard is to get to the heart of the problem, the truth, then we deal with a "culture" of spin, cynical at that because people in their own interest alone neglecting the goals of the company.

Hence, company boards have a role to play. They are one of the few bodies able capable to oversee the culture at that level, monitor it and act on deviations. Because they represent the interest of all stakeholders.

A board member should be, perhaps, responsible for culture and ethics. KPIs may be employed too to measure cultural performance. Like how many times have we had this type of behaviour in the last six months.

Essentially, a good culture helps a company compete better by enabling team work, innovation and motivating everyone to surpass themselves. But it takes time to make the culture work for you rather than against you.

Culture is notoriously hard to change though. You don't even have the privilege to start from scratch. And a good culture must be kept alive like the family silver.

Meritocracy and Ethics in Enterprise Architecture

https://it.toolbox.com/blogs/adriangrigoriu/meritocracy-ethics-and-enterprise-architecture-121619

Dec. 16, 2019

Meritocracy

When employees work together like a sports team or orchestra, they contribute, support and teach each other to deliver, recognizing each other abilities. Everybody wins because the reward is commensurate with the level of ability and contribution. This is the key of success for teams and in particular for Agile.

But, this seldom happens today in the average enterprise where ego and personal advancement dominate and demotivate. Today, even the "team work" paradigm is often used to hijack the results of hard working individuals. The talented delivers, the boss and the team get equally or better rewarded because they get to review the work and make precious suggestions. The "well done, mate" praise is the usual reward for the working horse. But, this dries the talent well renders it cynical.

Meritocracy sets up a reward system based on contributions. It guarantees success in the enterprise because it motivates employees to produce together. *I support my peers, the enterprise produces more and I get as such proportionally more.* Without meritocracy employees lose heart, fail to share and have to be pushed from behind, lacking self-motivation. Also, political correctness enforced as positive discrimination may often go against meritocracy unfortunately because promotion on merit is replaced by various socially correct criteria. But, a *Democracy without Meritocracy defeats its own purpose.*

Ethics in the workplace

Has it ever happened to you that your ideas or presentation had been pinched and shown around by others? I found once one of my concepts circulating around without my knowledge. It was indeed a concept I presented for feedback in a small professional circle, but it was not me spreading it around but one of my colleagues who had appropriated it. Because people chose today to conveniently think that once it is discussed or posted somewhere a concept is public property and as such appropriate-able. This is one of the reasons EU re-enforced the intellectual property rights, going a bit too far though.

To prevent such a thing happening in the first place and then again and again, the enterprise or place should have a code of ethics and a body that defends it. Because, if one breaks the rules without consequences, everyone feels entitled to do so, because otherwise the culprit would gain an unmerited advantage. But when it happens again and again in a collectivity it is the culture of the place at play.

Because people naturally employ the maths induction law which dictates that an assertion is true if it is valid for the first few and then the n and n+1 occurrences. Some call it today stereotyping for political purposes but it is still a fact of math and life. But in everyday life, this is the generalisation process we all use.

Coming back to our issue, if tolerated, the unethical behaviour spreads and damages the culture of the place. To prevent and fix its corruption, a code of ethics must establish the desired behaviour for everybody.

But, while a code of ethics is good at telling people what is right and what is wrong for a place, without proper enforcement not only that it would not yield, but it may end up encouraging the unethical, because while the ethical individuals naturally prefer to operate within the rules, unhindered by the additional burden of explicitly observing the code of ethics, the unethical individuals would still break the rules to take advantage because there are no repercussions. And, this may have adverse impacts on the collective by attracting the wrong people who milk the system at the others' loss. Unethical people may even become the dominant voice and culture since they unsurprisingly congregate to defend each other and turn vocal to cover their uncouth position.

Yet, beware, the enforcement of a code of ethics may cost more than its benefits.

Enterprise Architecture and Ethics

In the case of Enterprise Architecture, is EA itself sufficiently mature to mandate a code of ethics today? The answer is no, considering the fact that the EA is so poorly defined today that almost anyone can claim to be a professional by invoking a self serving interpretation of EA. If an organization intending to enforce an EA code of ethics cannot even determine what an EA architect really does and as such, establish the criteria of selection, how can it claim then that it represents the EA professionals at all? Is this even ethical for an organization that protects ethics?

Moreover, such a code of ethics organization that acts without a means of differentiation between so many types of enterprise professionals, as in Enterprise

Architecture today, may bring the profession into disrepute because it appears that it does guarantee EA professionalism not only ethics, while it doesn't.

The big problem for all of us is that, if such an organization turns strong enough to take enough control of the recruiting market, we may have to join, pay and play by its rules to be able to profess at all.

This is also the case of some standards today which, while they provide no returns, have monopolized the training and certifications market reducing them to worthless diploma mills. Having jumped at an apparently good cause, delivering standards to the profession, an organization may cause a lot of grief later on to all of us. Think of the cost on you for refusing to adopt the standard, be trained and certified in it.

The good old detective question "cui bono" illustrates if not solves the dilemma of such standards showing that the organizations promoting the standards get rich while the EA and its community are discredited and the ultimate customers, the companies on this world lose time and money.

Now, does EA warrant, as such, a code of ethics and an associated organization to police the entry to and the execution of the profession? Not in my view, not at this stage, at least because it may serve more the interest of a small group rather than that of the EA profession. Because the ethics code itself becomes a weapon against the non-joiners who may be accused of wishing to reserve the right to behave unethically. Similarly, those who reject today the EA training in certification standards today, are discriminated against by the recruitment industry.

Culture, a Barrier to Digital

https://it.toolbox.com/blogs/adriangrigoriu/culture-a-barrier-to-digital-080217

Aug. 02, 2017

Julie Goran, Laura LaBerge and Ramesh Srinivasan of McKInsey Quarterly, published in July 2017 Culture for a digital age in which they state that "*in a digital world, solving these cultural problems - Risk aversion, weak customer focus, and siloed mind-sets - is no longer optional*".

"Shortcomings in organizational culture are one of the main barriers to company success in the digital age. That is a central finding from McKinsey's recent survey of global executives, which highlighted three digital-culture deficiencies: functional and departmental silos, a fear of taking risks, and difficulty forming and acting on a single view of the customer".

Culture can be indeed a roadblock for the enterprise transformation. But still... while the deficiencies mentioned above are well known enterprise problems that do impede enterprise transformation, they have little to do with culture. In any case, "digital-culture" hardly exists today.

Still, "*risk aversion, weak customer focus, and siloed mind-sets*", depending on the point of view, are either problems or best practises. Yet, they are not "bad" in themselves.

"*Risk aversion*" comes from the experience of failure. It is common knowledge that today the IT projects record of failure rises to about 70%. In voting terms, this would be a landslide. Understandably, any new IT project poses risks. But, as a result, **risk aversion is a healthy attitude when badly managed projects are the norm**.

And, no matter the "*customer focus*", defective manufacturing, quality assurance, poor quality checks... may affect the customer satisfaction and relationships.

The enterprise must first make sure that its value chain delivers properly the product so that the enterprise is able to focus on the end to end customers' experience rather than working overtime to respond to customers complaints generated by products faults, queries...

"*Silo-ed*" mind-sets result from the desire to perform better as a unit which is not too bad in itself. In fact, siloes are the first step towards a service based organisation that enables autonomy, the catalyst for performance.

But siloes forego collaboration mainly because the enterprise does not properly coordinate and co-interest the units to support the bigger aims.

In any case the silos are not so much a cultural problem but rather an organisational and managerial one. If a unit consistently underperforms then it is normal for the rest of the enterprise to avoid depending on it, acting as such as much as possible independently.

Besides "lack of understanding of the digital trends", "lack of IT infrastructure", "lack of internal alignment - digital vs traditional business", "business process too rigid", lack of dedicated funding" enumerated by McKInsey... have little to do with the enterprise culture but rather with poor organisation, lack of vision... and, in general, everything to do with poor management.

Streamline to render the enterprise agile before addressing cultural issues (i)

https://it.toolbox.com/blogs/adriangrigoriu/discover-streamline-and-render-agile-the-enterprise-before-addressing-cultural-issues-i-080317

Aug. 03, 2017

McKinsey concludes: "Leaders hoping to strike the right balance have two critical priorities... One is to embed a mind-set of risk taking and innovation through all ranks of the enterprise. The second is for executives themselves to act boldly once they have decided on a specific digital play—which may well require changing mind-sets about risk...".

That is, McKinsey recommends you to change the "mind-set" of risk taking at both the layman and executive levels, that is change the enterprise culture with regard to... change and innovation. Yet, this is notoriously hard to change. While the enterprise is slowed down by a culture of fear of mistakes and subsequent risk aversion that postpones forever decision making, the truth is that the road to Digital is blocked by the enterprise own complexity, the architecture debt built for long and lack of agility that increase the fear to act and as such lead to cultural inertia.

Hence, to cope with the Digital assault

the enterprise must be modelled to uncover, document and assess the current landscape.

An Enterprise wide Architecture team should be created to take over the task and deliver the enterprise blueprint.

2 - streamline the enterprise to reduce its own complexity in order for you to be able to better control the enterprise and its transformation.

To cope with change, the enterprise should reduce its architecture debt - that is the unnecessary duplication, variation... It should also be reorganised on architecturally correct principles. The EA blueprint would be the key asset in the process.

3 - render the enterprise agile to change

As such, the enterprise has to be modelled around services (SOA like) and APIs identified in the modelling effort of the target architecture, so that it could agilely adopt the Cloud, the API economy and Business Process Outsourcing that all come with the Digital.

4 – evaluate what the Digital future has in store for it

The company should form a dedicated team, tasked to put together a technology roadmap that leads to the digital vision. Since stakeholders would have the opportunity to see the future and discuss their issues, the confusion and fear of digital should be alleviated to a degree. The team should begin by putting in place an Innovation and Emerging Technology process consisting of:

.a a Digital landscape survey and impact evaluation

.b elaboration of relevant Digital technologies value proposition assessment and recommendations

.c prioritisation, roadmapping, prototyping and, eventually, implementation within the overall enterprise transformation programme.

.d technology impacts should be evaluated on the current EA landscape. A tentative target EA should be sketched at this time.

5 - re-evaluate the enterprise business models as the result of the Digital

The Digital era comes with new models such as Online, Sharing/ Participation, network enterprise...

An architecturally correct target EA, based on services, that considers the Digital business models and vision, could be established at this time.

Once this out of the way, the mentioned issues can be tackled safely to make sure that such "obstacles" as mentioned in the paper, are dealt with even before engaging in the digital enterprise transformation which can be fast and furious. All the above steps should constitute the first phase of the transformation. Without them the transformation could prove to be a long and costly exercise.

On leadership, acting and deception

https://it.toolbox.com/blogs/adriangrigoriu/on-leadership-acting-and-deception-061614

June 16, 2014

Should a leader be pessimistic or at least look so? Should deception be employed to inspire optimism?

Yet a false optimism would lead to decisions that may render things worse because it conveys a false sense of security.

A leader may hide own emotions but not the reality.

A leader must be confident. Confidence though is more than optimism because it relies on abilities, knowledge and past experience, that is competence. Because a leader's wrong footed confidence can lead to disasters given the consequences of decisions. I witnessed that.

Should a leader have theatrical abilities? An actor plays a role, that is behaves like someone else.

Yet actors are at times elected leaders because of their performance in their roles because they are popular. Yet, in practice, are they competent enough for playing the role in real life? Take for instance a medical doctor would you consult an actor who plays the role of a doctor?

Appearance is often important though but no so important as substance because stereotypes upon which we judge people often exist. Men of substance may often be as such under-appreciated because of their appearance. But leaders selected on appearance alone may lead you to failure.

ON SHALLOW WORK AND INNOVATION

Deep versus Shallow work

https://it.toolbox.com/blogs/adriangrigoriu/deep-versus-shallow-work-080817

Aug. 08, 2018

In the 'Want to Create Things That Matter? Be Lazy', Cal Newport defines the concepts of Deep and Shallow work. Cal, of Georgetown University, knows, since he has published a book on the topic, called *"Deep Work: Rules for Focused Success in a Distracted World"'*.

'**Deep Work**: Cognitively demanding tasks that require you to focus without distraction and apply hard to replicate skills.

Shallow Work: Logistical style tasks that do not require intense focus or the application of hard to replicate skills.'

In essence, Deep work is the highly qualified work that requires focus, hence conditions for it.

Shallow work is business as usual work that can be performed amongst or is a result of frequent distractions.

Deep Work produces though the things that matter. While it is not in itself about innovation, it enables it. Because of its greater focus, it goes to greater depths that may lead to it.

But Deep work can be only performed in the absence of diversions. That is because changing work contexts from one task to another takes time and effort. By analogy, at interruptions a Real Time OSs (Operation Systems) must save the task state information in a stack only to retrieve it later, on resumption. And interruptions can be nested.

Amongst the many distractions today, increasingly enabled by the digital technology, most performance workers can hardly focus on their work. Not only meetings, phone calls, emails are culprits but also the abundance of irrelevant information, news, social media and, not least, the unduly loud office environment today. People feel that they have a right to meet, speak and... laugh loudly because it is open space after all and as such permitted. Guys and gals often put as such their calls on speaker to show off.

The Deep professional work is obstructed as such by the many distractions and the perennial noise today created by our co-workers, in particular those doing shallow work that does not require concentration.

Work used to be more focused, and as such effective, decades ago when distractions were fewer. Today the mobile and meeting mania, the email, social media... have crowded our agenda and diminished our productivity.

Deep and Shallow work compete for the skilled worker time (i)

https://it.toolbox.com/blogs/adriangrigoriu/deep-and-shallow-work-compete-for-the-skilled-worker-time-i-080917

Aug. 09, 2018

The problem is that, in the enterprise, the Deep and Shallow work compete for the same resource, the time of the skilled worker.

Deep workers are mandated in meetings and calls only to sanction the decisions and review the work done by the Shallow workers. But could such reviews be effective when the work is shallow from the very beginning? A certain amount of Shallow work comes naturally in the regular breaks every hour or so. Sometimes the breaks prepares the ground for deep work. Some other is necessary in an emergency.

The most consuming Shallow work comes in the form of "collaboration" which, unfortunately, grows on people since communications, team work and collaboration "skills" are highly ranked in CVs.

Shallow work of the collaboration kind, that keeps interrupting the Deep work while it is hard to quantify it fills the weekly work reports justifying in a way the lack of time for Deep work. The assumption seems to be that the employee really works in meetings, over the telephone, email and social media. Surely, such "collaboration" work has value, at least, in the eyes of its performers. But what is its value in comparison with the deep work of designing the product, writing software...

The truth though is that we cannot Deep work eight hours at a stretch. Any work needs breaks, such as the 10 minutes rest every hour, spent chatting by the coffee machine or an after lunch nap for refreshing the mind and recharging the batteries. These breaks are as such integral part of the Deep work. Even meetings, checking our email, socialising... are necessary in the end. But the percentage of Shallow to Deep work should raise to at most 50%.

Shallow work though, takes most of the workers' time, i.e. between 70% and 85% according to sources. What is the productivity of an enterprise where employees sit on the phone or in meetings most of their time?

Deep Work is not encouraged in the enterprise today (ii)

https://it.toolbox.com/blogs/adriangrigoriu/deep-work-is-not-encouraged-in-the-enterprise-today-ii-081017

Aug. 10, 2017

Deep Work is not really encouraged in the enterprise today. The deep workers are increasingly becoming a minority. That is because the Deep work, often regarded today as the province of the socially unadapted, is seldom lauded and promoted. Deep workers are not perceived as "team workers" any longer because they tend to work in silence and solitude while almost everyone today wishes to work with people, socially, in the administration of things and management of people rather than spent years learning, researching and sweating to go to the bottom of problems to offer effective solutions.

The truth is that few can do Deep work. It requires solitary isolation, reflection time, perseverance, patience and most importantly deep skills and sweat. And since deep work seldom leads to promotion people have no incentive today to study, and work hard. There is no reward at the end. Promoted are the shallow workers with people and political skills.

It is no wonder though that most of us do Shallow work. To begin with Shallow work does not require hardly acquired skills but rather a natural gregarious behaviour. Often people like to hear themselves speaking, chatting in meetings, "liaising" with customers and "networking" with peers. On top, those most vocal in meetings collect the spoils, no matter what they say if they say it loud enough.

The problem is that, if left at it, the shallow workers, administrators... may marginalise the Deep workers, the professionals, showing at times disdain for them because Deep workers, bent over their work, fail to socialise enough, to present themselves.

But isn't this as it should be today? After all, what is there so important that it deserves our full attention? Commercial enterprises may not be the right place for Deep work because business as usual work is rather common, repetitive, bureaucratic... Work mostly consists of monitoring, supervision, control, maintenance, updates... that is, that rarely needs deep thinking.

Fact is though that our productivity falls rapidly amongst the noisy pretence of the Shallow work. Email was often named as the culprit. Meetings going amok for lack of agenda and control are another suspect. Phone calls... are breaking our concentration every few minutes or so.

We suffer from a collaboration and communication overload that kills our capacity to work effectively. We just jump from one thing to another. The more interruptions we suffer the less work we do. We just change contexts. And get stressed from the overload from the inability to achieve anything deep enough. We do not solve our problems any longer, we employ a consultant who would do the deep work for us.

But, let's give a chance to the few deep workers we still have, those who still can immerse in deep thinking. We have to stop the ever increasing zoom "collaboration" and "communication" and social media waste our time.

We have to stop the Shallow work take over the last remnants of our deep work.

When 'collaboration' slows down your work

https://it.toolbox.com/blogs/adriangrigoriu/when-collaboration-slows-down-your-work-080417

Aug. 04, 2017

In *The collaboration curse* *(The Economist),* Harvard Business Review (HBR) discusses the issue of the "collaborative overload".

'Rob Cross and Peter Gray of the University of Virginia's business school estimate that knowledge workers spend 70-85% of their time attending meetings (virtual or face-to-face), dealing with e-mail, talking on the phone or otherwise dealing with an avalanche of requests for input or advice'.

"Many employees are spending so much time interacting that they have to do much of their work when they get home at night'.

'Tom Cochran, a former chief technology officer of Atlantic Media, calculated that the midsized firm was spending more than $1m a year on processing e-mails, - with each one costing on average around 95 cents in labour costs...,- the cost of a small company Learjet'.

'It does not take long for top collaborators to become bottlenecks: nothing happens until they have had their say—and they have their say on lots of subjects that are outside their competence'.

"A reason is that ...managers often feel obliged to be seen to manage: left to their own devices they automatically fill everybody's days with meetings and memos rather than letting them get on with their work." (The Economist).

"So organisations need to do more to recognise that the amount of time workers have available is finite, that every request to attend a meeting or engage in an internet discussion leaves less time for focused work".

I remember the first time I worked for a large corporation. My calendar had been already filled with meetings the day I joined. My initial attempts to sit at the desk, trying to put together answers to the problems I was to come with answers to, were regarded with suspicion.

People did expect me to be in meetings, on the phone or typing emails furiously. Worse, I still preferred pen and paper. I avoided phone calls as being disruptive. I turned down meetings where I had little to say... All at the risk of disconnecting myself from the rest and be forgotten as such.

Even so, the problem was that I never had the time to think in depth. Hence I did my work at home. But that was exhausting, a heavy burden for my family and indeed, not sustainable in the long term.

Only later, I realised that anybody in search of an answer or decision, called a meeting. As if the deep work was done in meetings. The problem was that at the end of the week I had nothing to report but meetings, phone calls, chats, emails...

But, when corporates or governments need to do some deep work they do employ external contractors and consultants. Because who can instantly go back to deep work, assuming it was able to do it in the first place, after years of soothing shallow work?

It is interesting though that long term contractors are soon dragged in the meetings routine too. It looks like to survive Shallow work drowns the Deep work in their collaboration and communication social activities.

"Peter Drucker argued that you can do real work or go to meetings but you cannot do both". (The Economist).

Talk about business model innovation or simply business innovation?

https://it.toolbox.com/blogs/adriangrigoriu/should-we-talk-about-business-model-innovation-or-simply-business-innovation-080515

Aug. 05, 2015

McKinsey Quarterly discusses in this article "*Disrupting beliefs: A new approach to business-model innovation*" The article categorizes and discusses new business models and proposes a process for business model innovation.

True, new ways of doing business increasingly disrupt the old ways. McKinsey comes with plenty of examples that changed the business world. Still, how many entrepreneurs or enterprises talk about their business models, know them or have them documented?

And how would that business model representation look like? A page, often called canvas, with a few unattached boxes, or, more exactly, a list of customers segments, channels, resources, partners and a value proposition? Is that good enough for the purpose?

I think we are making things more complex than they are. We always sought to increase profit by looking at new customer segments and channels and we often looked at minimising costs by looking at processes and resources. But we haven't called that business model innovation so far.

That is, we have always tinkered with the existing operating models without even thinking about it. We can keep doing that, changing the way business operates, without even calling it business model innovation. We must calculate indeed, the benefits of implementing change, that is we must build a business case whenever we do change our operation, so that we understand if it is profitable in the long run.

Back to the article though, how do we go about business model innovation? McKinsey says: take your industry dominant business model and reframe the long held beliefs. Here it is, your recipe for innovation.

Why people keep teaching us how to innovate, think creatively and so on? Innovation, like creation, is not really learnable. Not everybody can create, not on demand anyway. There is no process that automatically leads us to innovation. Same as with leadership, perhaps. But we do like to play with it.

What we can do is create the conditions for innovation through critical thinking, expanding the breadth of our knowledge and enabling cross-domain collaboration because ideas don't come from the blue sky but from other fields of activity through analogy and comparison. We can look at how nature does things. That is what a lot of innovators do.

About Business Model innovation

https://it.toolbox.com/blogs/adriangrigoriu/about-business-model-innovation-080715

Aug. 07, 2015

McKinsey Quarterly discusses in this article "Disrupting beliefs: A new approach to business-model innovation"

 Innovation by twisting the business model alone looks rather academic and limited in scope because innovation may happen anywhere in the enterprise as for instance in the re-organisation of the company.

But if you do wish to innovate your Business Model you may first have to understand what that is. A Business Model shows how a company goes about its business to be able to return value/profit. Representing the business model down on paper is a bit more difficult though.

In fact, I would say that on paper a business model, rather than showing a list or disconnected boxes on a canvas, we should illustrate a value chain, represented in sufficient detail to reveal costs and revenues for the calculation of profitability. That's not the case today though, not to my knowledge.

Hence, to be of any use, the representation of the business model should be built on the value chain. In turn, the value chain should be mapped on an enterprise wide architecture (EA) to enable the analysis of the chain of components that deliver the product.

A business model may be represented thus as a path through a full EA that illustrates the customer segments, channels, partnerships, processes and the resources that execute them and deliver the product.

A map of disjoint boxes would not do the job to illustrate the sequence of processes and the technology and people resources/partnerships that execute the links of the value chain.

The business model total cost could be as such calculated on the EA to establish the profitability of the model.

But true, there is not often that you see an EA blueprint today either.

As an observation though, profit appears to be the only value taken into consideration by a business model today. Still, there are other things though that matter to a company, such as the impact on the environment and in general corporate social responsibility and customer satisfaction.

Still, if you intend to change your business model and you are in the media industry, one of the most productive models today "sell advertising while giving own product away". That is, in effect, "marketing" other products while giving away own product. The model makes profit from marketing other products rather than selling one's own.

This is the main business model for public radio and TV, Google Search, Facebook...

Hence, marketing pays if your product, or rather service, has a wide reach. Rather than market your product, for which complex pricing and competition maybe issues, get revenue from advertising while offering your product for free.

On Business Innovation

https://it.toolbox.com/blogs/adriangrigoriu/the-business-innovation-process-081215

Aug. 12, 2015

McKinsey Quarterly discusses in this article "Disrupting beliefs: A new approach to business-model innovation"

Today the Business Model (BM) concept is not defined and represented as a business flow that generates value/profit, as it should. But how better can you analyse the BM and calculate the value/profit returned if not on its value chain flow?

The BM analysis is reduced at looking in isolation at the separate boxes in the BM list, such as customer segments, channels...

But today the BM concept includes neither the organization explicitly nor the enterprise support functions which may still contribute to the overall effectiveness of your enterprise.

Outsourcing of IT for example, does not touch customer channels or segments, production activities and resources... Since it does not make a profit either, it is not a part of a business model canvas. Still, the outsourcing may increase your profitability no matter the traditional business model.

Hence, even taking into account all business models (BMs) of an enterprise, you may still not cover the whole enterprise and the fields of potential innovation.

Anyway, innovation should not be implemented in isolation but in the context of your strategic planning so that it can be aligned to other developments.

To innovate today, do your Digital due diligence because, if there is innovation somewhere, it comes from the Digital revolution that brings new digital channels for sales and services interaction, mobility of workforce and customers, suites of applications that automate the enterprise, Cloud outsourcing and integration technologies, the Internet of things (IoT), new manufacturing technologies as for example 3D printing, real time business intelligence... and many more.

THE SERVICE BASED ORGANISATION, TRAGEDY OF COMMONS & HOLLACRACY

The Enterprise Organisation and the Tragedy of Commons

https://it.toolbox.com/blogs/adriangrigoriu/the-enterprise-organisation-and-the-tragedy-of-commons-111616

Nov.16, 2016

In "*The Tragedy of the Commons: How Elinor Ostrom Solved One of Life's Greatest Dilemmas*" David Sloan Wilson elaborates on "The design principles for solving the tragedy of the commons".

Garrett Hardin in the essay "The Tragedy of the Commons", published in 1968 in the *Science* magazine, used the parable of a group of villagers that share a common pasture. The farmer who adds an extra cow to the pasture gains an advantage while the community loses because of over overgrazing.

In fact today, we can talk about people, rather than cows, overgrazing, overheating, over driving... on the common resource, earth. Perhaps the principles enunciated here would help us protect our world.

By extension, we may also call it the tragedy of "common property" that gets over exploited today to the advantage of the unscrupulous few.

How can this be averted by a group is the crux of the above article that discusses the organisation principles of the group that help achieve that.

In my posts here, I'd like to apply these principles to the Enterprise Organisation.

Elinor (Lin) Ostrom (Nobel prize winner in economics in 2009) stated in the *Governing the Commons* book that *groups are capable of avoiding the tragedy of the commons without requiring top-down regulation if certain conditions are met.*

Here are, further explained, Lin's design principles (DP) for the group sharing the Commons:

1. Clearly defined boundaries (DP1)

that essentially means that a group is deliberately created and agree to use the below principles. That's straightforward.

2. Proportional equivalence of costs and benefits (DP2)

states that a member cannot benefit more than consumes or uses, that is there must be a direct proportional relation between contributions and common resource utilisation. This principle enforces fairness.

3. Collective choice arrangements (DP3)

demands collective decision making. That's the norm today even though in practice there is usually a leader of the group that may alter this balance.

4. Monitoring (DP4) the usage, the consume

Monitoring reports if principles are complied with.

The Enterprise Organisation and the Tragedy of Commons (i)

https://it.toolbox.com/blogs/adriangrigoriu/the-enterprise-organisation-and-the-tragedy-of-commons-i-112716

Nov. 27, 2016

In "*The Tragedy of the Commons: How Elinor Ostrom Solved One of Life's Greatest Dilemmas*" David Sloan Wilson elaborates on "The design principles for solving the tragedy of the commons can be applied to all groups".

.5. Graduated sanctions (DP5)

This rule enforces the principles. It establishes proportional penalties for those who do not comply with the proportional quota of usage or the rules.

Because principles unenforced, like laws, are usually ignored.

.6. Fast and fair conflict resolution (DP6)

is more of a (nice to have) behaviour. It never happens though unless it is regulated.

.7. Local autonomy (DP7)

means that the group has the autonomy to organise itself.

.8. Appropriate relations with other tiers of rule making authority (DP8)

states that the same rules that apply inside the group should apply among the groups of a larger group.

In our case this is the enterprise.

 Here are accordingly a set of principles, based on the above, which we can use to design our enterprise organisation in groups that

.1. are autonomous but have all adopted the enterprise resources usage rules

.2. pay is proportionally to skills, contribution and resource usage

.3. make decisions collectively

.4. monitor their activities

.5. apply proportional sanctions when the profit adjudicated by some are disproportional large to contributions

.6. apply these same rules between the groups of an enterprise

Anything out of the ordinary? That sounds a bit like an enterprise we would have devised. This is kind of enterprise we all want in fact. That is we'd love autonomy, benefits according to contributions and skills, collective decisions and policing the enterprise to keep all these endeavours honest.

The Enterprise and the Tragedy of Commons, governance groups (ii)

https://it.toolbox.com/blogs/adriangrigoriu/the-enterprise-organisation-and-the-tragedy-of-commons-governance-groups-ii-120216

Dec. 02, 2016

Yet the situation is much more complex today than in the cows' pasture example. What is missing? Hence, in addition to the enterprise organisation principles (see previous posts), there should be

.1. a governance function

.2. implementation of the service and contract concepts.

.1. a governance function that establishes

   - the organisation and its groups

   - the overall enterprise vision, goals and targets for each group

   - the communication interfaces to upper levels and between groups

   - assigns work to groups

   - monitors deliverables and proportionality of benefits

   - enforces sanctions in exceptions...

A Governance function is also necessary inside the group to institute

   - accountability for various common tasks and decisions

   - the basis of decision making, that is, the rules, policies, information... that must be taken into account

Governance may be though a collective function, that is decisions may be taken collectively.

The necessity for a governance function indicates though that we cannot abandon, after all, the top down regulation for the groups of enterprise, perhaps against the Tragedy of Commons specs.

No matter the principles though, the enterprise is usually organised hierarchically because higher level functions coordinate a number of related groups and take responsibility for their collective operation.

The coordinating functions organise the groups below, assign deliverables, monitor progress, coordinates activities between groups, oversee the end to end flows and take responsibility for the enterprise operation below and report above. This entity can also replace non-performing groups, re-organise... as long the deliverables to the rest of the enterprise remain unchanged.

The Enterprise and the Tragedy of Commons, the virtual enterprise (iii)

https://it.toolbox.com/blogs/adriangrigoriu/the-enterprise-organisation-and-the-tragedy-of-commons-the-virtual-enterprise-iii-120416

Dec. 04, 2016

To sum up, a governance function over a few groups is necessary though in either a virtual, collective or physical form to realise the cross groups coordination of activities, control of costs and assign budgets and assume accountability.

The number of hierarchical levels of an organisation depends on the number of groups at the bottom of the hierarchy and the optimal size of a group.

Assuming one has 100 bottom level groups and an average size of 5 (some say 7 is the magic number from a optimum governance point of view), and that for each ensemble of 5 groups there should be a governance function, then there are 20 coordinating groups at the level above, 4 at the next level above and 1 at the very top. The organisation has four levels as such top to bottom.

In case all bottom level groups below are "realised" or "operated" by partners, only the top governance entities are part of the "core Enterprise", while all together, they form the overall "Virtual Enterprise".

To build from scratch a manufacturing facility is near impossible and too risky. So today entrepreneurs come with the idea or design, get funding from crowd-sourcing, contract a firm to build them an ecommerce site, outsource production to an existing manufacturer, employ the services of a marketing firm, use the Cloud for IT power and ERP solutions and so on.

Effectively, the whole enterprise is virtualised with the exception of a couple of governance levels that coordinate the overall operation and control the budgets, costs and deliverables.

Take for instance the MVMT watches business started by two young entrepreneurs that began from an idea and implemented it by outsourcing most of the enterprise functions.

The Enterprise and the Tragedy of Commons, services & contracts (iv)

https://it.toolbox.com/blogs/adriangrigoriu/the-enterprise-organisation-and-the-tragedy-of-commons-services-contracts-iv-120716

Dec. 07, 2016

At the same time with the governance function for an ensemble of "Tragedy of Commons" (ToC) groups, the service and contract concepts were thought necessary and introduced here.

.2. Services and contracts

While the Tragedy of Commons principles makes sense, only concepts like service and contracts can make an enterprise work reliably in practice.

Without services and contracts, the interconnections between groups are tangled, access is informal, non committal, through various minimal and personal channels, relying on non-standard and unreliable procedures. Therefore potential misunderstandings and disputes are very likely.

The additional effort to specify the services and contracts will handsomely pay by clarifying responsibilities and eliminating the arbitrary and the unknown.

A service should define the mission of a group. It defines what it delivers, specifies the contact points, the APIs web sites, communication channels, protocols, testing procedures (repeat procedures in case of failure, time to response etc)...

Because autonomy motivates people, the internal organisation, governance, processes of a group should be hidden and not interfered with from the outside world.

Groups should interact over service interfaces rather than through all pores, so that interactions are formal rather than personal. As a result, the people, organisation, processes and governance... remain internal and autonomous.

The service concept enables interchange ability of services (that is the people and technology as the delivering entity) as long as the outcomes are similar and relation customer-supplier goes through the same interface.

Today though, many organisational groups in the enterprise lack interfaces. They are interconnected through a myriad of back doors and personal links that lessen the predictability and effectiveness of cross operation.

When services are based on good will and promises alone rather than interfaces, the deliveries maybe excuses rather than outcomes.

Hence we need contracts because they specify, beside the deliverable of the group and the description of its features, performance indicators, timetable and, among others, the sanctions to be applied in the case of non-delivery, poor quality and delays. Contracts legalise the service delivery.

On Holacracy, the organization paradigm

https://it.toolbox.com/blogs/adriangrigoriu/on-holacracy-the-organization-paradigm-090815

Sept. 08, 2015

Holacracy is a "system of organizational governance in which authority and decision-making are distributed throughout a holarchy of self-organizing teams rather than being vested in a management hierarchy" (Wikipedia).

A holarchy "is composed of holons or units that are autonomous and self-reliant, but also dependent on the greater whole of which they are part". Holarchy is described in the 1967 book *The Ghost in the Machine* by Arthur Koestler.

Holacracy seems to propose the teams' autonomy and distributed "authority and decision making" we all dream about. But is holocracy so different from a hierarchical organization?

While Holacracy sounds great in words such as "iterative governance, adaptive processes, self-organization...", is it any good in practice? Let's explore. Anyway, it is not my intention to criticise Holacracy but, to understand it and find out what it is after and translate it in terms of my trade, that is, business and enterprise architecture.

A holacracy is made of "circles" (aka teams). "Circles are organized hierarchically and each circle is assigned a clear purpose and accountabilities by its broader circle... Each circle has the authority to self-organize internally, to best achieve its goals".

But, in its own admission, Holacracy is still hierarchical. Also, each circle determines the purpose and perhaps even the existence of the circles below.

The fact that every holon is as part of a larger system and, at the same time, as made of smaller elements is nothing new. So far, Holacracy still looks like a hierarchy which emphasises the autonomy of its nodes aka circles/teams.

In Circles, such roles as "secretary", "lead link" and "rep link" are specified.

But such roles exist already in organizations. The "rep" (representatives) exist as PoCs (Points of Contact), even if not specifically mandated. The secretary is the working leader.

But is it really necessary to enforce these roles in practice? "Rep" roles, for instance, may and do often restrict the proper flow of information, communication and collaboration between circles and members.

On Holacracy, the organization paradigm (i)

https://it.toolbox.com/blogs/adriangrigoriu/on-holacracy-the-organization-paradigm-i-090915

Sept. 09, 2015

"A role is not a job description; its definition follows a clear format including a name, a purpose, optional "domains" to control, and accountabilities, which are ongoing activities to perform. Holacracy distinguishes between roles and the people who fill them, as one individual can hold multiple roles at any given time"

(Wikipedia).

Yet, what's new? Typically, all roles in an organization are defined around work items, deliverables, responsibilities, communications... rather than around people who fill them in. Hence, the role and the person are already separated to a large degree. In fact what is wrong with a job description (JD) that describes a role? True, many role JDs are poor, specified in a rather free format and incomplete at that.

Besides, the fact that people fill in several roles is not new even if the fact is not stated as such.

"Roles are defined by each circle —or team— via a collective governance process, and are updated regularly in order to adapt to the ever-evolving needs of the organization. Each circle uses a defined governance process to create and regularly update its own roles and policies" (Wikipedia).

Hence, the circle delegates and empowers the team members, most likely for a period of time, until a regular re-organization. But most enterprises do re-organize themselves and update their governance when necessary rather than on a regular basis. Holacracy though seems to wish to do so much more dynamically.

It is important to note now a key difference to traditional approaches. The "lead link", in this collective governance approach, is not, apparently, a manager role.

To the best of my understanding, there are no circle or team manager roles. All decisions are taken by the circle collectively.

Is then the circle working somehow like an Israeli kibbutzim collective farm?

Mandated collective decision making in a circle is, as such, a major variation from other governance and management approaches.

On the other hand, holacracy, how well does it work? We all know that decision makers, to escape accountability, often prefer to let committees, boards, teams take the decisions for them. But Holacracy proposes in fact responsibility without accountability because you cannot fine the whole group.

And, given the collective approach to management, who is held accountable for not delivering then?

On Holacracy, the organization paradigm (ii)

https://it.toolbox.com/blogs/adriangrigoriu/on-holacracy-the-organization-paradigm-ii-091915

Sept.1 9, 2015

"Holacracy specifies a tactical meeting process that every circle goes through usually on a weekly basis", Wikipedia.

That looks though more like a prescription of an agile software development process. Yet, should the meeting rules be prescribed to such a degree in the organization design principles?

That all being said, is Holacracy really another form of hierarchy? This statement from the Holacracy site says that *"Holacracy replaces the traditional hierarchy with a series of interconnected but autonomous teams ("circles")"* seems to contradict the previous findings that Holacracy is a holarchy which is a hierarchy.

The statement from the same site that *"distributed authority replaces delegated authority"* is hard to interpret too. After all, delegated may be distributed. Perhaps, it's too easy to interpret Holacracy, as convenient, in different or even opposite ways.

There are questions left though. For instance, given the autonomy of circles, would there be any shared enterprise support functions that circles would still depend upon such as IT, HR, Finance...? Is there a career path for people across circles?

What Holacracy seems to emphasise nevertheless, is that the team is collectively self managing and organizing, that is, if you ignore the roles already prescribed. That would enable initiative and innovation and motivate employees. Thus, the end justifies the means.

Perhaps, the aim of Holacracy is to make sure that teams (circles) have collective management and autonomy and are self organized. I many ways this paradigm reminds us a of services. This and the few specific "rep" roles specified in the Holacracy constitution are further implementing the rather more formalised interfacing mechanisms of services.

Yet Holacracy does look to me in some ways over specified, over-prescribed. Is it really part of an organizational design method to establish rules for meetings and "rep" roles?

Holacracy, as a whole, appears to me like seen through the looking glass of a team/circle member who is keen on autonomy, self determination but has little insight or even interest in the whole enterprise.

But I admit I have not read the book or the Holacracy constitution because Holacracy is not my primary objective here.

The Service Based Organization rather than Holacracy

https://it.toolbox.com/blogs/adriangrigoriu/the-service-based-organization-rather-than-holacracy-092015

Sept. 20, 2015

Holacracy looks like an Agile minded programmer's dream about the organization of a software development company. It has the feel if not the looks of Agile methods. To me though, Agile may work and render nimble rather small companies where everyone knows and trusts everyone.

For larger organizations where people did not grew up together, do not know each other by name, have various levels of skill or trust is in small supply, such Holacratic principles may not work at all.

Hence, while such autonomous type of organizations may ensure initiative and inner staff satisfaction, they may not exhibit enough transparency, synchronization and control mechanisms to assure the top management of large organizations of successful operation.

A hierarchical level could be added then to assume accountability and coordination of such autonomous units so that they work in synch to deliver to a common goal.

But, right, as with a Holacratic organization, complex organizations, to be effective, have to leave the organization and decision making to the right level, to the people in the know.

Whatever works best for the goal should be the choice, holacracy or not. For instance, an old hand in charge may streamline the process in comparison to the collective decision making because the majority choice are not always the best, as we all know.

Still, Holacratic Circles are not really autonomous entities since they may have dependencies, for instance, on enterprise support services such as procurement, recruitment, funding... that may obstruct their successful delivery and dilute their accountability.

Hence, we may have to push the autonomy even further.

The teams/circles have to be formally engaged through interfaces and contracts for deliveries that hide their organization and governance as opposed to Holacracy that specifies them in detail.

I would call this a Service Based Organization where the teams/circles deliver services under contracts.

Thus, we care no longer about team sizes, training budgets, recruitment... about circles/teams or Holacracy but about the service the entities deliver and the legal responsibility that comes with not delivering it on time, quality and budget.

The paradigm change is that the enterprise cares and pays for a service rather than the team/circle management that delivers it.

The Service Based Enterprise

https://it.toolbox.com/blogs/adriangrigoriu/the-service-based-enterprise-092415

Sept. 24, 2015

In a Service Based Enterprise, the organizational units would deliver well defined services to each other for which they would be eventually contractually bound. The enterprise would bother no more about the internal organization of the units or their inner governance as long as they do not impact the contractual bottom line.

The organization of the units/teams is in every unit's responsibility rather than enforced in detail as in Holacracy.

The units/teams/circles may be internal units but also companies in their own right, partnering with the enterprise to deliver the service.

The Service Based Enterprise ensures autonomy to the delivering units/teams, self organization, own decision making... all the nice principles of Holacracy but without its constraints. The units are mission driven to deliver.

To accomplish autonomy, the entities could be formally, if not legally separated from each other and from the enterprise. The separation should be formalised through as well defined interfaces, information contracts that establish deliverables, interactions and QoS.

This would reduce the endless discussions, tergiversations and eternal justifications between the departments of the enterprise.

By analogy, a Service Oriented Architecture often adopted in software today, proposes autonomous services that are deployed, discovered, catalogued, and may be replaced or modified independently as long as they are accessed over interfaces which are published and monitored against the quality of service delivered and specified in contracts.

But so are the functions of a Service Based Enterprise. A unit can be replaced as such at any time as long as it delivers the same service with similar interfaces. The unit delivering a Service can change its own technology and organization as long as it does not affect the outcome. All that matter is the specified delivery on time, budget and quality.

The organisation of a Service Based Enterprise

https://it.toolbox.com/blogs/adriangrigoriu/the-organisation-of-a-service-based-enterprise-092915

Sept. 29, 2015

Typically, enterprises are structured around a combination of function, product, location... criteria The usual enterprise representation is the organisation chart that says though so little about the enterprise, not even the products. Because most organizations have similar charts, no wonder, we cannot get much out of a chart.

Always the same, the Board, the CEO, COO, CFO, CTO, CIO, HR Director, VP of Strategy and their departments.

But true, we don't design much enterprises today. The construction of an enterprise is an organic process. We plan some, we build some then we grow the enterprise, we adapt it and specify a strategy that we rarely implement. More often than not, we re-structure the enterprise, in fact, mostly the people organisation.

Nevertheless, there is no real method to design the enterprise.

But how can we properly design an enterprise without Enterprise Architecture (EA), that is, without an Enterprise Model to show the logical structure of the enterprise, the interconnections, the material and information flows, the technology and networks, partners and suppliers...?

And how can we succeed in implementing the strategy when, rather than being mapped to the whole EA, the strategy is cascaded to the organisation chart, that is, only to a small part of EA, the people?

No matter how hard we try to implement the strategy, an obsolete or improper technology can hinder the efforts because, to a large degree, technology automates most functions and processes today.

Now, we discuss about the autonomy of teams, as in Holacracy, but, looking at the organisation chart, we have no idea what are the interactions and the dependencies on the rest of the enterprise described by an EA. That may render autonomy just sterile talk.

An Enterprise Architecture is a must for the change, re-organization and transformation of the enterprise.

A Service Based Enterprise organisation nevertheless would ensure that autonomy is real because a Service is delivered, in principle, by an "encapsulated" unit, reached only through agreed interfaces and protocols while the outcome and its QoS are formally contracted. The Enterprise, as the client of the service, does not need to know then about the internal organisation, governance, size, names and salaries of the team. In an Service Based Enterprise autonomy comes as such effortless.

How to re-organise the enterprise around services

https://it.toolbox.com/blogs/adriangrigoriu/how-to-re-organise-the-enterprise-around-services-100115

Oct. 01, 2015

To recap, autonomy empowers the enterprise departments to organise and govern themselves. Hence, an enterprise organised in autonomous units would promote motivation, stimulate initiative, manage resources and take ownership of the deliverables more responsibly. Holacracy is right about that.

But autonomy loses ground though with each dependency on the rest of the enterprise. Enterprise wide budgeting, planning, security policies, recruiting criteria, travel approval, working hours, technology choices... they may all constrain the unit's liberty of action. As autonomy diminishes so are its benefits.

A fully autonomous unit should have a minimum of ties with the enterprise, that is, essentially only a client-supplier relationship. That is, it should just provide a service to the enterprise for which it gets paid.

The enterprise should not concern itself with the unit's technology issues, headcount, costs, budget... No more cryptic explanations for delays in IT jargon. The cost to purchase, install, maintain, update, upgrade, customise a major IT system should be of no concern for the whole (service based) enterprise.

The enterprise pays for what it consumes, that is, for service usage.

The cost of the service may be higher though because the autonomous unit benefits no longer from the enterprise common shared services.

To develop the Service Based Organisation, we have to come with the current Enterprise Model first, i.e. a lean Enterprise Architecture that really covers the whole enterprise including business architecture and people organisation. We have to discover and document the present logical operation and structure, people organisation and roles, and the technology architecture.

Then, we have to design the target enterprise picture by specifying the atomic capabilities as services with interfaces. The good old Enterprise SOA approach helps.

To achieve autonomy, the business services that involve human operators, rather than being provided by the enterprise itself, could be outsourced to best of breed Business Process Outsourcing providers. Since more and more suppliers specialise in such services, they should offer a good QoS/cost ratio.

Services, such as SaaS, IaaS, PaaS, may be outsourced to the Cloud.

How to re-organise the enterprise around services (i)

https://it.toolbox.com/blogs/adriangrigoriu/how-to-re-organise-the-enterprise-around-services-i-100515

Oct. 05, 2015

There is no point in implementing all enterprise services ourselves when there are so many companies out there that do outsourcing as a business. They provide all such services as industrial design, manufacturing, sales, marketing, travel, reservations, payroll, recruiting...

We need to establish the services that are core to the business model, constitute a competitive advantage and, not least, are components of our strategic direction. But there is always a trade off between what we can do well and sufficiently cheap compared to what the market offers.

Choose what services you wish to keep in house to strengthen the core/strategic competencies and what you plan to outsource.

Specify services in collaboration with suppliers. Hence, do design from start your target enterprise services taking into account the offers available on the market.

Interfaces are key because they draw that boundary between the internal structure and operation and the "exterior" that ensures separation and as such, autonomy.

Ultimately, the success of the service based company comes from its capability to design the autonomous services, choose best of breed realisations and integrate and coordinate their operation as an effective value chain.

A service should be readily interchangeable even though, in practice, it is not that easy. The autonomy should work both ways, for both the enterprise and the service unit.

In order to minimise risks, do proper due diligence before engaging a company or Cloud service because it may ruin your Value Chain.

In the end, the enterprise, rather than own the organisational units delivering the services, may end up employing outsourced services from independent companies or a broker. The Services would become part of your Value Chain though. Because of that, strategic, long term, alliances are recommended.

The resulting enterprise, designed around services will be nimble, agile and lean and mean.

ON GARTNER'S EA HYPECYCLE , PREDICTIONS & EVENT DRIVEN STRATEGY

Gartner's 2010 EA hypecycle, a retrospective, definition

https://it.toolbox.com/blogs/adriangrigoriu/gartners-2010-ea-hypecycle-a-retrospective-defintion-090816

Sept. 08, 2016

Inhere I revisit Gartner's Enterprise Architecture hypecycle for... 2010 from my notes and this article, to find out what the EA world looked like, what were the predictions and what was achieved since then. Since the content at EA hypecycle on slideshare.net though has been removed, I do reuse my copy of that cycle. This will look a tad like a forensic examination.

In any case, best to start with the definition of EA.

In 2010 "Gartner defines EA as the process of translating business vision and strategy into effective organizational change by creating, communicating and improving the key requirements, principles and models that describe the organization's future state and enable its evolution".

Fast forward to 2016, Gartner's *Enterprise Architecture* (EA) is "*a discipline for proactively and holistically leading enterprise responses to disruptive forces by identifying and analysing the execution of change toward desired business vision and outcomes...*".

The wording has been turned around but, while in 2010 the priority was "translating business vision and strategy into effective organizational change", in 2016, it is "leading enterprise responses to disruptive forces by identifying and analysing the execution of change toward desired business vision".

Disruption rather than change, seems to be now the EA key reason to be. Still, disruption is still a change, a major unexpected change that may affect your business. And an EA key use is indeed to enable the transformation to vision. But "strategy" dropped from the definition.

The 2010 EA definition part about *"models that describe the organization's future state"*, which was relevant, has been left aside in 2016 though.

The modelling of the Current enterprise, the starting point for an enterprise modelling, is not mentioned either in 2010 or in 2016.

Who's going to do it then?

Hence, both definitions lack parts and may improve in clarity.

Because EA is, primarily, the discipline of modelling the enterprise, the EA deliverable is the Enterprise Blueprint.

But the EA can be used in many ways. For instance, EA may be used by employees to understand better the enterprise, to align terms and components, to set the context for solution architectures, to re-design the organisation chart, to identify capabilities, to effect change - from simple fixes to tactical change and enterprise transformations - to simplify the enterprise and to manage its complexity. Given the enterprise vision, strategy, goals... architects can model the future EA outlook.

And, if asked to, the EA team can indeed propose responses to disruptions, as per Gartner's definition.

Gartner's 2010 EA hypecycle, a retrospective (i)

https://it.toolbox.com/blogs/adriangrigoriu/gartners-2010-ea-hypecycle-a-retrospective-i-091016

Sept. 10, 2016

Gartner's Enterprise Architecture hypecycle for... 2010 from notes and this article (no longer available).

The message in 2010 was centred around an EA hypecycle with *"23 EA disciplines, practices and technologies"*. With so many EA "technologies", the field for Gartner looked positively teeming with activity.

To avoid confusion in the hypecycle, Gartner identified two generations of EA. The early one, the "technology EA" and the incoming "enterprise wide EA".

The "early-generation EA, situated on the right side of the Hype Cycle, is marked by long-standing and well-practiced approaches such as enterprise technology architecture (ETA)...".

Since neither in 2010 nor in 2016 architects use the same *"long-standing and well-practiced approaches"* for the IT EA, it's looks like each architect use their own mixture of experience and tools.

Yet, the EA technologies on the hypecycle, what happened to them?

"Visualisation, Simulation"

right at the beginning of the curve, is the first EA technology to climb the hypecycle. Visualisation progressed with tool technology but per ensemble it does not show us the enterprise top down from processes to resources, with end to end navigable processes.

It is still there on the hypecycle with regard to Simulation, at least.

"Hybrid Thinking" (HT)

was a way of merging design, marketing... and in general, the artistic, humanistic and technological thinking. Fashionable at the time.

The HT concept seems to be less used today, if at all. Design Thinking is still on though. The discipline advanced perhaps towards the end of the cycle, where is more mature, better understood, more used,

"Pattern based strategy"

is next on the curve. Not sure if it's a Gartner concept. By mapping patterns firms are able to model and predict trends before they happen. Only Gartner can tell how much it progressed or if it is employed at all. But I am sure it has nothing much to do with EA. Perhaps, it should have not been on the EA hypecycle in the first place.

Gartner's 2010 EA hypecycle, a retrospective (ii)

https://it.toolbox.com/blogs/adriangrigoriu/gartners-2010-ea-hypecycle-a-retrospective-ii-091216

Sept. 12, 2016

"Middle-out approach"

Gartner states that the "middle-out approach focuses on architecting interoperability by defining a small but rigidly enforced set of general, stable interface standards, while allowing complete autonomy of decision making for the specific technologies and products that are used within the solutions. This approach is highly suited for organisations and "business ecosystems," where the business units, partners, and suppliers are not under the direct control of a central EA team".

To me this appears like the revival of the good old SOA which was declared dead simply because it was confused for a software technology rather than the architectural style it is.

This approach advanced on the hypecycle past the trough of disappointment. Most probably because of the increasingly outsourced services and the advent of the Cloud which enforce interfaces and technology neutrality. That is an enterprise cares now more about the business service and its interface rather than about the technology behind it.

"Managed diversity":

With "managed diversity," "project teams can decide which product best fits the project needs, rather than having a single standard imposed on them" says Gartner. Best applied to the management of the many types of mobiles in the enterprise.

It may equally apply to anything. Diversity is always great. The problem is though the sharply increased cost of management - suppliers, stock, skills, compatibility, integration... The normal is to employ standards. Perhaps this should not have been on the hypecycle at all.

But "Gartner has further identified four basic approaches to EA - traditional, federated, middle out and managed diversity".

Anyway, these approaches seem to apply to any enterprise solution development. It appears that Gartner supports a mixture of many EA methods (managed diversity) which represents in fact the rather poor state of EA art rather than the ideal.

Most EA developments used volens nolens a mixture of EA approaches in 2010 and still use a mixture in 2016 in an artistically managed diversity. I'd prefer a framework that works.

"Enterprise solution architecture" and *"Enterprise information architecture"* disciplines have been happening for a long time now with or without EA, and independent of it.

But right, in my view as well, they are dependent on EA, if that's Gartner's angle. That is, they cannot progress without alignment or mapping to EA. For instance, a solution development should employ the same views as an EA. Perhaps because of this dependency they have not progressed on the hypecycle.

"EA governance"

It's just part of a process not really an EA discipline or approach.

It also depends on the specific the EA development method. There are though more general governance models like Agile that could be adopted in EA. Should this be on the hypecycle anyway?

"Business Capability Modelling" and "Enterprise Business Architecture"

They are elements or views and, respectively a layer of EA. A capability is represented as an EA view while the Business Architecture is the key layer of EA. Anyway, the business architecture lack of progress holds back the whole EA. Registered little progress on the hypecycle even though some Business Capabilities Maps appeared. But they look too much like the Business Process Maps we had for a long time now.

Gartner's 2010 EA hypecycle, a retrospective (iii)

https://it.toolbox.com/blogs/adriangrigoriu/gartners-2010-ea-hypecycle-a-retrospective-iii-091516

Sept. 15, 2016

"EA certification"

Since it's more like a service rather than a technology. Anyway, certification is mature but EA is not. With a disjoint body of knowledge and no two definitions alike, no EA efforts delivers comparable results. Hence, certification cannot guarantee EA but proficiency with a specific method. The TOGAF certified, for instance, would deliver TOGAF outcomes rather than EA.

Since, in the end, certification today does not guarantee the practitioner is able to deliver EA, it is an immature discipline so far.

"Business Driven Architecture"

It's just a principle, good practice... rather than a discipline or technology. Should not have been on the hypecycle at all, had you asked me.

 "EA Performance Management"

Performance management is general enough not be on the hypecycle.

Any development in the enterprise demands performance management as it needs governance. Once we define EA, have a proper process of development and utilisation, it will be hopefully clear what performance aspects and KPIs we have to measure.

It is at the top of the hypecycle curve though more in terms of the interest it raises rather than in terms of maturity.

Since we don't agree what is, we still don't know what EA performance covers, what its scope is... If it is about EA development progress, it depends on the approach process, team's capability and planning efficiency.

If it is about the value that EA returns, since EA enable many uses and each use may return value in different ways, we have to look first into the key uses of EA. Since this depends on the EA definition and intent, it is hard to quantify the EA performance which is at the peak of hype rather than delivery.

"EA frameworks"

is on the downside, falling quickly.

 We still go through the "winter of discontent" with them because each comes with own definition, frameworks are incomplete, fragmented, delivering at best their aim according to own definition etc.

"EA tools"

 at the "trough of disillusionment" in 2010.

How can they help though when we don't know what the overall deliverable is? They do provide though more advanced modelling, visualisation, reporting and planning capabilities.

What they do badly need though is the capability to easily configure any full blown EA framework and metamodel without costly tool development support. They'll stay in the trough for a while depending on the progression of the EA framework.

"Whole-of-Government"

EA is still at the long beginning that outlived a few presidencies already

Are there two government EAs that do look the same or have much in common?

I would say they are stagnant perhaps lacking that generic framework... The most advanced is DoDAF though, extended to NATO as well. It is still a bit too complicated, by design.

Gartner's 2010 EA hypecycle, a retrospective (iv)

https://it.toolbox.com/blogs/adriangrigoriu/gartners-2010-ea-hypecycle-a-retrospective-iv-091516

Sept. 15, 2016

"Enterprise Architecture"

itself, in the larger sense, appears, not surprisingly, at the bottom of hypecycle where it is in danger to stay until some true framework is agreed upon. Later on, on the hype flat, doing quite well in Gartner's view, is the "Traditional EA", IT I believe.

But since, after all, this EA consists of Information Architecture and Business Architecture which are placed on the climbing curve of the hypecycle, I believe that EA should be climbing on as well. But this being a hypecycle it shows , perception rather than progress or maturity.

"EA assurance"

Is climbing the plateau of productivity. When there are no two similar EA definitions, scope and frameworks quality assurance is indeed hyped. Also, if EA is made of so many "technologies" in different hypecycle phases how can the assurance be assured? I assume the assurance here is related to the traditional EA.

Federated EA"

seems to be doing well on the hypecycle. This was one of the ways of doing EA according to Gartner. It is natural though that the Business Units EAs be correlated, coordinated... There is no special discipline for that though, except the common framework indeed and its governance.

This particularly applies to the government approach which has to correlate many departments EA. A proper EA framework solves the issue.

Should not be a hypecycle technology in itself.

"Enterprise Technology Architecture"

seems to be productive already, according to the hypecycle. Technology denotes IT infrastructure, I guess, not just any technology. It is a sub-layer of the enterprise wide "traditional" EA. Not much progress though, even if there is a lot of hype, taking into account the increasing number of enterprise architects.

"Business Process Analysis"

at the hypecycle end, being productive. Nevertheless, not much to do with EA so far. It evolved independently. We may de-clutter the cycle by removing it.

Anyway has not made huge progress excepts that it tends to invade the Business Architecture space because the initials, BA, are the same.

We are at the end of the hypecycle. Let's recap Gartner's message of 2010: "As IT roles shift away from technology management to enterprise management, EA is suited to bring clarity to these blurred boundaries, and, by 2015, increased adoption of EA processes and uses by business will further IT's alignment with the organization's culture, future-state vision and delivery of business value outcomes..."

It ought to be so, yet it is not, not yet anyway.

"To prepare for 2015, EA practitioners need to ensure that EA practices are driven by a clear business vision and defined business context, and that their EA program has stabilized the practices and disciplines that are less than two years to mainstream adoption."

Had EA practices been driven by business vision, every enterprise would have own EA approach.

In reality, EA, once modelled and the governance established, should be used to support the implementation of the business vision an strategy to transform the enterprise, to evolve it according to principles as a whole, to fix the enterprise malfunctions, to understand it and communicate in same terms about the same things.

Gartner's 2010 EA hypecycle, a retrospective (v)

https://it.toolbox.com/blogs/adriangrigoriu/gartners-2010-ea-hypecycle-a-retrospective-v-091816

Sept. 18, 2016

Inhere I revisited Gartner's Enterprise Architecture hypecycle for... 2010 from my notes and this article (no longer available).

Some questions linger though. Why "EA governance" "EA Information Architecture"... are at the beginning of the cycle when "EA" itself is at the trough and "traditional EA" or Technology EA are nearly productive? Because the relationships between "technologies" or "disciplines" should be considered at the time of placing them on the hypecycle.

Perhaps, many should not have been on the EA hypecycle in the first place. Since EA covers the enterprise, many "technologies" could be perceived as related but they are just complementary.

Some are just principles or good practices, rather than technologies or disciplines..., such as Business Driven Architecture.

Some listed "technologies" such as Governance, Performance Management... are in fact common aspects of any development in the enterprise and only slightly related to EA.

Other are today rather self standing disciplines such as Information Architecture and Business Process Analysis. But since they are part of EA, in theory, would benefit from the EA modelling progress, rather than vice-versa.

Some "technologies" were not considered though like Archimate and Capabilities. Perhaps they were in their infancy in 2010.

The speed of technologies traversing the cycle appears very different though. As such, in a year's time some would get to maturity while some would still sulk at the beginning.

Technologies should not simple disappear from one hypecycle to another but exit at the trough.

There is still confusion if the cycle represents hype or maturity.

Anyway, EA "technologies" progress is hampered by the EA modelling lack of progress. And that partly because of the persisting disagreement on the EA definition and scope.

If we don't know what it is how can we model it, how can we govern and certificate it?

Yet, when even the EA standardisation and certification bodies are in business for themselves how can we expect EA for the masses of architects and enterprises.

"Overall, EA slipped into the Trough of Disillusionment, along with EA tools, because EA practitioners couldn't or wouldn't push EA efforts to become integrated with the business, drawing an invisible wall between the business and IT" said Mr. Allega in 2010.

This is still the case in 2016, even though efforts are made to promote TOGAF, Business Architecture and Capabilities.

Gartner's 2010 EA hypecycle (vi), outline

https://it.toolbox.com/blogs/adriangrigoriu/gartners-2010-ea-hypecycle-vi-outline-092016

Sep 20, 2016

In the end, the hypecycle turns out to be more of a Gartner's own perception of EA in that many "technologies" are really considered because Gartner thinks so rather than being really used or useful out there in the industry. But that's to be expected.

There were quite a few Gartner's promoted concepts at the beginning of the cycle that were not really mentioned by the EA community at the time or now. With concepts like "Patterns based Strategy", "Federated EA", "Managed Diversity" ... it looks like Gartner has almost created in 2010 an EA world of its own which did not eventuate. Many "technologies" rarely heard of today, if at all.

After all, this is a way to promote an EA view to make it happen. Gartner's

"Emergent EA", remember it?, was also lost in translation.

Perhaps, sticking to what everybody accepted would have been better.

Hence, all in all, the hypecycle illustrates a Gartner oriented view of EA which did not materialised. Technologies listed have not registered significant progress - partly because the EA modelling itself, has made little progress. But that is understandable when EA is more hype than reality. Organizations promote their own views competitively.

"We predict that by 2015, the marketplace of EA practitioners will find a landscape very different from today's environment," said Betsy Burton, research vice president and distinguished analyst at Gartner.

Well, not really. Same methods, same outcomes.

"The artificial walls between business and IT are crashing down, and EA is the bridge to integrate business and IT... by 2015, increased adoption of EA processes and uses by business will further IT's alignment with the organization's culture, future-state vision and delivery of business value outcomes" said Philip Allega, research vice president at Gartner.

Well, it's 2016 and the walls between business and IT haven't crashed yet and the EA processes and methods have not been adopted so far by the business.

Predictions were not fulfilled. After all the hypecycle was all about hype.

But EA is still in big demand, not only in concept but in practice. EA is not a hype. It started from IT because technology understands architecture. But the concept may return much more value at enterprise level.

What we still need is an EA framework that enables us all to understand what are the parts of an enterprise, how to model them, what are they key diagrams, modelling entities and relationships and how to fit them all in one whole navigable EA blueprint.

Then Information Architecture, EA governance, Business Process Analysis... will all find their place in the EA and will evolve in harmony to begin returning value at last.

Gartner's 2016 EA hypecycle in words (vii)

https://it.toolbox.com/blogs/adriangrigoriu/gartners-2016-ea-hypecycle-in-words-vii-092216

Sept. 22, 2016

Here is the textual description of Gartner's 2016 EA hypecycle

On the Rise:

Algorithmic business, The Economics of Connections, Economic Architecture, Human-Centered Design, Situationally Adaptive Behavior, Software-Defined Architecture, Business Ecosystem Modelling, Digital Ethics, API Marketplaces, API

Economy, Architecting Innovation, Design Thinking, Business Ecosystems, Platforms, Mobility Architecture

At the Peak

Customer Journey Analytics, Security Architecture, Application Architecture, Digital Business, IoT Architecture, Web-Scale Application Architecture, Workforce Planning and Modelling, IT/OT Architecture, Business Capability Modelling, Business Architecture , Information Architecture, Big Data Architecture, Cloud Computing Architecture, DevOps, EA Governance

Sliding Into the Trough

EA Certification, Solutions Architecture, Event-Driven Architecture, EA Frameworks

Climbing the Slope

Roadmaps, Enterprise Architecture Tools

Enterprise Architecture, Entering the Plateau, Web-Oriented Architecture

Suffice to say that few novelties have survived from 2010. But there are plenty of new ones.

I would not analyse each of the hypecycle "technologies" above at least because many don't seem to belong.

Significantly nevertheless, in 2016, no EA discipline entered the plateau of maturity except the Web Architecture which an enterprise development rather than Enterprise Architecture related one.

Obviously, EA has to take into consideration new enterprise technologies in the design of the target architecture. But new technologies, in particular in this digital era, should be separated from the EA discipline itself, which, essentially, is about modelling the enterprise and managing and using the EA model to serve all business stakeholders rather than inventory technologies.

A few key EA technologies are shown to slide Into the Trough: EA Certification, Solutions Architecture, Event-Driven Architecture, EA Frameworks. I doubt that in a few years they will succed to move past the trough.

It looks like key EA technologies are falling to the bottom of the disappointment trough. Not a good year for EA, 2016.

Solution Architecture though does well in practice and still lives happily ever after in my opinion, without EA.

Yet, the paradox is that Application Architecture, which often overlaps with Solution Architecture, is at the hypecycle Peak of Expectations.

"Business Capability Modelling, Business Architecture, Information Architecture" appear at the peak of hype, which I agree with but I would stress nonetheless that that does not mean maturity but the peak of marketing.

And Enterprise Architecture is still climbing the plateau. Let's hope it does not fall back in the trough like the boulder of Sisyphus.

One may ask though how can EA climb the plateau ahead of its key technologies such as EA frameworks...? But in the hypecycle that does not impede other EA related technologies prosper.

Gartner's 2016 EA hypecycle (viii)

https://it.toolbox.com/blogs/adriangrigoriu/gartners-2016-ea-hypecycle-viii-092416

Sept. 24, 2016

From *Gartner's 2016 EA hypecycle*

Some technologies in the hypecycle like *Design Thinking* and *Human Centric Design* are similar in intention, if not the same, but perhaps coming from different backgrounds. Anyway, they are not part of EA even if they may add to the EA good practices and architecture and design principles.

Mobility and *Big Data, Customer Journey Analytics, IoT, IT/OT are all* part of "Digital Business" evolution which is listed as well. Yet Digital Business is the outcome rather than a technology. It should not be in the hypecycle as such.

Like in the 2010 hypecycle, many technologies in the hypecycle do affect the enterprise but not its modelling and EA mode d'emploi. Since this is not an Digital Technologies hypecycle for the enterprise, these "technologies" should not be included in this EA hypecycle.

But let me comment of a few technologies:

Algorithmic business, the use of mathematical algorithms to improve process automation and business decisions. It looks so far off. It's not even AI which is based most on learning from practice. Well, the enterprise is not yet a self driving enterprise.

The Economics of Connections is more of a requirement from the Digital evolution to accommodate a multitude of connections to things, systems, economic agents. It happens anyway, perhaps under different names or no name at all, but, while it will be reflected in the EA blueprint, it is not an EA technology but, at best, an Enterprise technology, if not only a simple fact of life.

Economic Architecture, the concept to model the key markets, exchanges and institutions of an economy, the same EA does for the enterprise. It would be useful once we have a clear method to model a system, end to end.

Human-Centered Design (**HCD**) is a design that considers the human perspective in all steps of the problem-solving process. EA does not solve problems except, perhaps, the architecture debt, if required to.

Situationally Adaptive Behavior... self explaining

Software-Defined Architecture Application Design for Digital Business addressed by

SOA yet again. Applies to applications design rather than the enterprise

Business Ecosystem Modelling, applies to the strategy field rather than EA but from a modelling point of view it makes sense though.

Digital Ethics... may add to the design principles embedded in the enterprise decision making systems

In essence, the cycle, in classifying digital technologies, illustrates a mixture of hype and reality that leaves you kind of wondering which is the case: hype or maturity of a technology.

As stated already, many technologies affect the enterprise rather than EA, the approach to model the enterprise. Some of them address the greater economy modelling issue, not in scope of EA.

I, for one, would have stressed the enterprise modelling technology and tools, architecture languages, metamodels, generic enterprise models, business models, capability evolution and maps.... But I am no Gartner.

Another question is how much can we rely on such hype forecast in this quick changing technology landscape? Or perhaps, it is all hype as the name denotes.

And after all, what does Gartner quantify in the cycle: the hype itself, which maybe the result of marketing or the maturity of technologies?

Also, at first sight, there is little continuity between the yearly hypecycles.

In the end, it is not clear if Gartner stimulates the hype around some technologies or simply evaluates it. Perhaps both.

Besides how to use this hypecycle if it's mainly about hype rather than objective progress and use of EA enhancing technologies?

Talents for a Successful EA, from 'Smarter with Gartner'

https://it.toolbox.com/blogs/adriangrigoriu/talents-for-a-successful-ea-from-gartner-032518

March 25, 2018

From "Smarter with Gartner" where "Enterprise architects find answers to what keeps you up at night", sounds like vintage Gartner.

Here is what Christy Pettey says in 5 Talents Needed for a Successful Enterprise Architecture Team.

"Organizations no longer want their enterprise architecture (EA) practice to be focused on standards, structure and control," says Marcus Blosch, research vice president at Gartner.

I agree, it looks like giving up what we could not achieve may sound like a safe policy today. Anyhow, talking about the EA role, skills, organisation, collaboration, strategy and practices..., in the absence of the EA structure and blueprint the enterprise still expects, seems to be the best practice nowadays. As if EA modelling... has been all done and dusted. The reality is though that today, EA is still anchored in IT. But we talk about it as if it has already crossed the divide into business.

It is said here that EA has to be driven by business outcomes. It was said before. Yet, with EA meaning all things to all people, every interpretation is possible. Anyhow, that sounds wrong to me because the EA outcome is, essentially, the blueprint of the enterprise. The enterprise is discovered and documented with no business outcome in mind. But the EA model is indeed used by stakeholders to drive their own business outcomes.

But, on the whole, rather than specific business outcomes, EA enables complexity management and as such process efficiencies and cost savings and renders the enterprise agile to change.

The five EA talents according to Christy Pettey:

A talent for developing business strategy

"Successful EA teams will develop business architecture skills that can model their organization's strategy, goals, and business and operating models in detail, as well as tracking innovative technologies and business models," says Blosch.

EAs may be required indeed to come with the IT strategy today and, indeed, "can help, bringing together an understanding of the organization's strategy and business model with the opportunities of digital".

But, until EAs are able to deliver the EA model, rather than papers about what EA is, and until EAs are called to cover the entire enterprise rather than IT alone, such a business strategy talent would be hardly in demand today. In fact, it may invite questions about the role of EA and may even spread confusion because EA would be stepping in territories closely held now.

Talents for a Successful EA, Smarter with Gartner (i)

https://it.toolbox.com/blogs/adriangrigoriu/talents-for-a-successful-ea-smarter-with-gartner-i-032918

March 28, 2018

From "Smarter with Gartner" where "Enterprise architects find answers to what keeps you up at night"!

Vintage Gartner!

Here is what Christy Pettey says in *5 Talents Needed for a Successful Enterprise Architecture Team*

from Talents for a Successful EA, Smarter with Gartner

"A talent for designing new services and experiences"

This is not really an EA talent or task. Design thinking aims to improve the customer experience in the interaction with the enterprise, more like ergonomics targeted the improvement of workers interaction with the work environment. The Design Thinking (DT) task would be to optimize customers processes, user interface and interactions rather than model the current EA landscape or design the target architecture of the enterprise. DT is also more optimization than design. As such, Design Thinking team should be separate from EA.

In addition, the new services design is typically performed by Product Management rather than EA architects. The new service development follows its own process (NPD: New Product Development) in the enterprise and is manned by NPD teams rather than by Design Thinking. The NPD is though different from Design Thinking. NPD specializes in business process flows while DT in optimizing the customer interaction with such processes. The EA team just makes sure the work of the new service development and Design Thinking teams aligns to and fits in the EA picture but EA does not do the NPD or DT jobs. As such, EAs do not need specific skills in this respect.

Naturally, EAs must have an extensive knowledge of the enterprise but the EA architect is not though the enterprise factotum.

"A talent for innovation"

"EA and technology innovation leaders should focus on business strategy, innovation and collaboration..."

"Enterprise architects can drive this process by tracking innovative technologies, services and business models and creating a Hype Cycle for their organization".

The idea that *"innovation leaders should focus on... innovation"* is... precious. Innovation is not even a natural talent of an architect whose strength is the structured rather than the creative thinking.

A separate emerging technology team, working with the EA as well as with marketing, departments etc, may solve the issue though. Innovation is a full time job. EA is a full time job too.

Adding Business Strategy, Design Thinking, New Service Development and Innovation to the EA tasks only prepares EA for more failure.

EAs should focus on EA, yet to be delivered today, rather than anything but EA.

Talents for a Successful EA, from Smarter with Gartner (ii)

https://it.toolbox.com/blogs/adriangrigoriu/talents-for-a-successful-ea-from-smarter-with-gartner-ii-032718

March 27, 2018

From " Smarter with Gartner" where "Enterprise architects find answers to what keeps you up at night"! Vintage Gartner!

Here is what Christy Pettey says in *5 Talents Needed for a Successful Enterprise Architecture Team*

"A talent for orchestrating collaboration across the organization"

"In reality, architecture is 90% people and 10% architecture" Blosch says.

To me, it's more like 90% of EA efforts deliver just 10% architecture. The remaining 90% is perhaps communications, collaborations, chats, coffee time… In any case, any office work has a natural overhead. But when the overhead reaches as high as 90% perhaps it's time to ask questions. If I were the CFO, I'd ask what the Return on EA (RoEA) looks like.

Perhaps the architects should let the results, i.e. EA model, market itself rather than spending 90% of the time marketing EA…

We keep hearing that EA is all about people or it is all about communications, strategy… Yet, architecture is just architecture as the names says, not anything but architecture. But, since architecture modelling proves to be the hardest part, people do reinvent the term architecture. Sure, people, communications, strategy… have all a role to play but still, architecture is still architecture, that is a blueprint of nodes in interconnections.

And, since the full EA is ultimately delivered by stakeholders rather than EAs, with each stakeholder modelling own part, the EA role is "coordination" rather than "orchestrated collaboration". The term "orchestrated collaboration" sounds more like a half hearted attempt at saying coordination to me. That is because the EA architect today has little authority. The future of the enterprise depends on his power of influencing.

EA is too often advertised as the EA people connecting the enterprise, perhaps because EA, more often than not, is interpreted as activities rather than deliveries.

And too often EA delivers to TOGAF specs rather than the promised EA model. But had the EA people delivered the enterprise model, this would constitute the common repository, standards, blueprint, vocabulary, language… that enables the touted collaboration in the enterprise.

Talents for a Successful EA, Smarter with Gartner (iii)

https://it.toolbox.com/blogs/adriangrigoriu/talents-for-a-successful-ea-smarter-with-gartner-iii-033018

March 30, 2018

From " Smarter with Gartner" where "Enterprise architects find answers to what keeps you up at night"!   Vintage Gartner!

Here is what Christy Pettey says in *5 Talents Needed for a Successful Enterprise Architecture Team*

"A talent for navigating to the future"

It is hardly the EA job description today to *"develop a vision for the future, the business and the people, working practices..."*. For that there is the business strategy team.

Yet, in a brave new world, the EA may have to be called upon to come with the enterprise vision. For now though, the main task of EA is to discover and model the current structure and design the target blueprints of the enterprise at various future stages.

And, indeed, the EA job description specifies the review of solution architectures and elaboration of architecture standards, technology selection guidelines, the enterprise transformation roadmap and indeed enterprise change and transformation support. In any case, how could EA elaborate the business vision, strategy, innovation... when EAs today work still deep down in the IT weeds, trying to sort out the spaghetti like architecture?

Blosch says that "successful EA teams will develop business architecture skills that can model their organization's strategy, goals, and business and operating models in detail, as well as tracking innovative technologies and business models". Yet, EA teams should not have to develop business architecture skills, they should already posses such skills, by definition. How else can one do EA today?

With the exquisite "set of talents" recommended here, the EA architect would deserve to be nominated in a top position in order to be able to accomplish the mission of EA, the modelling of the enterprise, and integrate solutions architectures, business strategy, design thinking and UX design, new product development, digital evolution and innovation... in EA and the enterprise transformation.

Gartner's event driven business strategy, the 'secret sauce...'

https://it.toolbox.com/blogs/adriangrigoriu/gartners-event-driven-business-strategy-the-secret-sauce-110617

Nov. 06, 2017

CIOs must define an event-centric digital business strategy says Gartner in the title of its article. In the subtitle, Gartner emphasises though *Event Driven Architecture (EDA), to quote: "Event-driven architecture will become an essential skill in supporting digital business transformation by 2018"*.

The article continues then talking about "event driven application software": "Achieving broad competence in event-driven IT will be a top three priority for the majority of global enterprise CIOs by 2020, according to Gartner, Inc. Defining an event-centric digital business strategy will be key to delivering on the growth agenda that many CEOs see as their highest business priority...

"Event Driven Architecture (EDA) is a key technology approach to delivering this goal," said *Anne Thomas*, vice president and distinguished analyst at Gartner.

"Digital business demands a rapid response to events. Organisations must be able to respond to and take advantage of '*business moments*' and these real-time requirements are driving CIOs to make their application software more event-driven.""

To begin by defining the term, an event driven paradigm emphasises rapid response, real time, as opposed to polling for changes, for instance. It is a nice to have but like anything good in life, it costs.

But Gartner refers to "Event Driven Architecture" (EDA), event driven business strategy, event driven IT and event driven application software which paradigms are very different since they apply to different disciplines, like architecture, strategy, IT and software, each with its own ways and purpose to implement the event driven paradigm.

This lack of distinction may stir confusion because addressed are different audiences, different mechanisms and different outcomes.

Once again, while "event driven" is constant, the approaches are different because they apply to different enterprise domains such as "Business Strategy", "Architecture", "IT" and "Application Software" each with its type of events. That is, the events that Strategy, Architecture, IT and Application respond to are totally different in nature. The outcomes are too.

An event driven business strategy changes direction as events in the surrounding environment take place. For instance, market events. Events are likely to be processed by people, rather slowly at that.

In an event driven architecture, the enterprise architecture functions must respond to events generated by other nodes or external conditions in real time.

An event driven IT, limited to the IT technology or department, responds to events such as defects, requests for support, support calls, server generated signals (not enough memory...). Like above, events would be responded to by people and technology.

An Application may be driven by events coming from other software modules. The events are processed fully automatically in this case.

Which one is the "secret sauce" of Digital success?

Gartner's event driven business strategy, the 'secret sauce' for success...(i)

https://it.toolbox.com/blogs/adriangrigoriu/gartners-event-driven-business-strategy-the-secret-sauce-for-success-in-the-digital-era-i-110717

Nov. 07, 2017

CIOs must define an event-centric digital business strategy says Gartner in the title of this article...

Our journey to understanding Gartner's event driven world continues.

"A convergence of events generates a business opportunity, and real-time analytics of those events, as well as current data and wider context data, can be used to influence a decision and generate a successful business outcome".

Gartner also defines Business Moments: *"a business moment exploits the connection of people, business and things and allows companies to innovate for entirely new scenarios."*

If not sure what that is, Gartner offers an example. In "Business Moments", "Smarter with Gartner" talks about a household IoT alarm that alerts Mom, the custodian of our home.

But this sounds more like a Mom rather than business moment.

Not sure where Gartner goes with that. But it looks to me that they think that one or more "events", analysed in real time, may reveal business opportunities to put it in English. Yet, I thought we already knew and do that, even if not in real time.

Gartner states indeed that: "This is why digital business is so dependent on EDA. The events generated by systems — customers, things and artificial intelligence (AI) — must be digitised so that they can be recognised and processed in real time", states Gartner in the end.

To me though the problem is not so much the real time processing because it is

the people and their culture that usually stall developments taking forever to make a decision, but the correlation and collective interpretation of events which require more than an AI engine to be able to phrase business opportunities and actions. Perhaps, that will happen later, much, much later when the Market, Competition, Applications, IT, Architecture, AI... events will be all funnelled into a future enterprise intelligence engine which will generate a list of business opportunities while we linger by the coffee machine.

Gartner concludes: "EDA will become an essential skill in supporting the transformation by 2018, meaning that application architecture and development teams must develop EDA competency now to prepare for next year's needs".

Hence, Gartner talks about a real time, event driven enterprise where every tier of an enterprise ecosystem (market, external stakeholders, people, technology and processes) may generate events that are correlated, interpreted and processed by the enterprise intelligence engine to generate a list of actions and opportunities for us to follow up or, ... even act on them.

But really what we'd like now in more pragmatic terms, is a more responsive enterprise, prepared for the Digital change. For that we need to model the Enterprise Architecture and act to streamline it. Once this is done, we can discuss change as a result of various events, we can animate the model and play with it.

What Gartner wills is an agile Enterprise that would render our Enterprise nimble to evolve to the All Digital future.

Gartner's predictions for 2018 and beyond (i)

https://it.toolbox.com/blogs/adriangrigoriu/gartners-predictions-for-next-year-and-beyond-i-111117

Nov. 11, 2017

Gartner Top Strategic Predictions for 2018 and Beyond.

Here they are, commented. But to me they sound like the de facto situation of today.

1. Consumers Favor Visual and Voice Search

That was on the cards for a some time now with the constant but slow progress of speech and image recognition based on AI. I doubt though that they would replace the textual search given the state of AI neural networks today. It applies mainly to households rather any other market.

2. Digital Giants Self-Disrupt

This looks like business as usual dilemma of innovative companies but, true, in particular now, given the growing pace of digital change. But no "giants" would disrupt their own business unless they have a good business case or the competition overtakes them.

3. Blockchain taking over

That sounds pretty obvious to anyone who reads the news today. Hard to miss a "prediction" like that.

4. Increased Fake News

If no legislation is passed to stop the fake news proliferation, that may be turn very damaging to individuals, businesses and nations because fake news may have grave consequences such as changing elections outcomes. Failure to regulate them would be catastrophic. Too often fake news are published with a financial gain or revenge aim in mind in order to hurt another party. Tolerance now may give birth to monsters later. If I were Gartner, I would lobby governments to initiate serious work in this sense because social media "giants" stall the issue for fear of increasing costs.

5. Counterfeit Reality Overtakes Reality

"Counterfeit reality is digital media manipulated to portray events that never occurred or did not occur in the manner in which they are presented". That is actually fake news, as above. Yet, I believe that Gartner's business is to predict how AI would evolve to counteract this trend rather state a trend we all know. What worries me most is the lack of original content in our daily articles, papers, presentations which add nothing new but keep drumming and speculating about non-issues. That is what I might call "fake presentations, papers" that seem to increasingly take over our professional media.

6.- Bots Take Over

"By 2021, more than 50% of enterprises will spend more per annum on bots and chatbot creation than traditional mobile app development". Not sure how can one compare the two domains though, that is bots and mobile applications. Bots are applications which automate actions on the web otherwise executed by humans. Chatbots exhibit too verbal interaction with humans by employing AI technology. Examples are Siri, Alexa and Cortana which, I have to say, I avoid at all costs. But even so, why wouldn't we need mobile applications no more? Perhaps many applications would include voice interaction but that does not make them bots. Yet, as the bots are taking over, they are increasingly pestering the Internet attempting to access various sites as if they are human. That is why anti-bot systems are put in place. To be recognised as humans, we have to enter various recognition patterns when logging into a site.

"Post-Application era" sounds grand but more like a film about the end of the world, with (ro)bots having taken over. Perhaps Gartner should have made a few precious predictions about the evolution of the AI technology that mans the bots. As for instance, when would we be able to understand how a neural network based AI works?

7.- Versatility Wins Over Specialization

"By 2021, 40% of IT staff will be "versatilists" holding multiple roles, most of which will be business- rather than technology-related". That is so... to a degree.

The reason "versatilists"(?) take over from specialists is that technology is being increasingly outsourced to the Cloud. Anyway, few enterprises can still manage properly the growing complexity of technology today. Hence technology is outsourced "As a Service". Consequently, technologists move out into specialised enterprises that deliver IT and business services based on technology. While we will need IT and IT people in the enterprise no more, we'll need architects, strategists... to integrate and roadmap services. Thus, we'll need no more technology specialists but generalists who understand both the potential of technology and the business. While there would be more technologists in the companies offering technology services, their number would be smaller than that of the IT specialists present in the every enterprise today.

But, as always, as complexity in a domain grows, new specialised disciplines and organisations appear to cope with that. That is how, historically, the trade guilds have been created.

Gartner's predictions for next year and beyond (ii)

https://it.toolbox.com/blogs/adriangrigoriu/gartners-predictions-for-next-year-and-beyond-ii-111217

Nov. 12, 2017

8.- AI Creates More Jobs Than It Takes

It is a documented fact that technology evolution renders obsolete some jobs while creating new ones. But the newly created *"AI-related jobs"* must be further clarified because it has little meaning and as such it is hard to quantify.

Related jobs might mean jobs for developers of applications that employ AI technology as for instance medical diagnostics, financial advising, weather forecasts, self driving and flying things... to name the known few.

On the whole though, since a single application can replace tens of thousands of jobs at least, I do not believe that AI creates more jobs than it renders obsolete.

9.- IoT in Everything

Everybody talks about IoT today. No wonder because IoT is about digitisation of all things around so that we can monitor and control them on our body, at home, in the office, in factories, in town and in nature. Our cars seem to have tens if not hundreds of digital chips today. IoT spread is explained by the gains in processors power and miniaturisation and the ubiquity of wireless networks. The prediction is true but evident to everybody.

10.- Assume IoT Security Vulnerabilities

Perhaps this point here was just added to round the count to ten. IoT security should have been included in the point above because it tends to slow down the IoT adoption in "Everything". Because ,without security, IoT is simply dangerous.

Hence, what Gartner should have quantified is the increasing threat presented by IoT, in the absence of a security framework. That is because, in an IoT dominated world, an entity can remotely take control of the digital world around us - be it home, car, office, street...- and turn it against us. Hackers can track us using the street CCTV, lock us out of our house, take over our cars while cruising, light fires and provoke explosions by tinkering with our gas, heating and electrical systems and spy on us over our phone, TV connections with *predictable* consequences.

Most predictions above, such as blockchain, IoT, chatbots, AI... are already receiving the due attention in the daily press. Nothing much to predict because these things happen.

I would have expected Gartner though, as the top high technology analytics consultancy, to come with forecasts with respect to such domains as the new brave world of Everything as a Service, new business models enabled by the Digital (like sharing), the evolution of data centres or the enterprise to virtual, social media in the office, fintech, transportation...

Gartner predicts that EA will focus on Digital platforms

https://it.toolbox.com/blogs/adriangrigoriu/gartner-predicts-that-enterprise-architecture-will-focus-on-digital-platforms-040717

April 07, 2017

Gartner: "Digital is transforming organizations and EA itself, with digital business platforms emerging as a powerful approach to innovation. EA and technology innovation leaders are promoting these efforts, providing the skills and competencies needed to support innovation and architect the digital platform".

Yes, Digital is doing that, that is transforming the enterprise. But, this "digital business platform", what is it? An explanation is owed here.

To find out, Gartner recommends the purchase of this document for half a grand. In search of a cheaper answer, I found this from Gartner *How to Build a Digital Business Technology Platform*.

Quote:

"This report details how CIOs and IT leaders can use the five major platforms required to enable the new capabilities and business models of digital business.

- The Information Systems Platform

- The Customer Experience Platform

- The IoT Platform

- The Ecosystems Platform

- The Data and Analytics Platform

- The Complete Digital Business Technology Platform"

Well it appears that, in Gartner's vision, the enterprise can be partitioned in "platforms" we should focus on to succeed in the Digital transformation. Respectively, a "platform" for Information, one for Data and Analytics, another for Customer Experience, IoT...

But these "platforms" look like top level topics that the Enterprise Architect and Business should cover in order to organise their thinking around the impacts of the Digital evolution.

Translated in domestic terms, so we can understand one another, it looks like this list of five (I counted six though, perhaps the last one is not a platform after all) focus categories: Information, Analytics, Customer Experience, IoT, Ecosystems and Business Systems.

So far, so good. But so what?

In the digital enterprise transformation, the information, customer access, business systems would be all affected indeed.... Still, we are already aware of that. Yet, perhaps the art of stating that in new ways helps.

Problem is that we are talking about rather abstract groupings of functions or topics that do not easily map on systems. Take, for instance, the Information, IoT... present almost anywhere.

Yet, we have never called them platforms, perhaps because a platform denotes something like a framework supporting something else rather than a general topic as above.

Still, these general "platforms" are meant to draw our attention to the impact the digital transformation may have on such things like Information, Customer experience, Business Systems...

To recap in a different way, Gartner's "platforms" are neither nodes of an architecture nor technologies platforms per se but, perhaps, a top level tick list for checking the impact of Digital on the enterprise transformation.

Gartner predicts that BA will focus on Digital Platforms (i)

https://it.toolbox.com/blogs/adriangrigoriu/gartner-predicts-that-business-architecture-will-focus-on-digital-platforms-i-040817

April 08, 2017

Gartner predicts that Enterprise Architecture will focus on Digital platforms

Gartner says that by 2018, half of EA business architecture initiatives will focus on defining and enabling digital business platform strategies:

"We've always said that business architecture is a required and integral part of EA efforts," said Betsy Burton, vice president and distinguished analyst at Gartner.

Right, Business Architecture is a part of EA. Fortunately, we knew that for some time.

"...The increasing focus of EA practitioners and CIOs on their business ecosystems will drive organisations further toward supporting and integrating business architecture...

This is to ensure that investments support a business ecosystem strategy that involves customers, partners, organisations and technology... On average, the number of ecosystem partners they had two years ago was 22... two years from now, Gartner estimates that it will have risen to 86."

If you couldn't quite follow that, don't blame yourself.

I would sum it up though, to the best of my understanding, with the following: Business Architecture is found increasingly relevant, given the soaring number of partners in the business ecosystem.

My view has always been that without Business Architecture you cannot really shape the IT architecture. But today, Business Architecture is becoming increasingly important since the role of IT architecture is diminishing, with the technology moving outside the enterprise, to the Cloud.

With the digital progress, the enterprise IT is increasingly virtualised (IaaS, SaaS..., SDDC). Also, with the advent of microservices and the API economy, services make inroads in the enterprise.

These developments make possible the outsourcing of IT to the Cloud and of Business Processes to partners, in a BPO manner (i.e. related Process, Technology and People). Take for instance HR functions such as Recruitment, Expenses...

Consequently, the Value Chain is virtualised as we speak since its links are outsourced. Sourcing, Distribution, Marketing... are outsourced today to specialised partners.

While it coordinates the overall Value Chain, the enterprise may not own the individual value chain links any longer, as it did in the past.

Since IT and business processes are going to be further outsourced to third parties, the most relevant part of the Enterprise Architecture becomes indeed the Business Architecture that describes the enterprise independently of implementation technology and business function ownership.

Hence, with the progress of Digital, what matters in the end is the Business Architecture layer of EA because the Digital technology and Business Processes are increasingly outsourced to partners in a providers Cloud and, as such, they are no longer a matter of concern to the enterprise.

The paradox is that the more the Digital technologies progress, the less are we concerned about technology because Technology is moving into the Cloud.

While Digital brings new complexity, it also removes technology outside the enterprise to the care of partners, streamlining as such the enterprise management.

See article that outlined the trend a while ago and called it The Cloud Enterprise.

But, to be clear, today we still have technology in-house and "hybrid clouds". That is, we still own and manage technology in the enterprise.

ON MCKINSEY'S EA, DIGITAL TRANSFORMATION AND "TWO SPEED IT"

McKinsey's practical ideas for managing EA

https://it.toolbox.com/blogs/adriangrigoriu/mckinseys-practical-ideas-for-managing-ea-120615

Dec. 06, 2015

McKinsey's published its Ten practical ideas for organizing and managing your enterprise architecture

 Perhaps, the article should have started though with a definition of what EA means for different organisations and what are its methods and activities in practice. Because different approaches have different management criteria. And there are so many different EA development approaches, never mind "EA management", whatever that is.

 Comments point by point:

 "1. The organization of enterprise architecture should reflect the organization of the business"

If this is about EA structure and Organisation chart it is true. Otherwise

 "2. The company should be clear about who is accountable for EA decisions"

Specific rather than diffused or committee accountability is a governance principle that applies anytime, anywhere and not only to EA. Such a lack of accountability was shown in our major banks that rigged the interbank rates, the exchange rates and... while the scapegoats were constantly a few mid level employees empowered, perhaps, for that very reason.

#2 is yeah, sure we know it already but it is hard to realise in practice...

 "3. The EA department should collaborate closely with the business and the IT organization"

That goes without saying. Perhaps the item was added just to make the count of ten.

#3 is unattainable as long as there is nothing in EA for the business or even for the rest of IT.

McKinsey's practical ideas for managing EA (i)

https://it.toolbox.com/blogs/adriangrigoriu/mckinseys-practical-ideas-for-managing-ea-i-120715

Dec. 07, 2015

"4. The EA department should keep strategy-related tasks separate from operational ones"

That's a given in most companies. Anyway, EA does not or should not really have operational tasks. But in practice, EA members plug anywhere they can, projects for instance, to justify the existence of their function.

EA does operate an Architecture board and reviews solution projects but that's it, in terms of operations.

#4 is right, EA does not/should not have operational tasks.

"5. The company should give the EA department approval rights"

"for instance, approving new IT-related projects or changes to the technology landscape".

EA does approve architecture developments in the ARB (Architecture Review Board). This approval is an input to a more Business oriented change board that sanctions the IT budget as well.

The final outcome, the decision, depends very much on the EA reputation though.

But I don't think a technical IT EA can or should approve budget for projects. Moreover, developments should be prioritised, roadmapped and planned at the enterprise level rather than approved by IT departments like EA.

EA should enable good governance/decisions of the organisation through principles, standards, roadmaps and EA artefacts, commonly employed, such as EA blueprints.

While EA is involved and should produce guidelines for the decision process, it should not make decisions on behalf of the business.

 #5 EA, definitely, should not have, in my opinion, this responsibility of approving business developments.

"6. The company should keep accountability for elements of the enterprise architecture in one group"

This is right. Still, EA is very much about the agreed governance (principles...) it puts in place, rather than through its team members opinions.

#6 is right and evident.

"7. The company should analyse and measure the effects of enterprise architecture on the business"

A common sense point made long ago. After all, what you cannot measure, you cannot control or improve for that matter.

But measurements could be performed by key architecture indicators only if the EA delivers what it is suppose to, the organisation blueprints, architecture principles, checkpoints etc. and the outcomes are currently in wide spread use.

Rather than creating a pilot, apply the metrics for the pilot to the key developments.

Any evaluation is rather ballpark indeed, either a kind of opportunity lost analysis, what would have happened if we did not have EA or, business case like, done beforehand, like what would be the benefits if we have EA.

#7 definitely yes, but ball park, and not through a pilot evaluation but with metrics applied to key developments.

McKinsey's practical ideas for managing EA (ii)

https://it.toolbox.com/blogs/adriangrigoriu/mckinseys-practical-ideas-for-managing-ea-ii-120815

Dec. 08, 2015

"8. The EA department should keep it simple"

Just try to explain TOGAF to the Board or show them an Archimate diagram. It would be jolly good to watch.

Yes, the EA team should keep it clear rather than simple, first in their practice and then in communications.

Simple does not equal Clear. KISS (Keep it Simple, Stupid) should be KIC(lear)S, in fact, because the opposite of simple is complicate, which is an objective state of a system you can do only so much about, while of clear is confuse, which is a state of mind.

#8 Keep it Clear would be the good practice.

"9. The company should use one tool to rule all elements of the architecture"

That's right. But honestly, just a few would utilise that tool which is too IT oriented, never mind so expensive. Most will visualise the outcomes generated on the Intranet.

#9 straightforward for IT, but start with a free one to find out, first hand, what you are after. Otherwise you may end up paying the dear license fees per user when you barely use the tool.

"10. The company should invest in EA leaders"

A good piece of advice, like most others, which applies to any company, any situation..., including McKinsey's own. The definition of the leader is worth further refining though. Perhaps, a can do person, a professional with charisma.

Otherwise, we may end up with another survey on what an EA leader is.

#10 yeah, we kind of always end up with that.

It happens too often that analyst companies conceal their views or lack of thereof behind executive surveys.

But one can hardly trust the results of a survey if, in the first place, no interviewee uses the same definition and deliverables of the discipline, EA in our case. The survey assumes that EA is an established discipline and practice that consistently returns value. That's not the case today.

McKinsey's nine questions for the digital transformation

https://it.toolbox.com/blogs/adriangrigoriu/mckinseys-nine-questions-for-the-digital-transformation-how-relevant-are-they-030316

March 03, 2016

Here is a McKinsey's (MK) article on the "Nine questions to help you get your digital transformation right".

To quote, "corporate leaders understand the need to raise their Digital Quotient, but many are struggling with how to do it."

Right. Now, the nine questions and my comments:

"How well do you know where change is occurring?"

McKinsey suggests that "leaders review the new frontiers where big changes are happening, the core elements of the business affected by change, and the foundations needed to support the change (Exhibit 1)".

While, "exhibit" sounds a bit pretentious, like an work of art in an exhibition or a piece of evidence in a court of law, the artefact illustrates a mixed bag of things, starting from

-   New Frontiers, a rather general list of technology domains affected by the digital progress, which may have little to do with your enterprise or industry, take for instance the "Smart Grid", "e-Health", "e-Government"...

- continuing with a few "Core" elements or, perhaps, impacts on the business which, essentially, refer to automation and customer interaction, otherwise rather bare bones

- and ending with a list of rather obscure enterprise "Foundations" such as "Agility", "Data Security", "Devices", "Connectivity"... that may or may not have a loose relationship to the topic, the Digital. In any case, the "foundations" are not really technologies or domains but more like Critical Success Factors for the enterprise transformation to succeed.

I don't really see business executives reviewing this.

In fact, what the leaders should review, is alternative target operating models or end game big pictures and new business models for the enterprise, so that they can understand how the business will be changed and then be able to make decisions.

That is, the top management doesn't need to see the raw unprocessed information on various technologies but how the enterprise would look like as a whole when the technologies are implemented. They need to see then the business cases for the few alternative technology scenarios and new business models.

Now, is this "New Frontiers-Core-Foundations" technology taxonomy relevant and do we need it at all? That's for you to decide.

And where in Exhibit 1 is the Cloud that, paradoxically, takes the technology out of the enterprise and solves to a degree the problem that the Digital creates?

McKinsey's nine questions for the digital transformation (i)

https://it.toolbox.com/blogs/adriangrigoriu/mckinseys-nine-questions-for-the-digital-transformation-i-030616

March 06, 2016

Comments on McKinsey's article on "Nine questions to help you get your digital transformation right".

"Do you know which customer journeys matter?"

What they (McKinsey) say is that the Digital transformation must include the outcome of the analysis of customers' journeys. Fair enough, the customer journey matters, indeed.

Anyway, care must be taken that the digital transformation does not lump all the analyses, solutions and developments that have no connection to Digital and have not been performed before for lack of will or funding.

And, while the question seems to suggest that some customers' journeys do not matter, it does not seem to answer the question "which".

Still, the customers' journey is just an aspect of the many interactions with the enterprise stakeholders that have to be investigated from the points of view of emerging technologies. For instance, the interaction with partners and suppliers through B2B, interaction automation with the outsourcing providers and the Cloud, the financial institutions, regulators, the government...

"Are your teams collaborating across functions?"

Coopetition, cooperative competition, has been the word of the day for quite some time now. That makes even more sense for the collaboration between units of the same enterprise, or to the point, the cross boundary teams that McKinsey refers to.

This is the case though for any enterprise wide transformation, Digital is no different. Most advice points in fact, seem to apply to any kind of transformation.

Then they recommend self management teams. While this sounds fine, before even organising such self managing teams, handsomely rewarded, accountable for profit and loss etc you really need to put together that end game enterprise model big picture so that the teams partition their work judiciously while avoiding overlap and worse of all, internal competition.

To succeed, cooperators must agree, even before that, on the common components, terminology, protocols, communications...

At the centre of it all, it should be the enterprise blueprint and the Architecture team that works with all stakeholders to establish a common Digital transformation picture, governance and strategy.

McKinsey's nine questions for the digital transformation (ii)

https://it.toolbox.com/blogs/adriangrigoriu/mckinseys-nine-questions-for-the-digital-transformation-ii-030916

March 09,2016

Comments on McKinsey's article on "Nine questions to help you get your digital transformation right".

"Do you have a disciplined 'test and learn' approach?"

McKinsey says that you have to 'iterate until you get it right' and 'keep testing with customers'.

This approach is not dissimilar to an Agile approach where the outcome is delivered in iterations having often feedback from customers. It looks like this is what McKinsey implies without saying it. Got it. But it was better if they have said so because we would have got the gist faster.

Obviously, any new technology capability must be trimmed after polling the customers' reaction. But that is typically after deployment, because you need the customers' to use it in the first place.

But you may deploy a Beta like platform for a few select customers before full deployment. You may deploy on a smaller scale as well to test the waters. Prototyping is expensive, only to be used as last resort when risks are high and the technology is immature and little understood.

 "Are your budgets tied to progress?"

That is just good project practice, Digital or not. Go/No-Go milestones with budget decisions, re-assessment of value, costs and directions at each stage, is the practice for risky and large projects.

The budgets should be indeed tied to an iterative agile approach, as in the previous point, with often deliverables that attest progress.

In most cases though, the idea of pulling the funding plug, as exemplified, is not palatable except for venture capitalists which are investing in rather brand new, high risk/high reward early technologies in small startups. Established enterprises seldom play with technologies at this early stage in the maturity curve when the technology is not proven.

Besides, an enterprise realises its digital transformation as an integrated programme rather than as a number of individual projects each implementing a technology. You won't pull the plug for the programme.

And enterprises only experiment with technologies in the concept definition phase rather than in the product/capability development process.

McKinsey's nine questions for the digital transformation (iii)

https://it.toolbox.com/blogs/adriangrigoriu/mckinseys-nine-questions-for-the-digital-transformation-iii-031116

March 11, 2016

Comments on McKinsey's article on "Nine questions to help you get your digital transformation right"

"Do you have mechanisms to challenge ideas?"

In fact, everybody should challenge a technology at every stage of its life cycle. But, with Digital, it's not so much about challenging the technology but its efficiency, business outcomes and the total cost of deployment and replacement of the current.

In any case, there should be a concept phase where the technology is proposed and experimented with, standalone, after its initial value proposition has been approved.

Afterwards, the technology should be validated against vision, current strategy, target business picture, architecture principles and technology standards, integration issues, potential duplication...

Then the technology implementation becomes part of the overall Digital transformation programme. Once this established, the decisions are made by the governance board

A governance framework must be established to ease and standardise the decision making process rather than leaving it to individuals and the ad hoc debates of a company board meeting.

The framework should consist of standards, principles, rules, policies, roadmaps...

"Are your people empowered to act?"

Managers should not be empowered to act alone in such transformations that affect the future of the enterprise, let alone fire other managers. But any professional should have a right to dissent, on the record. This is not the military, after all. Imagine when the future of your enterprise lies in the hands of a single manager. Inevitably, (they become your biggest risk as such.

Transformations can be disastrous if relying on the command of a single super empowered manager that the top management trusts. I witnessed such trust and subsequent failure.

Rather than a hero manager, the cross boundary transformation governing board should take decisions based on the governance framework.

Anyway, the transformation, rather than being implemented by a plethora independent projects that deliver separately at different times, each lead by a fully empowered dragon slayer, should consist of a single programme that oversees all technology implementation projects. realising hence the target architecture in synch.

Separate projects would create from start duplication, overlaps, gaps, incompatibilities, data consistency issues and system integration problems.

McKinsey's nine questions for the digital transformation (iv)

https://it.toolbox.com/blogs/adriangrigoriu/mckinseys-nine-questions-for-the-digital-transformation-iv-031416

March 14, 2016

Comments on McKinsey's article on "Nine questions to help you get your digital transformation right"

"Is your IT operating at two speeds?"

As much that sounds weird today, when Gartner talks about a "two mode IT", McKinsey's "two speeds IT" appears insufficient, at least in comparison to the approach of DevOps concept that integrates the IT operation and development at the same fast speed.

If you ask me, DevOps is right while IT "Two Speed" is just a first step towards it, in that it speeds only the development and not the fast deployment part.

Because, no matter how fast you develop IT, you still have to deploy at the same speed, to take advantage of the new functionality. For that, you need not only agile development but agile operations as well.

For each development iteration you need customer acceptance tests and fast change and release management cycles, suitable for delivering features often rather than full capabilities once in a long while.

A capability would have to release functionality faster, in planned iterations that each go through development, testing, integration, staging, customer acceptance and deployment to the live environment.

"Are you coordinating a portfolio of initiatives?"

Every transformation today consists of a few aligned projects that is of a portfolio of initiatives. The Digital, due to its intempestive progress on many fronts, enters as well this category.

Digital today means that one has to automate and IoT enable the business operation, deploy new social media channels, on-line sales, virtual reality product experience, alternative payment systems, new business intelligence technologies, new logistics technologies (drones, self driving cars)... new business models, new digitally enhanced products... and migrate to the cloud at the same time.

An Emerging Digital Technology function should create a knowledge database that selects, proposes, tracks technologies of the concern to the whole enterprise till deployment.

The Enterprise Architecture team(s) has to devise the big target operating picture taking into account the new technologies and other developments and produce the roadmap while assisting the project teams and the programme coordinating the projects team implement the transformation.

McKinsey's nine questions for the digital in short (v)

https://it.toolbox.com/blogs/adriangrigoriu/mckinseys-nine-questions-for-the-digital-transformation-in-short-v-031616

March 16, 2016

Comments on McKinsey's article on "Nine questions to help you get your digital transformation right"

"Becoming a digital enterprise requires fundamentally changing the way you run your business."

Yet, the business operation essentially remained the same for centuries, millennia perhaps.

What changes with the Digital though are the business threats, reach, scale, complexity and agility that are grow fast. Due to this, the lifetime of a business is shortening.

Businesses still have the same good old processes, functions, same architecture but a rather different, more capable, automated and distributed implementation eventually realised in the Cloud.

The value chain still consists of the Develop, Plan, Source, Make, Sell and Service links but it is virtualised. There may be digitally enhanced products and new business models. And there may be more efficient ways to govern the business given the progress in communications, business intelligence, decision making and machine learning.

What is really different now is the amount and pace of change that has to be better planned and well organised to be achieved at the same pace as the industry. To be change ready, the companies have to be architected for agile change and easy complexity management and be documented in sufficient detail. They must be built out of Lego like blocks simple to interchange.

Businesses must be designed for change. Otherwise they may fall behind and fail.

The recent competition between the incoming slim fintech firms and the massive traditional banks illustrates the Digital peril well.

Nevertheless, to sum up, the nine questions, where the last is in fact a closing statement, I reproduced them here:

"Do you know which customer journeys matter?"

"Are your teams collaborating across functions?"

"Do you have a disciplined 'test and learn' approach?

"Are your budgets tied to progress?"

"Do you have mechanisms to challenge ideas?"

"Are your people empowered to act?"

"Is your IT operating at two speeds?"

"Are you coordinating a portfolio of initiatives?"

"Becoming a digital enterprise requires fundamentally changing the way you run your business."

The lot emphasises a disciplined collaborative portfolio approach to transformation that empowers the people and releases the budget on progress alone. The transformation starts from the customer journey.

In preparation, one has to be able to robustly challenge the new technology concepts and operate at two speeds the IT, McKinsey says.

With exceptions, it is common sense and reflects the principles of the Business as Usual transformation we already do know if not implement. There is little transformation advice specific to Digital though.

McKinsey & Co on the role of EAs in the digital transformation

https://it.toolbox.com/blogs/adriangrigoriu/mckinsey-co-on-the-role-of-enterprise-architects-in-the-digital-transformation-080916

Aug. 09, 2016

In "*How enterprise architects can help ensure success with digital transformations*" *Oliver Bossert and Jürgen Laartz* state the importance of EAs in the digital transformation of the enterprise.

So true but already stated since long.

Close to a truism is that

"...IT organizations may need to do a lot of systems and applications rework and reengineering to enable even the most basic digital activities. Companies may be slower to market with new products and services, and less able to react quickly to changing customer demand".

That is, to be able to agilely transform, organisations have to re-architect their enterprises, streamline them by reducing the architecture debt.

McK & Co concludes that "the enterprise-architecture (EA) department can play a central role in reducing the complexity associated with digital transformations" but "more than 40 percent of respondents in our survey say that the business leaders in their companies are not aware of what the EA group does...

"...our research indicates a general lack of awareness of enterprise-architecture groups within most organizations—who they are and what they do... "

The research is right, regrettably.

What McK & Co then says as an advice, is that:

"We believe that to improve the odds that a digital transformation will succeed, CEOs and CIOs need to raise the profile of enterprise-architecture departments...".

Hence, McK & Co recommends:

#1. Empower the EA group

#2. Company leaders in traditional organization... must engage more deeply with enterprise-architecture

#3. Attract EA talent by incentivising EAs

with "interesting challenges", "recognition" of the EA function, "structured career path"...

Therefore McK & Co asks:

- "Give them more responsibility... for certain big-picture decisions...

- Measure their performance... enterprise-architecture team to routinely provide the business units with the "technology costs" of any important decisions they make"

I hope someone listens.

McK & Co then concludes:

"CEOs and CIOs should consider the benefits of pulling enterprise architects closer to the center: bringing them to the table with business leaders, devising metrics that reveal the value of their work, and creating the type of incentives that will challenge them and prompt them to stay for the long term...".

It's a good summary of what the EA community has debated in discussion groups, blogs... for the last ten years or so.

Yet, it's McKinsey & Co speaking. And that weights.

Without EA, the avalanche of digital technologies could be hardly rationalised and adopted in time to survive the assault of technology on the businesses.

For complex change, we need first the enterprise blueprint. To enable a fast enterprise transformation without unintended consequences, delays and surprises, we also have to prepare the enterprise by streamlining it employing EA.

McKinsey & Co on EAs in the digital transformation (i)

https://it.toolbox.com/blogs/adriangrigoriu/mckinsey-co-on-enterprise-architects-in-the-digital-transformation-i-081016

Aug. 10, 2016

In "*How enterprise architects can help ensure success with digital transformations*" *Oliver Bossert and Jürgen Laartz* state the importance of EAs in the digital transformation of the enterprise.

Caution though, while McK & Co speaks convincingly about EA as a valuable development, in practice, the EA Body of Knowledge (BoK) has made little progress since inception. It is fragmented, incomplete, stuck in IT. It employs unproductive oldish methods, more like unglued collections of practices or general thinking tools.

There still are conflicting and confuse definitions for the EA discipline, process, terms and deliverables while EA still produces little in the way of usable and useful outcomes.

The audience is at best limited to some part of IT.

In the public domain, we haven't even seen yet a business case, a sample EA that illustrates how EA looks like, the navigable enterprise blueprint that describes all parts of the enterprise in terms of business process, function and information and the technology and people resources that support them.

Hence, until EA matures, it is hard to promote it to the higher echelon of the enterprise to gain support. EA would still come with endless justifications, sale pitches, colourful success stories rather than with results. That is, it will not deliver to expectations.

McK & Co pleading doesn't bring anything new to the table. Everyone understands the potential of EA as the Schematics of the Enterprise.

Nevertheless, even if McK & Co is a new comer to EA, it is good that they simply come to the table since they approach it from the business academy and consultancy angle. As such they can prop the EA case from the business standpoint.

Yet, it is not clear the scope of EA for McK & Co: IT or the whole enterprise.

A note though. There are so many Enterprise Architects and so few Enterprise Architectures.

Thus, Enterprise Architects must first deliver the Enterprise Blueprint which will serve as reference for all further developments and transformations.

EA would help all stakeholders discuss on the same picture and same parts, systems and roles, expressed with the same symbols and diagrams employing the same terminology.

Employing EA, architects will be able to enable the enterprise evolution to the Digital enterprise.

On McKinsey's Two Speed IT Architecture and Digital Business Models

https://it.toolbox.com/blogs/adriangrigoriu/on-mckinseys-two-speed-it-architecture-and-digital-business-models-030717

March 07, 2017

In a "A two-speed IT architecture for the digital enterprise", McKinsey's (McK) Oliver Bossert, Chris Ip, and Jürgen Laartz stated that "*delivering an enriched customer experience requires a new digital architecture running alongside legacy systems...*

And that "Digital business models have become essential for companies across a range of industries".

It all sounds good. Yet, if "legacy systems" are not in scope of Digital Architecture (DA), what is the remit of a Digital Architecture, what is Legacy and what is the difference between Digital and IT after all?

Since a business architecture is the logic of a business and abstract at that, essentially independent of technology, the term Digital Architecture mainly refers to the technology tier of an Enterprise Architecture.

But let me go back to definitions. Here is how an article in DZone defines IT and Digital:

IT is "the technology and management required to deliver computer systems to support the internal operations of a business or organisation"...

Digital "today it's commonly used to mean the technology within an organisation that is outward-facing, usually Internet-based"...

From a few websites being managed in the marketing team, the digital realm has expanded quickly both in terms of channels (smartphones, tablets, social networks...) and importance (from being a medium for communication to being a route to market to generate revenue).

These definitions seem to align with McK's Two Speed IT Architecture concept, that is one speed for Digital, yet another for "Legacy".

Therefore, for McK, there is the Digital, the Internet oriented Frontend, and the Legacy, the traditional Backend. Both are IT but, mind you, not all IT is Digital while Digital is more than IT - take for instance the Digital (enabled) Products.

The Two Speed Architecture refers to the speed of development of the Digital Frontend versus the Legacy Backend.

But right, the Frontend by employing new programming languages, web services, microservices, the API economy... and new communications and social apps evolved much faster than the Backend, still relying on classical now technologies.

I would argue though that, even if this definition is not uncommon, Digital, for many, has a much larger scope than the customer interfacing Internet technology.

Digital affects the whole enterprise in many more ways.

The Cloud, for instance, that takes over (and even renders irrelevant the IT inside the enterprise), is not really mentioned at all.

Missing too are such technologies as Artificial Intelligence, Virtual Reality and Social Media... that surely change the enterprise governance processes and, respectively, the marketing, shopping and sales experience.

On McKinsey's Two Speed IT Architecture and Digital Business Models (i)

https://it.toolbox.com/blogs/adriangrigoriu/on-mckinseys-two-speed-it-architecture-and-digital-business-models-i-030817

March 08, 2017

In a "A two-speed IT architecture for the digital enterprise" McKinsey's (McK) Oliver Bossert, Chris Ip, and Jürgen Laartz stated that *"delivering an enriched customer experience requires a new digital architecture running alongside legacy systems..."*

If we look at the client-server paradigm or the good old MVC (Model-View-Controller) software architecture model, Digital may apply to the Client or respectively the View (presentation) while the Legacy to the Server or Model (data) and Controller (business logic).

True though, the Client (View/Presentation) evolved much faster than the Server (Model-Controller) since the Internet technology took off.

The next question is what is a Digital Business Model.

In trying to find out, I pruned out the text and extracted the points McK wanted to make. It appears that to implement a Digital Business Model, companies have to:

"First... companies need to become skilled at digital-product innovation that meets changing customer expectations...

Second, companies need to provide a seamless multichannel (digital and physical) experience so consumers can move effortlessly from one channel to another...

Third, companies should use big data and advanced analytics to better understand customer behavior.

Fourth, companies need to improve their capabilities in automating operations and digitizing business processes".

To sum up, for McK a Digital Architecture and Digital Business Model are realised by such Digital technologies as "Digital Products", "Multichannel", "Big Data/Analytics" and "Automation" but not the IT legacy.

First, I would argue that, Digital or not, the harmonisation of the multi channel experience, automation and analytics had been a must since long before the Digital and Two Speed small talk took off. They hardly qualify as Digital news.

Also McK includes "automation", instead of mentioning the raft of technologies which implement it. Moreover, both automation and big data/analytics that are rather associated with the enterprise backend.

Hence this approach, which scopes Digital to these four categories above, associates Digital with more than the Internet Frontend and cuts into the territory of the legacy Backend with the automation and analytics categories.

Thus, while McK's Digital domain has rather conflicting definitions, either as an Internet Frontend or as four Digital categories, that also step into the Legacy domain, it is still true though that the Internet Frontend evolved much faster than the legacy Backend because of the Internet technology take off.

But that may not hold true for too long though.

On McKinsey's Two Speed IT Architecture... (ii)

https://it.toolbox.com/blogs/adriangrigoriu/on-mckinseys-two-speed-it-architecture-ii-031017

March 10, 2017

McK comes to the conclusion that a Two Speed architecture, one for Digital and another for Legacy, is a must to "help companies develop their customer-facing capabilities at high speed while decoupling legacy systems for which release cycles of new functionality stay at a slower pace". See "*A two-speed IT architecture for the digital enterprise*".

The concept looks like a re-iteration of Gartner's Bimodal IT concept defined as:

"the practice of managing two separate but coherent styles of work: one focused on predictability; the other on exploration. Mode 1 is optimized for areas that are more predictable and well-understood. It focuses on exploiting what is known, while renovating the legacy environment into a state that is fit for a digital world. Mode 2 is exploratory, experimenting to solve new problems and optimized for areas of uncertainty".

While the enterprise Internet Frontend may be seen as the implementation of the "V" View/Presentation in the MVC architecture paradigm, the enterprise "legacy" Backend realises the Control logic and data Model, that is, the C and M.

Yet, it is a fact today that the enterprise Internet Frontend development, using Agile methods and web technologies, is faster than the "legacy" Backend that must follow a more formal cascade process to realise the mission critical data schema and processes because they are core to the enterprise operation.

Hence, since the Two Speed Architecture is already the state of art in any enterprise, no action is required. The Two Speed architecture concept states what we already know and do.

With the progress of Digital though, the enterprise Backend development and deployment is sped up as we speak by such sweeping technologies as virtualisation of computing, storage, networking, Software Defined Interfaces (SDI), Open Computing Project (OCP), Cloud (...PaaS, iPaaS), ... and microservices/SOA applications architecture, that break and conquer the complexity of the backend monoliths in agile services developed independently.

Anyway, with the emergence of the Cloud first paradigm, that is, Rent > Buy > Build in that order, the development activity in the enterprise becomes the last option. That is because IT development takes usually too long compared to product lifecycles today, costs too much and is too prone too failure.

About McK's Digital Architecture.

The term "Digital Architecture" seems to cover for McK either the Internet Frontend or the four categories of technologies listed, some of which (i.e. automation and analytics) belong to the Backend rather than the Frontend blurring McK's definition between Digital and Legacy.

An observation is that Backend does not necessarily equals Legacy even though it may have a longer lifecycle than the frontend due to its complexity and cost to change.

But while a disjoint architecture of four "digital" technology categories makes little sense, the term Digital used only for the Frontend severely limits its scope.

The Digital evolution touches, not only the Frontend or the four McK technology categories, but also the Backend, as shown above, and in fact, all of the enterprise.

 Hence, in my view,

 - Digital evolution touches the whole enterprise, rather than the Internet Frontend alone

 - Legacy is only that part of IT that is based on older technology.

McK associated the Backend to Legacy perhaps, because it implements the enterprise Business Logic and Information Management which being complex and core to the enterprise, and as such under severe change management constraints, change at a slower pace.

On McKinsey's Two Speeds of Development... (iii)

https://it.toolbox.com/blogs/adriangrigoriu/on-mckinseys-two-speeds-of-development-iii-031417

March 14, 2017

I noticed that the insertion of the term Digital in front of known enterprise concepts such as *architecture* and *business model*, bestows these "digitally enhanced" terms no additional meaning while rendering them rather ambiguous.

I also propose the terms Frontend and Backend to substitute McK's Digital and Legacy concepts because Digital covers much more than the Internet customer interaction and the enterprise technology is not really Legacy.

Hence, what McK proposed in terms of Two Speeds, a speed for Digital and one for Legacy translates into a speed for the Frontend and another for the Backend.

But I observe that the development of the Frontend is, in its nature, faster today that than the Backend, given the progress of the Internet technologies. Yet, the Backend implementation speed catches up quickly due to such technologies as virtualisation and fast hardware platforms and in-memory databases (like SAP HANA).

Hence, there is not much point in recommending Two Speeds of Development one for the Frontend (McK's Digital) and another for the Backend (McK's Legacy).

Further on, McK states that "*the ability to offer new products on a timely basis has become an important competitive factor*". "That kind of speed (i.e. for developing new products) can only be achieved with an inherently error-prone software-development approach".

Yet, the fact that new products offer a competitive edge has been true since the dawn of time... No news here.

Still, the speed of product or capability development should not come from a deliberate "*error-prone*" environment that may result in defective products and faulty interactions with the customer that may harm the profit and brand.

Error prone enterprise Frontends would do no good to a company. Huge damages may be incurred by companies which customers are unable to success a site during online failures.

Besides, the development of any capability or product is inevitably an end to end process that touches both its Frontend presentation and Backend production.

Hence, a DevOps development model, rather than a Two Speed one, integrates capability/product development and deployment in a smooth one speed cycle that crosses the enterprise Frontend and Backend, i.e. the Digital and Legacy in McK's terms.

Nevertheless, speed of development should come from an enterprise architecture design based on such principles as separation of concerns, modularity and encapsulation embodied in SOA, microservices, web services and APIs, that break complexity in independent blocks with APIs to enable re-use and parallel development... and as such a faster development.

Also, to speed up the process, the development should use:

- Agile processes delivering often in iterations, frequent customer consultations and testing and reduced project overload

- High level, business friendly languages and collaborative Integrated Development Environments do help.

- separate development, testing, staging and operational platforms

- re-use with API economy, Cloud services (SaaS, FaaS)...

On McKinsey's Digital Business Model... (iv)

https://it.toolbox.com/blogs/adriangrigoriu/on-mckinseys-digital-business-model-iv-032617

March 26, 2017

Next, according to McK, a "two-speed architecture... implies a fast-speed, customer-centric front end running alongside a slow-speed, transaction-focused legacy back end".

Yet, the different speed of Operation of the Frontend versus the Backend is an entirely different proposition from the speed of Development of the Frontend versus the Backend.

There should be no confusion between these two. The speed of Operation of the two has nothing to do as such with this discussion about Two Speeds of Development.

In any case, with the advent of such platforms as SAP HANA, that rely on fast hardware and in-memory databases..., the difference in operational speed between the Frontend and Backend is reduced to nil because transactions and analytics happen in real time.

About the "Digital Business Model"

in McK's view, the "Digital Business Model" seems to be nothing more than the existing Business Model of an enterprise which employs as resources more digital technologies, in fact, the four listed: "Digital Products", "Multichannel", "Big Data/Analytics" and "Automation".

Yet, a new Business Model must show how the enterprise returns value/profit in a different way which may not be the case here because the Digital Business Model does not really change that. These four new technologies do not change the way the enterprise returns profit or value.

Nevertheless, there may be new Business Models as a result of the Digital adoption. Uber, for instance, and the sharing industry in general, may claim the employ of new Digital Business Models because they employ Digital applications to coordinate the operation of the "participants" and their shared resources in their interaction with the customers which is key to their profit making.

The term Digital added by McKinsey in front of the existing Business Model only denotes that the enterprise has introduced a more effective Digital technology rather than a new Business Model.

On McKinsey's Two Speed IT Architecture Digital Blocks... (v)

https://it.toolbox.com/blogs/adriangrigoriu/on-mckinseys-two-speed-it-architecture-digital-blocks-v-040217

April 02, 2017

McKinsey argues in the *"Implications for Enterprise Architecture"* section, that the enterprise is de facto siloed and its channels are not integrated. That's right.

Also, that "the legacy IT architecture and organization, for example, which runs the supply-chain and operations systems responsible for executing online product orders, lacks the speed and flexibility needed in the digital marketplace".

Right again, but the speed of operations of the supply chain... has little to do with the speed of "development" of the Frontend or Backend. Perhaps, we should keep separate the issues of speed of Development from that of Operation.

Then McK lists then the Digital "blocks" of Enterprise Architecture:

" - Two-speed architecture. This implies a fast-speed, customer-centric front end running alongside a slow-speed, transaction-focused legacy back end.

- New microservices ... should be deployable in an hour rather than...

- Zero downtime.

- Real-time data analytics.

- Easy process configuration.

- Product factory,... need to decouple the products from processes...

- Automated scaling of IT platforms

- Secure architecture".

A couple of notes though

- these are not blocks in the architectural sense but rather non-functional requirements

- the points rather apply to IT rather than specifically to Enterprise Architecture or to a Two Speed or Digital architecture.

As with any good article, McK does proceed at last with the business as usual implementation recommendations:

" Manage a hybrid target architecture with very different platforms.

- Plan for ongoing software delivery with blends of methodologies

- Develop the low-speed architecture, too.

- Build a new organization and governance model in parallel with the new technology.

- Change mind-sets".

But we do already manage hybrid architectures,... and change, so there is nothing you don't already know or do.

On McKinsey's Two Speed IT Architecture and Digital Business Model (vi)

https://it.toolbox.com/blogs/adriangrigoriu/on-mckinseys-two-speed-it-architecture-and-digital-business-model-vi-040317

April 03, 2017

McK ends up recommending an approach to the two speed architecture transformation:

"Run waves of change in three parallel streams.

- a digital-transformation stream builds new functionality for the business,

- a short-term optimization stream that develops solutions that might not always be compliant with the target architecture

- an architecture-transformation stream is the third necessary component".

I would not recommend this "parallel" development strategy though. One of the benefits of EA is that it enables a holistic transformation approach in that all streams, the architecture, optimization/tactical, Digital transformation and strategy implementation (missing above) should be part of the enterprise evolution programme, all correlated to act as one rather than parallel streams that compete for resources and operate changes independently to the same systems.

I would also note that, ideally, the architecture modelling stream has to deliver some time before the rest so that the transformation can benefit from EA.

McK's "Digital Business Model" remains still defined though as the way of operation of an enterprise that deployed Digital technology. Yet, a Business Model may not really change only because we use Digital technology for automation for instance.

But Digital can introduce new Business Models where technology becomes core to producing and delivering the product to the customer. An example is the Sharing industry.

To render the enterprise agile, both the Frontend and Backend architectures should rather be working at the same speed in terms of Development and Operation as opposed to dropping the standards of errors for the Frontend for the sake of rapid development.

To conclude the Two Speed architecture which seems to refer to the two speeds of Development of the Frontend and Backend is already the state of the art today for many reasons. Yet, the speed of Operation of the two is too often illegitimately introduced in the discussion.

In the end, I am not sure to which of the two, the Two Speed Architecture concept really applies to.

Nevertheless, the optimum is realised when the two speeds of Development and Operation for the Frontend as much as the Backend are matched. There is no real reason to be otherwise.

But true, today the web technology at the customer Frontend is faster than the complex Backend which lags because of its complexity which impedes fast change that may introduce faults. That changes though with the introduction of microservices, APIs, the Cloud etc.

Also DevOps, as opposed to the Two Speed concept, integrates software Development with Operations so that the quick methods of Development are balanced at each iteration with the requirement for robustness needed for deployment in Operation.

GOOGLE ON EFFECTIVE TEAMS AND GOOD MANAGERS

What Google thinks a good manager is

https://it.toolbox.com/blogs/adriangrigoriu/what-google-thinks-a-good-manager-is-011316

Jan. 13, 2016

Here is how Google underlines the "eight skills to look for in its managers".

"*One day* in July 2001, Larry Page, the founder, decided to fire Google's project managers. All of them... Since Google hired only the most talented engineers, he thought that extra layer of supervision was not just unnecessary but also an impediment. Page explained that he didn't like having non-engineers supervising engineers. "Engineers shouldn't have to be supervised by managers with limited tech knowledge".

Page, indeed, had to fight the eternal culture of the "professional manager" or "manager by profession" which alleged that a manager, no matter the experience, can lead any company, in any domain or industry without having specific domain knowledge.

So what Google thinks a good manager is?

1. "is a good coach"

A team consists, usually, of domain experts. To be able to coach at that level, a manager has to be a thorough professional. Hence, project managers could hardly coach the people in the know, Page was right. This criterion as such, excludes project managers from managing engineers.

Still, project managers are good administrators that should support the manager and team deliver, by planning, liaising with the team to check progress, milestones, collect information, issue reports, signal delays, bottlenecks and risks and organise meetings.

2. "empowers teams and does not micromanage"

This is a common sense governance principle. No manager can do the work of a team alone. The manager has to assign, by definition, work to the team and then coordinate their collective delivery. Micromanaging, while at times necessary, should not be the case for a team of professionals that one trusts.

But, mind you, coaching might be confused at times, with micromanaging.

3. "expresses interest/concern for team members' success and personal well being"

This is an attitude that cannot be really commanded. Anyway, the interest shown may not be genuine most of the time. What is genuine though is the manager's mutual interest in keeping his performing members happy.

I would change the trait to the effect, and I'd call it behaviour, that a manager must make sure that the team members are motivated, otherwise, expressing interest in the team personal well being may be seen only as political correctness, performed for the sake of the managers' manual.

4. "is productive and results oriented"

Sounds good but means little. Anyhow, a manager should not attain results by whatever means.

To be successful, everyone has to be productive or results oriented, manager or not.

Google's discovery about effective teams is not so surprising

https://it.toolbox.com/blogs/adriangrigoriu/googles-surprising-discovery-about-effective-teams-is-not-so-surprising-063016

June 30, 2016

Here is the Google's surprising discovery about effective teams. But Google has done extensive research too into the skills and character traits of a good manager. Let's digest these findings.

"In 2013, the Internet giant decided to explore this issue. After all, of its 37,000 staff members, only 6000 of them were managers or directors... Their findings could not have been further from their initial assumptions. It turns out that the secret to a high-performing team lies less in the individuals that make it up and more in the wider team dynamics... Who is on a team matters less than how the team members interact, structure their work, and view their contributions".

The answer to these questions was perhaps intended to help them establish what a great team looks like and how to select a manager for a team of talented people yet grand egos, often selected on such lateral thinking criteria as answering such questions as "how many golf balls fill a school bus".

"Over a period of two years, a group of researchers at the company analysed more than 180 teams and interviewed hundreds of employees".

High-performing teams, they found, almost always displayed five characteristics:

1. Psychological safety

"Team members feel safe to take risks and be vulnerable in front of each other".

That perhaps, says something about the work environment today, about the raw competition in the workplace that prevails in front of team collaboration.

Obviously, in an unsafe world, people would avoid to take risks from fear of making mistakes. It all comes down to office politics. Yet, no pain, no gain. At the end of the day, no safety means little innovation, which Google seems to crave for, considering its range of products and activities.

But how do you create "safety" in the workplace? Ultimately, the manager dictates the team culture, as per the proverb: " the fish begins to stink at the head".

Perhaps the Command should be *"Cut on the office politics"*. Yet, easier said than done. This is a topic Google could have investigated as well because it may severely alter the team behaviour.

Google's discovery about effective teams is not so surprising (i)

https://it.toolbox.com/blogs/adriangrigoriu/googles-surprising-discovery-about-effective-teams-is-not-so-surprising-i-070116

July 01, 2016

2. Dependability

"Team members get things done and meet Google high bar for technical excellence"

This *"Google high bar for technical excellence"* sounds a tad patronising nevertheless, even intimidating... The point is that team members must be excellent professionals so that they can be trusted, depended upon.

In English, this means "professional competency" which is quite a normal and elementary requirement. No news here.

It is upon the manager though to recruit the team members according to this, his and various other criteria such as political correctness, for instance. The question is, is the manager sufficiently enticed to select a candidate that is, professionally, better?

3. Structure and clarity

"Team members have clear roles, plans and goals."

That comes down to the manager yet again who establishes the job description, work breakdown and individual goals plan for the year.

The manager establishes the work structure to minimise the potential gaps that leave things undone and overlaps that may generate team conflicts and waste.

4. Meaning

"Work is personally important to team members"

True, that means again that the manager would have to assign work that is in line with individual skills, as much as possible, to get the maximum out of and motivate the team.

The manager should also make that the work assigned is aligned to personal goals as well.

The above team's ideal traits are still dependent on the manager.

5. Impact

"Team members think their work matters and creates change".

To create change, work and deliverables must be aligned with the higher vision and strategy of the company.

The manager is responsible for this, yet again.

Each individual member should be really involved in realising the mission and vision of the company, rather than only think they are. For that, each piece of work should be captured in the context of the greater picture. It looks like, for that, one needs an Enterprise Architecture, indeed.

Google's about effective teams and the manager's role

https://it.toolbox.com/blogs/adriangrigoriu/googles-about-effective-teams-and-the-managers-role-070216

July 02, 2016

The elaboration of the traits of the ideal team is the easy part. Just ask your employees. And that's what you'll probably get. It should not come as a surprise though that the role of manager, representing the authority, is minimised or even eliminated. Nobody likes them, really.

Moreover, in theory, everyone is fair and well mannered, without own agenda, while funding is bottomless and promotion is available for everyone. But that's life.

So, how can Google make sure that the team traits they uncovered after such an extensive research are realised in practice though?

Ideally, a team that exhibits all the above traits, delivers and realises the potential of its members to their own and company's satisfaction.

In practice though, things can go wrong many ways altering this perfect equilibrium. So far, we haven't even talked about money which fuel all our ambitions. Team members should collaborate and couch each other. But do they in a reality where knowledge is a competitive asset that creates differentiation? Budgets are limited and hence not everybody gets the tools, the support they need, the appraisal they deserve or ultimately the bonus.

What's out there to deal with the fact that, in reality, this is not a team of equals? Not even democracy works in practice, not for long anyway. Unless there is a governance framework that keeps things balanced and fair. Perhaps, a good subject for investigation.

Anyway, the ideal "One for All" team model looks more like "All for One" in real life.

A team can govern itself for a while in some cases but that's not common. It is the manager who is responsible and ultimately hold accountable for team deliverables, who is the point of contact for the team, who arbitrates debates, who makes decisions and who motivates the team and inspires it, by example.

But here is how Google, in the "eight skills to look for in its managers", further underlines the virtues of a good manager.

What Google thinks a good manager is (i)

https://it.toolbox.com/blogs/adriangrigoriu/what-google-thinks-a-good-manager-is-i-070416

July 04, 2016

- "is a good communicator"

That's right. In practice though, too often this is used in office politics against recruiting or promoting professionals/engineers in manager roles. Since, professionals, allegedly, cannot communicate so well, perhaps because they are so busy doing rather than communicating, they are not good managers. But Larry Page was not a good communicator, according to this, but created and still drives Google successfully. Yet, it is much easier to improve communications rather than professional skills.

A major cause of IT projects failure is failing to set at the helm a professional rather than an administrator.

- "helps with career development"

Overlaps with, continues and perhaps, should be merged with point 3, "expresses interest/concern for team...". But both can be seen as part of the team motivation effort a good manager has to do.

- "has a clear vision/strategy for the team"

The team should implement the vision and strategy of the company which should be cascaded to the team.

Still the team may have a strategy of its own so that it may grow, return rewards and ensure a career path for members. But I am not sure what this item is exactly about in Google's mind.

8. "has important technical skills that helps him/her advise the team"

This last point should have come first. That makes possible point 1 with regard to coaching.

Without technical skills a manager has to rely on somebody else to make decisions.

Because, without that, a manager cannot fully understand the problem, envisage the solution, cannot arbitrate technical disputes, perform work breakdown, assess quality of deliveries or make sure that deliverables of the team assemble in the whole. The manager has to have the wide knowledge that binds the deep expertise of the team together.

About managers, leaders and Google manager's traits, cntd

https://it.toolbox.com/blogs/adriangrigoriu/about-managers-leaders-and-google-managers-traits-cntd-070516

July 05, 2016

In the end, I think there could have been made a distinction between managers' and leaders' skills. Management is a science while leadership is mostly an art, rather unexplainable at that. It just is. While management organises people and work, leadership is inspiring people to act and follow.

A manager needs mastery of professional skills, clarity, structure and sometimes, attention to detail. Leadership demands pathos, imagination and vision. But seldom people have both.

While, ultimately, no matter how good the team is, the manager's role remains important in keeping balance and realising the potential of the team and each member, in practice there so many ways a manager can fail the team and the enterprise that we so often want to get read of the role altogether. But the democracy in a team has to prove too good for too long to be able to give up the manager role. On the other hand, an unworthy manager can make things awful.

It looks to me though that the eight points are rather an employee bottom-up point of view (take for instance "helps with career development"...) rather than a management top down viewpoint which is usually the view that counts at recruitment and promotion.

Too often though the manager recruits in his own image, leaving aside perhaps these traits.

Another observation is that Google's ideal team seems to revolve around a programmer's view of the world. Still, an enterprise is often much more than the programming team that delivers a product.

And, more importantly, a research in how these ideal teams' and managers' traits can be realised is recommendable. Otherwise they will just remain on paper as many of our good endeavours.

How can individuals excel in these traits beating the office power politics?.

MIT SLOAN & DELOITTE ON DIGITAL MATURITY & DECOUPLING

On digital maturity, research from Sloan MIT and Deloitte

https://it.toolbox.com/blogs/adriangrigoriu/on-digital-maturity-research-from-sloan-mit-and-deloitte-071617

July 16, 2017

The "*findings from the 2017 digital business global executive study and research project*", a Deloitte collaboration with MIT Sloan Management Review, "*based on a global survey of more than 3,500 managers and executives and 15 interviews with executives and thought leaders*", "*reveals five key practices organizations best able to achieve digital maturity employ—and the lessons all companies can learn from their success*".

"Lessons for companies that want to improve their own digital efforts, include":

-1 . "Implementing systemic changes in how they organize and develop workforces, spur workplace innovation, and cultivate digitally minded cultures and experiences."

This looks like a multiple (triple) point. In fact, it is only a preparatory step. It suggested the organisation of cross functional development teams and stimulation of a "*digitally minded*" and innovation culture. But we have been talking about digital and innovation culture for long now with little realisations though.
- 2. *"Playing the long game"*

Same again, we already aim to do that. When you ask the same old questions you get the same answers. Thus, I am not sure if this exhaustive research is news, so far.

In addition, in the case of accelerating Digital change, long term is harder if not impossible to predict. Hence, rather than "playing the long game" we should prepare the enterprise for agility to change so that, no matter the predictions, we should be able to change the enterprise at short notice.

 - 3. "Scaling small digital experiments into enterprise-wide initiatives that have business impact."

Perhaps, we should rather clarify this. Rather than *"scaling small digital experiments"*..., we, perhaps, have to implement an innovation and emerging technology development process and database beginning with the research, recording and evaluation of technologies, assessing their value proposition in the context of the enterprise architecture, prototyping and placing them on the tentative enterprise transformation roadmap.

We need though the Enterprise Architecture function that analyses the impact of technologies on the enterprise.

On digital maturity, research from Sloan MIT and Deloitte (i)

https://it.toolbox.com/blogs/adriangrigoriu/on-digital-maturity-research-from-sloan-mit-and-deloitte-i-071817

July 18, 2017

- 4. "Becoming talent magnets."

Sure we have that in every recruitment newsletter and strategy discussion. But not quite implemented in practice. Does Digital add anything new though?

Anyway, talent is hard to retain since it needs challenges and ongoing reward. Unless you are Google or Facebook you can hardly get and, in particular, retain the best. There is simply not enough of them and not enough for them. Anyway, digital skillsets in demand turn obsolete every few years unless constantly upgraded through hard work.

A much more practical proposition is to monetise the innovation capabilities you already have since, the case is, that most of the time your innovation is simply ignored, usually because you never had the time or funding for it, there is no innovation process to make it happen or you paid little attention having other priorities.

- 5. "Securing leaders with the vision necessary to lead a digital strategy, and a willingness to commit resources to achieve this vision."

We had this leadership issue since the dawn of time, digital strategy or not. Anyhow, executive Digital literacy has been highly desirable since IT has become so crucial to the enterprise because CEOs, Boards... had to understand to a degree what they approve, that is, the increasingly expensive IT investments. Besides, IT change brings business disruption, the risk of which must be understood beforehand.

But nobody can expect the top management to understand the avalanche of new technologies.

Hence, an emerging technology function has to be created in order to continuously evaluate technologies, communicate them, assess risks and opportunities and propose action in terms Boards can comprehend.

This ET function should closely work with Enterprise Architecture because technology impact can be meaningfully assessed and roadmapped only in the enterprise wide context.

To sum up, to achieve the status of Digital maturity Deloitte says, more or less, that we need cultivate the enterprise innovation culture, have a digital strategy, a kind of emerging technologies process, digital talent and leadership.

Yet, enterprises already know that but true, few execute this properly. But the secret of successful consultancies is, apparently, not to tell customers anything new, but rather what they want to hear, what they already approve off, so that customers adopt their services believing they employ a consultancy that implement their own great ideas.

About 'MIT Sloan's Digital Decoupling'

https://it.toolbox.com/blogs/adriangrigoriu/about-mit-sloans-digital-decoupling-073118

Aug. 20, 2018

"Technical Debt Might Be Hindering Your Digital Transformation", Adam Burden, Edwin Van der Ouderaa, Ramnath Venkataraman, Tomas Nyström, and Prashant P. Shukla in MITSloan Management Review discusses the technical debt in the digital transformation. It looks like papers today are written in teams of about five. Less work, more credit perhaps.

They state that "Companies seeking to expand their businesses across the globe may find themselves hindered by an untenable IT environment - a patchwork of hundreds of different systems that slow collaboration and make it difficult to scale innovation".

That sounds more like Architecture Debt to me rather than Technical Debt, which typically happens in software. Anyway, since Technical Debt is the result of implementing expeditive solutions at the expense of proper solutions, it covers the Architecture Debt territory as well.

We all know that technical debt is no good because for expediency we sacrifice quality. Debt hinders other developments one. To move on agilely, any enterprise must pay its Debt first. In the end, one has to pay the cost of the temporary solutions turned permanent.

A problem I can see is that the article seems to address Legacy systems as Debt: "*Some 67% of executives we surveyed said they would like to replace all of their core legacy systems*". Yet, Legacy is not Debt, it is just old technology going obsolete. The legacy was properly designed at the time rather than expediently. There was no Debt created when the technology was implemented.

Anyway, to get rid of technical debt, the authors come with the "digital decoupling" concept: "*decouple the critical parts of old systems and make them work harder for you by building new digital systems on top of them*". I would have thought that the critical parts of old systems are also up for Digitalisation. Well, the Decoupling solution addresses the Leaders, as always for such companies, rather than the Architects.

To "get out of debt" the authors propose to:

1. "*Decouple data from legacy systems...* i.e. move it into "data lakes", centralized repositories.

Translated in our terms, the recommendation seems to address data lakes that is BI, data warehouses, Big Data instead of the transactional and Master Data Management. Data lakes are nice but, what has this all to do with Technical Debt? Please explain.

2. " Decouple applications from the legacy infrastructure"

This looks to me like the good old Application Virtualisation or the move of the legacy infrastructure to the IaaS cloud. Yet, we do that for a long time now.

MIT Sloan's Digital Decoupling to Cope With the Technical Debt That Hinders Your Digital Transformation (i)

https://it.toolbox.com/blogs/adriangrigoriu/mit-sloans-digital-decoupling-to-cope-with-the-technical-debt-that-hinders-your-digital-transformation-i-090218

Sept. 02, 2018

In "Technical Debt Might Be Hindering Your Digital Transformation", Adam Burden, Edwin Van der Ouderaa, Ramnath Venkataraman, Tomas Nyström, and Prashant P. Shukla in MITSloan Management Review discuss technical debt in the digital transformation. The authors state that leaders "*say technical debt severely limits their IT function's ability to innovate (70%), greatly limits their ability to migrate to new technologies (72%), and makes their IT function much less responsive to changes in the market (69%)*"... "*Companies seeking to expand their businesses across the globe may find themselves hindered by an untenable IT environment - a patchwork of hundreds of different systems that slow collaboration and make it difficult to scale innovation*".

Giving it straight for a leaders audience, the Debt ultimately consists in the changes that should have been but, for expediency, have not been operated in a solution. I, myself, have created debt while assuring everyone and believing that it's only a quick and dirty local try and not a solution for production. But then I was asked to come with a quick with a dirty solution. Soon after it was adopted by another group company. Hence, I had to travel to fix it every now and then and then train somebody to take over. But the solution had a lot of holes, that is debts.

Debt materialises when we implement a solution that works without covering exceptions, hidden dependencies or other planned developments..., that is, when we implement cheap and quick solutions at the expense of proper ones. We do save time and cost. Yet, we rather postpone the full and proper realization for later and more unfortunately, for others. We do not even document what's left over so that people would know what to later expect. Often, we do it because we are under pressure from a chief or the business. But there are plenty of other reasons to do it on the quick. We have to soon leave the company for instance.

Yet, the Debt incurs the later costs of finishing the job properly. In conclusion, whatever we save for the moment we have to pay later, perhaps at a really bad moment. Next time we change our system, thinking it is straightforward, we uncover the underlying Debt, the work leftover, the missing parts of functionality in certain cases... That may derail our project. To proceed, we need to fix them all or, to save our skin, bury them deeper, if possible, for the next comer creating a further debt.

As it happens, we often pay the debt during key enterprise transformations. Hence, debts then must be fixed first. Because a small project can unexpectedly grow large because of the accumulated debt that surfaces in your project.

About MIT Sloan's Digital Decoupling for the Technical Debt (ii)

https://it.toolbox.com/blogs/adriangrigoriu/about-mit-sloans-digital-decoupling-for-the-technical-debt-ii-050119

May 01, 2019

In Technical Debt Might Be Hindering Your Digital Transformation", Adam Burden, Edwin Van der Ouderaa, Ramnath Venkataraman, Tomas Nyström, and Prashant P. Shukla of MITSloan Management Review discuss technical debt in the digital transformation.

Debt materialises when we implement cheap and quick hacks at the expense of proper solutions. We do it to save time and cost. Yet, we rather postpone the full and proper realization of a solution. Often, we do it because we are under pressure from the chief or the business or because we are going to leave the company. Debt is created when the solution project allows for departure from the norms of architecture practices and principles.

The Debt ultimately consists in the changes that should have been operated but, for expediency, they haven't.

Since we do seldom document the debt exceptions, the debt comes typically as a surprise at later transformations time. But, if, during an enterprise transformation, it is properly documented, the Debt appears just as additional work that can be planned upfront. If not documented as it is often the case, the Debt appears as unplanned work which can double your costs and timetable at transformation time.

Since it accumulates, the Debt can paralyse the enterprise development because of the fear of the Debt left behind by the short cuts taken by the projects before. Also, paying the technical Debt is not about replacing obsolescent systems like legacy as in the paper discussed here, because legacy was well thought and served us and still do for many decades.

As an example, while working independently at a mobile software, I used to turned on and off the existing software configuration switches which in change, turned on and off functional features. But, quite often, the switching was accompanied by side effects that had nothing to do with the feature. That is, the software was suffering from Debt. I had the choice of figuring out what went off after switching and fixing it in the existing package, at the risk though of introducing an unexpected behaviour for existing uses if my changes were to be included in the basic package , or attempting to fix the side effect in my own code by creating back doors in the existing package. Neither solution was too tempting but, as always, I had to deliver sooner rather than later. Anyway, not only that the existing debt tripled my development and testing times but I created new debt that rendered the existing software more unreliable.

About MIT Sloan Digital Decoupling

MIT Sloan's Digital Decoupling to cope with the Technical Debt that hinders your Digital Transformation (i)

To recap:

1. *"Decouple data from legacy systems"* *says them,* i.e. move it into "data lakes", centralized repositories.

The recommendation of data lakes for BI processing, does not address though the real time inline Transactional and/or Master Data Management. Data lakes are nice to have but they have little to do with a technical Debt that really impacts the operation and the transformation of your enterprise.

2. "Decouple applications from the legacy infrastructure"

This looks to me like the good old Application Virtualisation we are already doing. No need to reinvent the concept though.

3. "Decouple the business process systems from one another".

"The days of building software as one large, unified system — where everything runs on one machine — are over... As technology evolves, such bundling makes less and less business sense, and it actually prevents each system from providing the most value" they rightly say.

But are the authors are referring to the mainframe and client-server applications of the past? Yet, while a thing of the past, they are still working hard for us. Or are the authors reviving the good old enterprise SOA calling it here "Decoupling"? Or are they talking about Microservices and APIs we already implement?

Nevermind, in the end Decoupling is just an Architecture Principle, well known and applied since the dawn of architecture. We have been applying "decoupling" for a long while now in concepts such as layers, services, IT virtualisation... We need not reinvent the concept here. While the principle and realisations are old, term "Digital Decoupling" is new. MITSloan really takes on Gartner at defining new catchy buzzy terms for things we already know and do. And, after all, why call the Decoupling... Digital because there is nothing digital about it.

4. "Decouple IT talent"

Here the article goes into people and organisation. It's hard to say though what this has to do with the Technical Debt.

Anyway, this recommendation goes straight against the grain of "digital decoupling" theory. That is, rather than de-coupling the IT, the recommendation seems to be to couple the IT with the business units.

For some time now, we kept doing IT reorganisations by coupling and decoupling the IT to business units. We separated the IT function from the business for cost effectiveness. Then, we merged specific IT functions with the business units for responsiveness. Yet, the solution is, as always, somewhere in the middle.

Anyway, how does decoupling mend the Debt in fact? Decoupling is an architecture principle and Debt is paid by implementing our architecture obeying architecture principles. But since Decoupling is already implemented by the Cloud, SOA, web services, microservices and APIs, we'd better adopt these paradigms rather than starting from scratch from MIT Sloan's "Digital Decoupling".

Moreover, for the Debt to be paid, the team needs an Enterprise Architecture not only enforcement of an architecture principle such as decoupling. And the preparation of the enterprise for the Digital Transformation demands more than paying the technical debt - which I would rather call architectural debt to be precise.

Besides, for the Digital Transformation to succeed, the enterprise needs to adopt the Cloud First paradigm so that it can outsource the technology issues and skills to those in the know, outside the enterprise. Hence no more technology decoupling problem.

IOTAND 5G

What is, in fact, IoT about?

https://it.toolbox.com/blogs/adriangrigoriu/what-is-in-fact-iot-about-072515

July 15, 2015

IoT is alerting the business world because it receives so much attention recently. But few can really appreciate what IoT is and what are its impacts on business. Is IoT a technology, a simple concept, a trend? How mature is it?

To begin with, today, it's like IoT is defined bottom up based on domain specific applications rather than top-down, from concept to technology needs.

Many articles make me feel rather uncomfortable because, from most, I still don't know what the big issue is and what do we have to do to prepare for it or make it happen. Hence, this.

This article from McKinsey's is a good read though.

So, what is IoT?

In a simple general view, the term denotes a concept and trend to connect Things, beside computers, to the Internet to remotely control them.

But once Internet enabled, the Things can communicate to other Things, to automate their collective operation over the network. The end result is the Internet of Things.

The IoT evolution is on-going but it is still at its beginning. But it's moving fast.

 IoT enables as such remote control of appliances and digital automation of physical processes. Information and events from sensor like Things are processed to command digitally enabled output devices such as valves, actuators, relays, devices... that act on the physical world.

The role of IoT is to link the realm of nature to the digital processing world through digitally enabled Things. Things act as convertors between the physical world and digital realm of computers and networks. As a result we shall be able to control the physical world around digitally.

The world is full of things that man built or nature created that we may digitally enable and then act upon. The scope of IoT may grow to cover, in time, every single Thing.

There are few limits to the types of Things that can be connected.

There is no limit to the kind of IoT applications but the current technology and our imagination.

What Does IoT Need to Do First?

https://it.toolbox.com/blogs/adriangrigoriu/what-does-iot-need-to-define-first-072715

July 27, 2015

IoT, in a short definition, is the digital enablement of the world around so that it can be acted upon from computers over the network.

If Things are to talk to other Things and be remotely operated, then they would need to exchange information and command/response pairs over the net. As such Things would have to embed:

- a digital chip, low power, low cost, that can be accessed over the Net and act on the physical world around. The interface between things and digital chips would depend on the nature of Things

- a unique digital identity in a domain

- downloadable and updateable software... for command and own management such as Start/Stop, Act... Report-Log, Repair, Self-Diagnose, Download...

- mechanisms to authorise access and monitor security...

Standards are a must at these early stage in order to regulate communications and establish a minimum set of APIs for a Thing, any Thing.

A scheme to identify uniquely a Thing is mandatory. IPv6 will do for now.

Wireless protocols have to be standardised for various environments differing through range, scale, power consumption, speed, amount of data transmitted...

Ultra-narrow band and Weightless standards use radio whitespace or spectrum left over between TV channels. WIFI, Thread, 6LoWPAN, IEEE 802.16P, IEEE 802.16.1b, Zigbee, Bluetooth, Alljoin (see this) are already options. It might well be that the wireless access would depend on the specific domain (home. factory, defense...).

A standardisation body currently IEEE P2413, ITU-T Y.2060 (06/2012) proposes standards for the overall IoT architecture. ITU defines it for any Thing, any Place, any Time and includes mobility, roaming...That means that Things that move can be discovered and connected to.

The IoT, in this form would have to be the network of networks

Companies cannot wait though given the typical pace of the standardisation bodies. They will innovate quickly and furiously.

The private sector would soon come up with digital enabled Things and applications as soon as they become cost effective.

Applications would be specified per vertical domains, as for instance: home, office, health, automotive, aviation, procurement, warehouses, commercial, manufacturing, mining, utilities, banking, transportation ... Domain specific standards may appear.

IoT security and regulation

https://it.toolbox.com/blogs/adriangrigoriu/iot-security-and-regulation-072915

July 29, 2015

Well, it is somehow worrying that your fridge may talk to the milk machine at the vendor to order a drone deliver the bottle on your roof and deduct the cost from your account without your intervention. The world of Things may end up playing tricks on us.

Obviously, a framework for access and security is paramount from start to define what can access what, who or what grants access and permissions etc. We had the same security problem with the Cloud. We still have it but things get gradually better. And we were worried when paying wireless with NFC but threats were mitigated though.

Access control standards are important because there may be so many Things to access over the Internet. How to control the interactions between things, who sanctions these actions?

IoT regulation must be specified at this stage. Here is a site discussing such issues. An international body to watch IoT critical developments in various IoT fields is perhaps welcome. ISA (Internet Security Alliance) is looking into the mobile and IoT security.

The IoT progress must be carefully monitored for every specific application domain. Threats, risks and mitigating frameworks must be considered for each domain, depending on how critical or how severe the damage can be. Take for instance the health, automotive or transport industries.

Because Things can get out of hand quickly. Hacking is a strong possibility. Large scale unauthorised interactions must be prevented because malevolent hackers can take over a whole network of Things.

Imagine a hack taking hold of Things and playing them against each other or us. Once the communication between Things is intercepted ("man in the middle" attack) the possibility for mal-action is also great. See this, for instance.

Disaster recovery plans are a must.

If standards do not move fast enough, industries will take things into their hands. The results would be a fragmentation of approach and many de facto standards.

IoT is the result of the Digital technology evolution

https://it.toolbox.com/blogs/adriangrigoriu/iot-is-the-result-of-the-digital-technology-evolution-073115

July 31, 2015

IoT already exists. We have telematics, SCADA, machine to machine and remote controls over the Internet.

The car technology and engines are digitally enabled now. The car is controlled by interconnected digital chips that communicate through CAN, the car network, to achieve fuel economy, stability, optimal breaking, driving and turning on any surface... We can even control the car from a distance.

IoT was made possible by the progress of Digital though. And, like anything digital, IoT is coming faster, and faster. It may soon grow to affect every aspect of life and the enterprise.

Moreover, the Digital, besides IoT, enables the Intelligent Thing, which, with the developments in neural networks can even learn and adapt like us.

IoT relies on

- the increasingly powerful, low power and low cost processing chips which evolution still obeys the Moore's law.

- advances in networking such as mobility, virtualisation, edge networks...

- progress in software portability, plug and play, fault tolerance, distribution...

- the Digital enablement of other technologies, take for instance the car technology.

IoT will affect our environment, transportation, entertainment... It will change the enterprise in many ways we cannot even foresee, that's clear. Automation for example. Fine tuning of processes. New customer channels and business models...

But, like with anything digital, it is the IoT "ubiquitousation" that matters, the pace of it, the acceleration of IoT because its rate of progress may overwhelm us. What we can do though is prepare the enterprise for IoT.

Thus, plot the IoT long term roadmap, watch the IoT growing and act when necessary.

And do prepare for Digital which is grander than IoT itself.

IoT is the new normal

https://it.toolbox.com/blogs/adriangrigoriu/iot-is-the-new-normal-080215

Aug. 02, 2015

What is an IoT Thing? It is a manmade object endowed with a sensor or an actuator, a valve, a motor... Before IOT we had electrically commanded actuators that changed states when submitted to an electric or magnetic field. IoT added the intelligent things that can interact or be controlled over the Internet. But soon it could be people with digital implants.

Ultimately, an IoT Thing could be anything, natural or manmade, alive or not... as long as it can be digitally connected and controlled. The Internet of Things (IoT) adds the digital interface to Things so that they can operate together or be remotely controlled.

IoT is as such, the connector between the digital and the physical realms. It connects us to the world around so that we can understand and better manage it. We, as a result, can sense, control and automate operations in the world around.

The presence, the location and the status of a Thing can be sensed or transmitted to other Things. Ad hoc networks between Things can be formed as such, enabling communication, collaboration or aggregation of capabilities such as processing power, networking capabilities...

The glue between all Things is the ubiquitous Internet. True for the network in the middle. But most of the time, the access network would be wireless so that we don't tie all things around in knots of wires. But connectivity may come over any network, for instance the existing power lines. IoT specifies in fact just the internet protocols which can operate over any network.

IoT, in time, would become the new normal as digitisation of the world around progresses. IoT is just the umbrella for the many applications in various domains. It may come as such under different categories and names, such as Car and Home, networks depending on field or industry. Since each application field has different requirements, standards may differ. But it is important to have that IoT framework that enables secure communication between them all.

IoT, in the absence of a framework, will go for a while through a process of trial and error. Anyway, we don't want to have the privacy and security problems we have in the Internet today in the world of IoT.

The Mobile Broadband Growth Law and Moore's Law

https://it.toolbox.com/blogs/adriangrigoriu/the-mobile-broadband-growth-law-and-moores-law-081819

Aug. 18, 2019

"Moore's Law is the observation that the number of transistors on integrated circuits doubles approximately every two years. This aspect of technological progress is important as the capabilities of many digital electronic devices are strongly linked to Moore's Law".

"More importantly for us is that the power and speed of computers increased

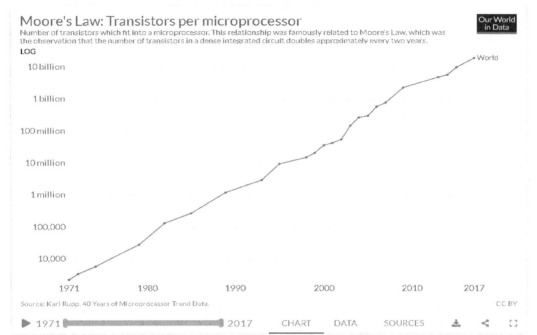

exponentially; the doubling time of computational capacity for PCs was 1.5 years between 1975 to 2009." from Technological Progress by Max Roser and Hannah Ritchie https://ourworldindata.org/technological-progress#

Now, the 5G itself is made possible by the Digital technology rapid evolution. That is, it is the Digital fast progress that enables the 5G industry. The exponential increase in clock, speed, number of transistors per chip heavily support the signal processing necessary for 5G performance: signal coding/decoding, multiplexing/

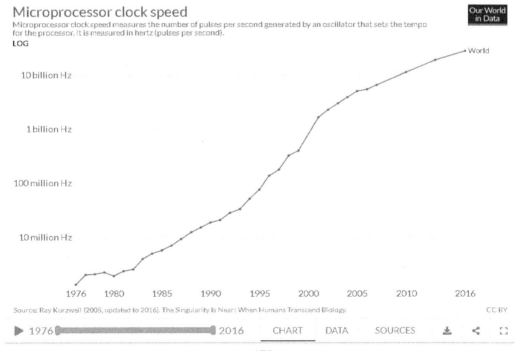

demultiplexing, encryption/decryption, parallel processing...

And also illustrated is the projected computing performance for top 500, the 1st and the average the top 500 fastest computers.

from https://www.top500.org/statistics/perfdevel/

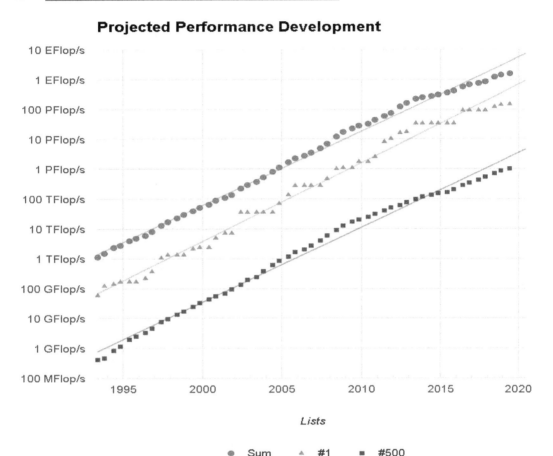

Projected Performance Development

Anyway taking into account the mobile bandwidth growth in the past and the projected growth in processing flops, I concluded that the mobile bandwidth grows as fast as the processing power, that is it doubles every 1.5 years, that is the download speed grows even faster than Moore's Law.

Here it is, the bandwidth I projected in what I called Adrian's Mobile Broadband Law.

I put it together around 2005 or so while working in mobile telecoms, in the desire to forecast the rates to come in the mobile arena, so that everybody could understand what kind of mobile products, applications and terminals should be available in the near and far terms so that one could take advantage of it. It was a good indication what your phone could and should do in the future. The law is still valid now after 15 years.

The Law states that, essentially, the mobile bandwidth (at download) doubles every 1 and 1/2 years.

The average mobile downlink speed though would be around an order of magnitude lower compared to that of the co-existing fix broadband. That is

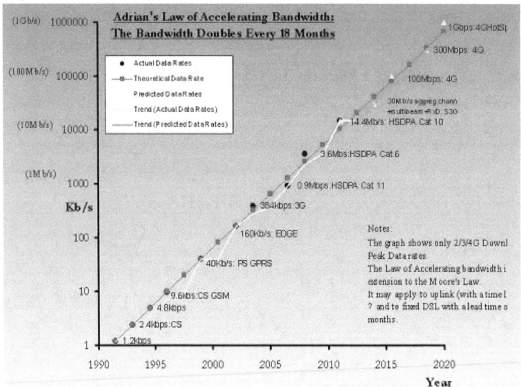

because the air transmission media is much more susceptible to noise and as such the information must be padded and increasingly heavily coded to be corrected at the other end. Besides, transmissions, received by multiple antennas, MIMO, must be processed in parallel today on eventually more frequency channels to increase the signal bandwidth and as such the speed of transmission.

And, just as an indication, according to my calculations then (now lost in the space of time), to be able to get the same capacity for mobile broadband on a similar scale with the fix line broadband, it is necessary to quadruple the number of base stations in the network.

Essentially, Adrian's Law is an extension of Moore's law.

The bandwidth growth is not only supported by the number of transistors on a chip, but by the increasing clock speeds, the new parallel and cache computer architectures and also the exponential growth in memory and its response time.

Essentially, since the broadband speed depends today almost entirely on the processing power in the network elements and terminals, the speed of download grow proportionally with the processing power even faster than Moore's law.

This Law was verified to a certain degree in practice. as you can see in the broadband bandwidth picture.

How many people remember that in the 1990s the speed was good if amounted to 9.6kbs over Circuit Switched GSM?

Then GPRS offered about 40kbp/s, EDGE, an improved version of 2G GPRS, enabled a theoretical speed of up to 160kbp/s.

Then we had the 3G with 384kbps initially and various ulterior HSPDA speeds (for download) of up to1Mbps.

4G today is supposed to supply between100Mbps to 300Mps and 5G 1Gbps in hot spots.

The mobile speed growth line is exponential as you can see on the logarithmic graph.

The purple line is the theoretical speed as illustrated by Adrian's law, the yellow represents the real growth in terms of practical speeds achieved in practice.

But how can we use this Law? Who in 1990es or the beginning of the second millennium would have thought that we are going to have a mobile broadband speed that may reach over 1Gbps in 2020s? That means very fast, almost instant downloads, streaming... Hence the mobile networks would be able to sustain multimedia services. New players may join as such the mobile media market.

10 June 2019: "Three UK has today announced it will launch 5G in August with a 5G home broadband service in London. Three will then launch both mobile and home broadband offerings in 25 towns and cities across the UK before the end of the year.

The law will not apply at infinitum though. Nor is Moore's Law because there are physical limits. But so far, solutions to discontinuities were found. The idea is though that the growth of capabilities and communications bandwidth may still be exponential if discontinuities can be defeated.

Knowing this law, would Nokia have been so economical with their phones design, insisting on the small but mass market phones then rather than on the large screen Internet terminals with a lot of processing power and memory as Apple's, had they understood that the phone capabilities would increase from 2005 to 2020 in practice from a few hundred Kbps to hundreds of Mbps and their processors would support advanced GUIs...

Had they understood the exponential growth of capabilities, this here mobile bandwidth growth law they may have invested in the future rather than giving in. They would have understood then not only the processing power at their disposal in the near future and the mobile bandwidth available but also the type of applications the phones would easily execute, the type of application the public would need on the move. They could have built the terminal of the future rather than procrastinating in the present. Same can be said about today's players. Has any phone supplier predicted the phone capabilities, the bandwidth and the kind of applications they could support in 2030? The laws above, eventually updated. would help them do this exercise.

To put all this into perspective,

"*The latest phones typically have 4GB of RAM. That is 34,359,738,368 bits. This is more than one million (1,048,576 to be exact) times more memory than the Apollo computer had in RAM. The iPhone also has up to 512GB of ROM memory. That is 4,398,046,511,104 bits, which is more seven million times more than that of the guidance computer. The Apollo 11 computer had a processor – an electronic circuit that performs operations on external data sources - which ran at 0.043 MHz. The latest iPhone's processor is estimated to run at about 2490 MHz. Apple do not advertise the processing speed, but others have calculated it. This means that the iPhone in your pocket has over 100,000 times the processing power of the computer that landed man on the moon 50 years ago*".

What 5G Means for the Enterprise

https://it.toolbox.com/blogs/adriangrigoriu/what-5g-means-for-the-enterprise-070919

July 09, 2019

5G is the 5th generation of mobile networks. While the G generations before covered voice/video calls, messaging and data, 5G has much greater ambitions. It is being designed to meet all the latest needs of the modern society and economy. For the first time, the mobile networks will aim to cover the business needs of various industries.

A key requirement indeed is too provide significantly faster data speeds and greater capacity to keep the world connected. As such, 5G will initially extend the existing 4G networks to essentially offer much faster rates of data transfer and, increased capacity and density at lower latencies.

Latency is the time taken for devices to respond over the network. 3G networks had a typical response time of 100 milliseconds, 4G is about 30ms and 5G will be as low as 1ms, that will ensure real time responses.

Key use cases for 5G:

A. Fast mobile and fix broadband data and streaming media beside voice

to serve the public and multimedia entertainment industries. 5G may well deliver, in some cases, the wireless internet access for homes, outdoor broadcast applications. As a replacement for the fixed broadband access, 5G may bypass the coding that ensured mobility but slowed down the rates and reduced capacity. Hence 5G may offer fixed access networks in some cases. But the speed, in my own estimation, may be ten times lower than that offered by their fixed counterparts while the base stations density may have to grow at least four times to accommodate the same density of users.

B. Massive IoT (Internet of Things) machine to machine (M2M) communications

to serve application like industrial processes, manufacturing, mining, agriculture, health monitoring, fleet management, meter reading.... Mobile networks will interconnect billions of devices. No one knows so far how many, perhaps nobody will ever know. For that, the network will need spatial extensions such as provided by Cat-M1 and NB-IoT technologies.

C. Critical IoT for Ultra Reliable, Low Latency Communications (URLLC)

for mission critical applications such as real-time control, robotics, safety systems, autonomous driving, health monitoring...

Both B and C though will depend on the security and separation the 5G will be able to provide at operating such applications in parallel. In any case, remote meter reading applications already are installed in our homes with the advent of the smart meters.

To implement the above use cases the Core Network must be able to

1. Provide quality of service for various services and use cases

2. Reduce latency for critical IoT processing at the access network edge and for Content Delivery through Content Cashing at the delivery edge of the network

3. Provide on demand separation and isolation of the network traffic for various industry applications. This is called Network Slicing and requires remote dynamic configuration.

4. Reduce network footprint (base station space and antenna sharing) and radio electricity consumption to reduce energy bills (currently close to half of the network operation costs). This is achieved through grouping and moving the baseband processing from the radio antenna locales to local baseband processing centres.

5. Extend coverage reach for IoT applications (Cat-M1 and NB-IoT)

Core Network technologies that support 5G or 5G must support

1. Network elements configured dynamically from a Management Centre. The Software Defined Network (SDN) effectively separates the Control/Signalling Plane from the Data Switching Plane over an API such as OpenFlow.

2. NFV - Network Function Virtualisation enables the Control Functions implementation in Software that may execute remotely in Data Centres standard servers. That enables easy scaling, upgrading, configuration...

3. Technology that enables Content caching to be able to store copies or 'cache' the popular content in local arrays of servers for faster access times for such applications like Video on Demand.

4. Enable the Edge and Fog Processing Data Centres connection to the mobile network at junctions closer to then users so that the information from the machines at the edge of the network is processed with minimum latency.

Radio Access Network (RAN) evolution

1. Split RAN

employing SDN and NFV principles so that the user and control planes are separated. The baseband hardware in nodes will be separated and grouped in local baseband processing centres located not more than tens of miles from the radios.

2. Radios will employ Massive' MIMO (Multiple Input, Multiple Output) antennas with beam steering technology

3. Operate in much higher spectrum to increase capacity and implement access over free spectrum with collusion avoidance protocols like Ethernet

4. Employ Cat-M (LTE-M) networks and NB-IoT technologies used to extend the reach of the mobile network for various IoT devices.

In conclusion

The part of 5G that increases the fast broadband availability for the public is almost on the market. Yet, the part of 5G that serves the business/industry is a long way off and it will take time to mature. The Network Slicing and Virtualisation is more on the bucket list rather than reality. SDN and NFV are doable but still immature.

In the future, 5G or perhaps 6-7G will be able to deliver to the enterprise your own virtual networks. In other words, with 5G the mobile operators aim to become network providers for business communications and IoT networks for various use cases such as Health, Utilities, Transportation...

Would the 5G operator be able to provide to each enterprise its own virtual 5G networks? I don't think that would be possible in the near future. It would be possible though for 5G to provide some separation based on QoS and for such general interest applications like Meter Reading, Electricity Grids, Health Monitoring...

But there is also WIFI-6 on the horizon. And, from my experience, at a certain time, the fixed networks will always have as much as an order of magnitude broadband speed advantage over the mobile networks.

Hence 4G-5G will provide basic IoT support to the enterprises in such industries as Utilities Meter Reading, Electricity Grids, Health Monitoring, Transportation.... In the future 5G may support Video on Demand content delivery and, perhaps, some critical IoT cases.

For some of these use cases 5G must be expanded to cover the enterprise space with LTE-M and NB-IoT technology up to distances of 100km.

Technologies That Support 5G

https://it.toolbox.com/blogs/adriangrigoriu/technologies-that-support-5g-072019

July 20, 2019

5G represents a live history of the mobile network evolution from the analogue radio (1G) to today's 5G. The heavily embedded telecom equipment of the first generation evolves now on the IT visualization path to the service paradigm and APIs, leaving in the field just the radio and switching equipment. Hence control functions can be grouped in mini control centers or clouds.

To accommodate the IoT, critical applications, their separation (slicing) and security requirements use cases, the 5G network has to be much more agile. For that, ideally:

The Control Plane should be separated from the data/switching plane.

The network Control Plane functions should be virtualized that is, realized in software so that they can be deployed and easy configured on general purpose hardware executed in Virtual Machines.

API's have to be introduced between the Control Plane executed now in software in data centers, and the Traffic Switches that should remain in proximity to the traffic.

API's must be introduced between the Control Plane and The Operations Management Software in central locations so that the network can be configured for various traffic and applications.

Separation of the mobility and quality of service managing functions.

The above principles essentially shape the look of the NextGen Core Networks and RAN. Technologies are already in place to ease the evolution to the virtualised network.

Network Functions Virtualization (NFV) is an initiative to virtualise network services traditionally run on proprietary dedicated hardware. With NFV, functions like routing, load balancing and firewalls are packaged as virtual machines (VM) on commodity hardware. Individual virtual network functions, or VNF's are an essential component of NFV architecture. Because NFV architecture virtualizes network functions and eliminates specific hardware, network managers can add, move or change network functions at the server level in a simplified provisioning process. Basic NFV benefits also include reduced power consumption and increased physical space, since NFV eliminates most traditional hardware appliances. NFV can then help reduce both operational and capital expenditures. Part of the challenge for NFV adoption is the number of standards and open source projects being conducted to promote NFV development. For example, a short list includes ETSI, Open Platform for NFV, Open Network Automation Platform, Open Source MANO (Management And Network Orchestration) and MEF -- formerly the Metro Ethernet Forum."

Software Defined Networking (SDN) and NFV are complementary technologies. But, instead of the physical network equipment -- which is programmed at the hardware level -- driving network control, Software Defined Networking (SDN) introduces a software-driven controller that handles these tasks and enables the changes to happen remotely. *"Architecturally, an SDN controller sits between the higher-level network applications -- like security, load balancing or firewalls -- and the lower-level physical network devices, like switches or routers. By sitting in the middle, the controller can manage the network more efficiently using SDN protocols. It sends information about the physical network below up to the applications and pushes the application control data down to the individual network devices."*

Because it's located in the middle:

"The SDN controller communicates up to the network applications via northbound API's -- like *REST* -.

And down to the network devices through southbound API's -- like *OpenFlow*. *Southbound APIs* facilitate efficient control over the network and enable the SDN Controller to dynamically make changes according to real-time demands and needs. *OpenFlow*, which was developed by the *Open Networking Foundation (ONF)*, is the first and probably most well-known southbound interface. It is an industry standard that defines the way the SDN Controller should interact with the forwarding plane to make adjustments to the network, so it can better adapt to changing business requirements. With OpenFlow, entries can be added and removed to the internal flow-table of switches and potentially routers to make the network more responsive to real-time traffic demands."

The 5G New Radio, 5G NR 5G new radio is the new name for the 5G radio access network. Using a far more flexible technology, the system is able to respond to the different and changing needs of mobile users whether they are a small IoT node, or a high data user, stationary or mobile.

Frequencies of above 50GHz are being introduced even though this is challenging in terms of circuit design and distance they travel since these frequencies do not travel far being absorbed by small obstacles. Given the availability of spectrum, 5G allows that different countries are allocating different spectrum for 5G.

Free spectrum frequencies are available if employing the principle of collision detection.

Fixed access to 5G NR.

Access points to be introduced for Edge Computing centers so that the signal does not have to travel the whole network, but can be processed as close as possible to the source.

Dense Networks: Reducing the size of cells provides a much more overall effective use of the available spectrum. There is a significant challenge though in adding huge numbers of additional cells to a network, and techniques are being developed to enable this.

Radio Modulation and Multiple Access: Formats that are being discussed include: GFDM, Generalized Frequency Division Multiplexing, as well as FBMC, Filter Bank Multi-Carrier, UFMC, Universal Filtered Multi Carrier and OFDM which has been used very successfully in 4G LTE.

Massive' MIMO (Multiple Input, Multiple Output) Antennas with beam steering technology which will consist of multiple elements or connections that send and receive data in parallel over more frequencies eventually. To be able to cope in real time, baseband digital processing must happen at both the network and terminal ends at very high speeds in the latest generation parallel digital signal processors.

"LTE-M" is the best option for mission-critical applications, since it supports communication in real time. This includes voice, emergency data and precision tracking data. However, be aware that although LTE-M technology supports voice, it will be up to each network operator as to whether or not it gets implemented on their LTE-M network.

NB-IoT is ideal for smart city applications which send small amounts of data periodically, such as waste management, smart metering or street lighting". https://m2mconnectivity.com.au/products/modules/cat-m-nb-iot/

THE DIGITAL ENTERPRISE TRANSFORMATION

The "digital" enterprise trendy frenzy

https://it.toolbox.com/blogs/adriangrigoriu/the-digital-enterprise-trendy-frenzy-112614

Nov. 26, 2014

I raised my eyebrows when I saw the recent ramp-up in the "digital" rhetoric and all the sudden frenzy surrounding it. "Pay attention", "beware"... of the Digital enterprise transformation or ignore it at your own peril.

But what is it all about? Is "digital" the new dotcom or Year 2000 scare? Many sources don't even tell us what they mean by digital. But they let us assume and, as such, fret about our own worst worries.

What we do know though is that the enterprise and its products have been digital for a long time now. And we, personally, are surrounded by so much "digital" today.

According to Kurzweil, technology change grows exponentially. That we know already but, perhaps, the frenzy raisers don't since it is the business sector that raises the issue rather than the IT.

The new business pundits seem to be taken aback but the extent of the digital pervasiveness. They brusquely realise that the business is so digital today while they know so little about it. They worry perhaps that they haven't got the skills and the understanding to act accordingly and drive the enterprise to its digital future.

See this article: "Digital Business; teaming a 'Digital' Leader with a 'Business Manager'"

In actual fact, the term digital means much more than IT since it includes electronic devices, appliances... at least, in combination with other technologies indeed. It means IoT, self-driving cars...

But how does "digital" affect our daily life though?

We have the web. We listen to music and watch films on mobile terminals and on line. We read electronically now. We do things online: read the newspapers, get timetables, shop, work...

We all have mobiles that grow again bigger than our pockets. They do replace a few other digital gadgets though: Portable Digital Assistants, documents storage, ebook readers, web access, media players and game players, GPS, map navigators, note takers, sound recorders, game players, radios, compass, remote access to the enterprise... Did I miss anything?

In Finland they even want to remove the good old hand writing and calligraphy from school even if Nokia is rather gone now. In the digital era, handwriting would be frowned upon. This obeys the law of unintended consequences.

We have digital watches that take our pulse and send signals to a hospital if need be. Cool!

We have anklets that send digital messages to the police that we have over stepped our zone. So uncool.

We pay wirelessly. We have online maps and our location at all times.

Digital technologies identify us, scan our eyes, face etc.

We smoke and chat electronically. We don't drink electronically so far..

We watch digitally animated films. We talk to things and they listen and execute. Dolls talk and walk. Drones fly.

We all search the Internet with Google and get ads in return.

But digital weather predictions still show sunshine when it rains.

We print tri-dimensional objects, that's interesting.

The internet of things is in its infancy. A lot still to happen in terms of automation of intelligent intercommunications. Fridges order your cheese when you run off! But they don't quite have that in supermarkets as yet.

Or the Microsoft robocops, that, more newly, patrol and spy their campus.

This affects indeed our customers' lives and as such the products you offer, the way you sell them...

Still, there is nothing out of ordinary happening now in digital, nothing new to worry about. It's just more and more and faster and faster.

Questions you have to answer though: how would this affect your products, your operation, your sales, channels, business models, value chains... Quite a lot of questions.

You have to watch the landscape and prepare for these changes because disruptive innovation, so much based on digital today, is fast and furious and will surely take you by surprise.

Don't rest easy because you created a digital function. You have to have the right skill to be able to react in time because, from concept , to realisation there is a whole value chain that has to be executed.

It is not so much the digitisation of the enterprise but its acceleration

https://it.toolbox.com/blogs/adriangrigoriu/it-is-not-so-much-the-digitisation-of-the-enterprise-but-its-acceleration-061715

June 17, 15

Everybody talks about digitisation of the enterprise today. Pundits make their business in alerting you that digital is coming like a storm, that you have to do something about it, best nominating a Chief Digital Officer (CDO) to solve the big issue. There would be already plenty of them out there, most exhibiting in their CVs years of digital experience. Does that help though?

We had technology since the first enterprise though. Did we have to worry about it? Not really, not more than necessary. Because it is the normal course of things.

Still, the first to have a better tool or weapon had a decisive advantage.

The first enterprise to have an effective technology would have a competitive advantage.

The enterprises that choose and properly integrate the increasing plethora of technologies would perform best.

What is digital technology though? It all starts from the transformation of information and analogue signals into a digital representation of "0/1s". Complicated algorithms in software can then process the information. General or special purpose computers and microprocessors host the information processing. The faster and smaller the hardware, the more capable is our digital world.

Our life has already been digitised. Our watches, media, players, phones, tablets, GPSs, laptops, radios, TVs, ... are all digital. All networks and transmissions are digital, our pets are micro-chipped, our cars are increasingly computerised..., we are equipped with digital pacemakers and hearing digital aids. We have complex digital instruments, airplanes and weapons.

Since digitalisation happens since long then, what's different now?

The progress of technology accelerates. Change took a long time in the past. In the 1950s we had the first TVs and computers. But technology evolved so much that a mobile phone today has many times the power of the first computer. The hardware that occupied rooms now is hosted in a bankcard chip or SIM.

According to Ray Kurzweil, the rate of change doubles every ten years or so. The progress of digital technology is particularly fast, probably even faster than that.

Hence, it is not so much the digitisation of the enterprise but its acceleration.

And it is the Moore's Law that explains the Digital revolution. It states that processing power doubles every two years or so. Hence computers have increasingly the capacity to execute our complex algorithms in real time.

"Moore's law is the observation that, over the history of computing hardware, the number of transistors in a dense integrated circuit has doubled approximately every two years...

This exponential improvement has dramatically enhanced the effect of digital electronics in nearly every segment of the world economy.

Moore's law describes a driving force of technological and social change, productivity and economic growth in the late twentieth and early twenty-first centuries". From Wikipedia.

The ten commandments of a successful digital transformation

https://it.toolbox.com/blogs/adriangrigoriu/the-ten-commandments-of-a-successful-digital-transformation-021015

Feb. 10, 15

To begin with a quote from one of my previous posts, "while in every day operation the lack of proper management practices is easy to conceal, it would however most likely fail the next large company transformation."

But here is a summary checklist for a successful transformation.

One has to make sure that:

1. the digital leadership is properly chosen on professional rather than political criteria, so that is aware of the business problem and company culture while understands the technology solutions

2. the transformation process

consists of standalone phases and projects, with Go/No-Go milestones and criteria, so that the process can be rewinded or stopped in order to limit losses when risks materialise

- o is agile enough to take into account the ever appearing new requirements and dependencies
- o is risk tolerant in that risks are continually evaluated and the associated contingency plans are in place since start

3. the transformation governance ensures that:

- o authority comes with accountability
- o principles, guidelines, policies and roadmaps are in place to guide the decision making and makers
- o the experts are empowered to make decisions rather than the committees of administrators

4. problem evaluation and solution design are double checked by a third party

5. the problem is analysed and the solution designed in the Enterprise Architecture context. The EA blueprint should be available before the transformation starts rather than modelled at the same time

6. a staging platform is created before changes go live in order to avoid late business malfunctions, dissatisfaction and operating losses

7. change roll back is embedded in procedure and planning.

8. Recording change history, to find out, where and what things went wrong, is a must.8. before the transformation, antidotes for the existing poor enterprise practices and culture are embedded in process and practices.

9. Communications with stakeholders and enterprise employees is adequately performed to poll for support and feedback

10. Security, backup, scalability, availability, systems management... are considered in the transformation right from the beginning

Fail to prepare this means you may have to prepare for the transformation failure.

Ultimately, success is the responsibility of the management, that is, of those that govern, organise, nominate and control the transformation as Peter Drucker once said:

The productivity of work is not the responsibility of the worker but of the manager

and

Executives owe it to the organization and to their fellow workers not to tolerate nonperforming individuals in important jobs

Architecture does not equal transformation but it enables it

https://it.toolbox.com/blogs/adriangrigoriu/architecture-does-not-equal-transformation-but-it-enables-it-072114

July 21, 2014

Jason Bloomberg writes or more appropriately quotes a few architects writing for Forbes on the role of EA in "Is Enterprise Architecture Completely Broken?".

Jason is right in saying that EA has achieved "paltry" degrees of success... but not for the reasons stated. Note: quotes are shown in " ".

"*Digital transformation is a fantastic way to rethink Enterprise Architecture,... as Angelo Andreetto reports*". But this is not the solution though to the EA paltry results though. Rethinking the EA as Transformation even if it sounds convenient, means changing the definition of such an established term as architecture to "transformation" . This rethink may introduce major confusion in the discipline.

EA, as any architecture, is about the structure of a system and its description while transformation is, in a Business Dictionary definition, "*a process of radical change that orients an organization in a new direction...*" .

Hence the two terms are different in nature. EA denotes in practice, the description of the enterprise while transformation is the process of changing it.

Yet enterprise transformation existed long before the EA has even been born.

Sure, EA can and should be used in the transformation of the enterprise today, but transformation is only one of its use cases. Because EA can also be employed to discover the enterprise, understand it, analyse it, manage its complexity, fix operational malfunctions... amongst others.

Take for instance the city architecture used for orientation, finding places of interest, repairs and for transformation.

The EA exposes the parts, dependencies and recommends transformation architectural principles and guidelines.

"The fundamental quality of Enterprise Architecture is its vision of the future".

That is simply not so. It is the business that determines and validates the vision and strategy of the enterprise, not the EA. This kind of statements and interpretations can only raise objections from business strategy and stakeholders further hindering as such our effort to raise the profile of EA.

""EA is often synonymous with the practice of documenting one person's viewpoint of their company's IT," Griesi bemoans."

That's again right but only because the current EA frameworks, while quite dissimilar and ignoring each other, do not ensure analogous, comparable and predictable results. Everyone in fact creates own EA framework and EA as such.

"Frameworks like TOGAF and Zachman "tend to become self-referential, where EAs spend all their effort working with the framework instead of solving real problems" according to Andreetto."

True, self-referential they are, because filling in the cells in Zachman's matrix or following the TOGAF process do not return EA, contrary to expectations, but a set of disjoint artefacts.

To build an EA though, one has to fill in the parts of an EA modelling framework, which by analogy looks like a skeleton, a chassis or a contents page, which none of the above frameworks is.

And EA is not supposed to solve the "real problems" itself. The stakeholders solve these problems in the EA context employing the EA. The architect has not suddenly become the trouble shooter of all the problems in the enterprise, doing the jobs of all the business people.

"According to Griesi, "EA fails when enterprises are treated as discrete systems that can be reduced into smaller problem sets...".

EA treats the parts in the context of the big picture and not in isolation. Looking at parts in separation is what we do now, without EA.

The EA looks at parts as cogs in the big picture.

There are architects who feel more comfortable talking about EA as transformation. That is because the issue of how to model the enterprise is still debatable and less glitzy.

But EA does not equal transformation even though one cannot transform an enterprise properly without an EA blueprint in the first place.

The EA is used to find out what are all the elements involved, what are the relationships and what is the impact of strategy on them.

The Digital Transformation should be lead by the Enterprise Architect

https://it.toolbox.com/blogs/adriangrigoriu/the-digital-enterprise-transformation-should-be-lead-by-the-enterprise-architect-112714

Nov. 27, 2014

While, at first sight, it looks like "digital" is much ado about nothing new, the sheer multitude, size and rapid progress, accumulation and penetration of digital technologies in the enterprise accelerates the urgency of the issue.

Enterprise may be wasted over night because of the fast evolution of digital. Take, for instance, Nokia. They simply failed to respond to the digital pace of innovation in digital terminals banking on their voice terminals for the mass market.

Businesses have suddenly woken up to the realisation that the world goes rapidly digital.

To succeed, new competencies are needed such as a wide technology command and a comprehension of the impact on the enterprise.

To survive in the digital enterprise space, the management needs to understand how all these technologies affect the enterprise at the same time and how do they work together to serve a customer that already lives in a world of digital entertainment, on-line purchasing, personal cloud services... and digital gadgets.

Here are only some of the digital developments in the enterprise:

 - virtualisation of processing, applications, storage and networking

 - proliferation of legacy technologies such as databases, portals, CRMs, ERPs, and new technologies in the data centers

 - the Cloud in its various forms IaaS, PaaS, SaaS...

 - mobile remote access to enterprise applications and information and as such, mobility

 - proliferation of terminals such as PCs, mobiles, tablets... and OSs iOS, Android, ChromeOS... Linux

 - web technologies with faster interactivity, search and standardisation of HTML5

 - big data analytics

 - open source technology

 - social networking such as Facebook, Tweeter... but not limited to them

 - robotics, automated production bands and workflows

- digital identification and security...

It is hard, if not impossible to consider all technologies and trends and then make sense and understand impacts in the context of your enterprise. But someone in the enterprise has to do it in a structured manner.

Can the current management handle the massive digitisation of the enterprise at such a rate?

Many recent articles, such as UK needs an ethics council and digital chief in every department – tech experts, What is digital transformation? Finding your digital sweet spot, Leading Digital Transformation seek solutions to the problem such as a new digital CIO or digital manager in tandem with the business manager...

More often than not though, the traditional CIO and IT department are not part of the solution space at least because of the legacy of slow delivery and poor communication and collaboration.

Still, the Digital Officer we seem to be looking for, is already there. the conceptual Enterprise Architect. Because the EA architect, as part of its job description, not only has to discover and document the enterprise structure and operation but has to align technologies to business mission and vision so that the strategy is achieved.

Today, the EA is best positioned to establish the digital enterprise vision and coordinate the transformation to achieve it.

But the right EA architects have to be raised to the level where they have a mandate to do the job.

The Enterprise goes digital

https://it.toolbox.com/blogs/adriangrigoriu/the-enterprise-goes-digital-121914

Dec. 19, 2014

The major game changer today is technology.

The core business has not changed much in millennia. Its value chains and streams remain about the same. Customer and partner relationships are still, as always, core to the business.

According to Kurzweil though, "an analysis of the history of technology shows that technological change is exponential, contrary to the common-sense intuitive linear view".

So we won't experience 100 years of progress in the 21st century — it will be more like 20,000 years of progress (at today's rate).

The direct "returns" such as chip speed, density and cost-effectiveness, also increase exponentially." And that enables a world of applications.

Most new products, services, applications, infrastructure and networking are enabled by technology.

Technology enables much greater scale of business, complexity, reliability, diversity, rapidity and cost efficiency. Applications like ERP and CRM deliver huge chunks of functionality Off-the-Shelf. Many enterprise services are delivered in the Cloud over the network.

The Cloud enterprise, where most of its functionality and technology can be delivered by partners in the Cloud, coordinate by an enterprise governance is possible since marketing, IT management and even manufacturing can be done by other parties today.

In a "A strategy for strategy: Figuring out how to figure out what IT should do next" it is revealed though that "*most C-level colleagues don't see IT as a business game changer*".

That is true because they are in charge of the status quo to minimise risks but it is unfortunate.

So, how can we deal with the digital disruption of the enterprise?

https://it.toolbox.com/blogs/adriangrigoriu/so-how-can-we-deal-with-the-digital-disruption-of-the-enterprise-122714

Dec. 27, 2014

"Speaking at CloudWorld Boston, Wang examined how the convergence of a host of technologies is powering digital disruption... Digitalization of business is a key factor in this accelerated pace of change... Businesses differentiate themselves by using the technology to create new strategies of such disruptive power that they can wipe out entire markets"...

Ray Wang is founder and principal analyst at Constellation Research in *Ray Wang: Cloud Is The 'Foundation For Digital Transformation'*.

So how can we deal with the digital disruption of the enterprise?

Certainly, it is not sudden but its rate of change is already overwhelming the enterprise.

The problem is that the today's management of the enterprise is not "digitally" equipped to respond properly to the challenge. Since digitisation has a strategic dimension neither is the IT equipped, focused as it is to keep the IT lights on.

So, who is going to manage the evolution of the enterprise to digital?

We need a new function to make sense, rationalise and integrate the emerging digital technologies of the present and future in the enterprise.

The function should be able to understand what are the technologies out there, their business cases, their integration in the enterprise and their collective roadmap and strategy. It would have to understand the big picture, the architecture of the enterprise, to see how technologies add value and link into the picture. This function should combine the emerging technologies with the business architecture and strategy acumens.

Yet, this is what an enterprise wide architect does today: describes the enterprise, roadmaps new technologies and developments and produces the strategy to get there.

The Enterprise Architecture would be crucial to the integration of technology in the enterprise since it allows the analysis of technology impacts on the enterprise functions and systems. The EA would enable the business to transform the enterprise from what it is to what it is envisioned to be, the digital enterprise. Without EA, the digitisation of the enterprise would be ad hoc, random and mail fail to deliver while costing more than it is worth.

Today though, many EA architects are working for and delivering into IT alone, mainly policing IT developments without ever producing the EA, the reference description of the enterprise. Since they do not work at the business level, they are unable to produce the business and the enterprise wide architecture. The IT architecture they come with, looks like patches of machine execution of an unknown overlying business architecture.

Since the digital officer function should be able to oversee the all the developments in the enterprise to be able to apply them to the whole enterprise, align and roadmap them and deliver in concord without duplications and waste, the scope and authority of the work should be enlarged to a function reporting to the CEO, or at least sit at the same level with the strategy, operation and IT chief officers.

Perhaps, solely the enterprise architects are, able to produce the EA from the business to technology and people tiers will be able to play the Digital Officer role. They should have though the management skills demanded by the role.

But if one of the usual business managers is appointed to the role, they would not bring the synoptic view and the architecture, business, and digital technology skills required by the job with all the risks this incurs.

Why the digital enterprise, is it inevitable?

https://it.toolbox.com/blogs/adriangrigoriu/why-the-digital-enterprise-is-it-inevitable-022515

Feb. 25, 2015

Do we have to take the digital enterprise path?

The digital enterprise is happening nolens volens, that is, there is no choice. The enterprise cannot really escape the technology progress. We cannot avoid the digital revolution. And it is a revolution indeed, because the change is significantly larger now and increasingly faster. Moreover, we are already engaged on the digital path.

According to Ray Kurzweil, "technological change is exponential, contrary to the common-sense "intuitive linear" view. So we won't experience 100 years of progress in the 21st century — it will be more like 20,000 years of progress (at today's rate)... We're doubling the rate of progress every decade".

Even though the digital future is inevitable, we can still make choices and actively control the digital evolution from as early as possible to get what we want, in accord with our vision, rather than accept what comes.

The digital revolution will enable

- the business be in control of the enterprise operation and evolution with capabilities purchased or configured on-line and mounted only for the required period
- the designed enterprise, architected from parts or services, given their increasing availability in the Cloud, at business process outsourcing providers
- the business to manage capabilities rather than technology
- more reliable planning and predictable costs owing to the availability of ready-made capabilities, rather than relying on in house development and deployment cycles as today
- technology expertise to be relegated to service provider firms rather than the enterprise
- quick scalability, configurability, reporting... agility to change, features inherited from capabilities
- Instant decision making based on Real Time Business Intelligence
- Model Driven Manufacturing where the design to manufacturing process is automated due to with 3D printing,

The digital gradually renders the enterprise virtual with most parts residing in a cloud of partners that participate into the Value Chain. What matters most and identifies the enterprise is the Governance function that coordinates the enterprise Operations, Development and Support activities that can and are increasingly outsourced. See also "The Cloud Enterprise"

Technology evolution would enable Business to be in control of the enterprise rather than continue to tinker with technology like today.

The digital enterprise at all costs does not pay

https://it.toolbox.com/blogs/adriangrigoriu/the-digital-enterprise-at-all-costs-does-not-pay-022815

Feb. 28, 2015

The Digital road is long, without an end in sight. In fact, we have already embarked on this road long ago. But the technology progress accelerates today at an unprecedented pace.

Since it affects now the whole enterprise, technology becomes a key competitive differentiator. Hence, we have to prepare the enterprise for the digital road because technology could make or break the enterprise.

What do you do though to make sure your enterprise evolves on the right digital path? Digital adoption can be expensive or ineffective if not properly thought. Not all digital technologies, for instance, would be productive for your chosen evolution. And, without proper integration in your operations and vision, the digital can create an additional weight. **Digital at all costs does not pay off.**

To succeed in the digital transformation today, we have to project the big picture at the end of the tunnel, the digital enterprise, the same way we do in enterprise architecture.

You need a true and strong digital team that operates at top business level to cover the whole enterprise rather than IT alone.

Yet, what we do today is embark in implementing the digital step by step, technology by technology. and hope for the best. Yet this path does not allow us to control the final outcome but strands of it.

What makes the difference is not so much the technologies employed but the degree of integration into your enterprise operation and vision so that technologies offer your maximum benefit at minimum cost and render the enterprise competitive.

The digital technologies may also transform your vision of the enterprise though and more, change its business models.

The paradox we live today is that the progress of IT leads increasingly to the outsourcing of the very technology that enables it. Perhaps because the effort to manage properly its increasing complexity becomes too costly and steals the focus of your enterprise. With the Cloud, the enterprise would own less and less technology.

The information technology is also increasingly hidden under virtualisation layers. Note the growing reliance on processing, storage and network virtualisation and the services paradigm in software.

Does Enterprise Architecture really enable enterprise transformation?

https://it.toolbox.com/blogs/adriangrigoriu/does-enterprise-architecture-really-enable-the-enterprise-transformation-041415

April 14, 2015

In theory, EA enables the enterprise transformation, the same way the blueprint of your house or town enables its change. Without a blueprint, laying cables in the wall or under the pavement is a risky endeavour because you may break the existing electricity wires and the water and gas pipes. In practice though, few EA efforts deliver the EA blueprint. As such, EA may hardly enable the enterprise change or transformation today.

Moreover, EA does not deliver business benefits directly because its aim is to deliver the blueprint of the enterprise. EA defines the process, the enterprise components and terminology.

The business itself must transform the enterprise, employing EA, to achieve vision, implement strategic directions (mapped to EA components), reduce duplication in processes, platforms, projects, to streamline operation, fix malfunctions...

The enterprise architect as such should deliver the "big picture", propose architectural transformation principles and assist the enterprise change. But without delivering the big picture, EA fails.

The paradox today is that while there are plenty of EA architects, there are few Enterprise Architectures.

That proves in fact that architects do not deliver EA but rather stories about it and engage in never ending efforts and self important discourses. Most architects sell the EA benefits rather than do EA.

In practice, without an EA blueprint, the architect can use only own experience to try to advise the transformation. Which is a risky proposition.

The EA architect arguments are baseless without the reference EA. And "influencing" everyone, given the current lack of authority of the architect, is even harder without the blueprint, standard components and terminology.

The EA architect cannot guide an enterprise transformation without the EA blueprint as a reference for all stakeholders and projects. And the blueprint must exist to a certain degree before engaging in the transformation rather than be modelled on the run, when it is too late.

Anyway, business stakeholders today hardly know what to expect from EA. They are quite pessimistic about it, noting the disaccord between practice and EA claims. In this void, the EA field is fertile for parties that, for own commercial good, sell their own "EA".

The subsequent paradox is that even if EA does not deliver, business customers do not complain because, for most, EA is still an internal IT effort of little consequence to the wider enterprise.

But that does not help remedy the EA situation.

In any case, it is not so much the architect but the architecture and proper principles that matter to a transformation.

As with a building, the blueprint is what matters after the original architect is long gone.

Consider Digital evolution in your enterprise strategy

https://it.toolbox.com/blogs/adriangrigoriu/consider-digital-evolution-in-your-enterprise-strategy-061915

June 19, 2015

With the acceleration of Digital progress, the enterprise technology landscape changes faster and faster.

Networks, disks, storage and processors grow more powerful, faster and cheaper. Information storage capacity soars at an unprecedented pace. ..

Virtualisation enables the separation of applications, processing, storage and network entities from the physical hardware, enabling as such easy online resource creation, configuration, scalability, availability, portability... and, hence, business operation agility.

In-memory databases enable instant processing and real time analytics.

On top of the infrastructure, more applications and suites such as Portals, Information and Document Management, Access Control, Orchestration and Enterprise Integration Buses, CRM, Call Centres, ERPs - Finance, HR, Procurement...- are increasingly automating, off-the shelf, the enterprise.

The Web added powerful and standard interactive technologies based on complex UI languages like HTML5 and scripting.

Mobile technology ensure fast access to the enterprise functions from anywhere.

Social Media facilitates bi-directional contact with customers and prospects.

This is where we are today. I remember nevertheless the10MByte disk that looked like a fridge in the early 1980s.

And ultimately, enabled by the Digital progress, the Cloud changes the paradigm of IT ownership. The IT goes back to the shared data centre. We rent from the data centre processing power, storage and networking rather than buy, maintain, upgrade, discard and recycle.

Paradoxically, the Cloud, by outsourcing the IT services over the net, offers us a degree of insulation from the digital technology rapid evolution. We don't have to master it all any longer.

In fact, the Cloud makes our digital evolution easier.

Because we manage our business functions and processes independent of technology and its location.

But why do we care about Digital?

Because of the impact of Digital on the business operation: faster responses, more intuitive UIs, more agile configurations able to respond to market changes, more scalability, more integration of processes, information and technology, more off-the-shelf choices, more automation... more of everything.

But we have to control the Digital evolution rather that the vice versa.

Adopting a technology frantically, one at a time, without the benefit of the big picture, may ultimately contribute to failure rather than success.

How would the digital enterprise look like from a business angle?

https://it.toolbox.com/blogs/adriangrigoriu/how-would-the-digital-enterprise-look-like-from-a-business-angle-022315

Feb. 23, 2015

Pundits have already embarked in campaigns of the kind "do digital or die". Right, but how would a digital enterprise look like?

And why should we do it, only because some say so? Businesses existed for hundreds of years before the "digital" technology was born.

In any case, the digital technologies evolution or perhaps, revolution, is on our cards for the long run. It is an ever on-going process. We just have to drive the enterprise on the right digital path, that is to make best use of digital developments. Because others would do exactly that.

For convenience, here are some of the digital developments that affect your enterprise. Still, there are many more and more to come. We can only skim the surface today.

- Virtualization of digital processing, applications, storage and networking
- Outsourcing SaaS, PaaS, IaaS... to the Cloud
- Mobile and remote access
- Social media
- Tele-collaboration and conferencing technologies
- Application suites and services increasingly expanding to automate the whole enterprise operation
- Electronic B2B transactions with partners and suppliers
- Customer Data Integration (CDI) and Master Data Management (MDM)
- Big Data, advanced business intelligence for Decision support
- Business applications and flows Integration based on business rules
- In-memory databases for instant processing of information
- Virtual reality
- 3D printing
- Internet of Things, self driving cars, robots, transport drones etc.
- And perhaps, sometime, in the future, the teleportation technology would let us materialise into the office before the boss or the customer arrives.
- But how would the digital enterprise ultimately look like? In this vision, the enterprise could be
- **Virtual,** stretching over the boundaries of a few physical enterprises owing to the Cloud and business process outsourcing enabled by fast digital communications, collaboration, B2B and transport technologies
- **increasingly Lego** like, assembled from parts such as SaaS services that would

be remotely plugged in and out and configured, scaled... over the net.

- The new paradigm would be **leasing capabilities rather than buying** and owning them.

- **Automated** end to end, with applications covering all enterprise functions and workflows and transactions executed without manual intervention due to the increasingly expanding application suites, services, IOT... beside robots, assembly bands

- **Small office footprint** due to remote working, mobile access and ubiquitous communication technologies

- On-line sales, payment, marketing and customer interaction based on web social media technologies

- **Virtual shops** manned by virtual reality technologies, decreasing physical shop footprint

- **Information, integrated, normalised, consistent...** due to MDM, CDI, integrated application suites...

- Real time business intelligence, due to in-memory platforms

- On-the-net data store and back-up on the Cloud

-

The Digital enables new business models and the "Virtual Value Chain"

https://it.toolbox.com/blogs/adriangrigoriu/the-digital-enables-new-business-models-and-the-virtual-value-chain-070415

July 04, 2015

The progress of Digital technology brings in the enterprise new business models.

Companies increasingly market, sale and service over net channels, rent their resources from the cloud and let partners provide the processing links of the enterprise value chain. But the customer channels, resources and partners are the key elements of any business model.

Take the example of so many firms today that outsource manufacturing, sales, marketing or, on the other hand, the product design and development, with most of them outsourcing now the enterprise support functions.

New companies appear, mainly comprising of management staff who assemble the pieces of the business from services that execute the links of the value chain, from sourcing to making and delivery over various channels.

The companies may just have a web site, hosted and designed by somebody else at that. But, the enterprise still owns the product and manages the whole production chain.

The new business model is of the "virtual value chain" kind. Both business processes and technology are outsourced to partners and cloud providers. The Digital progress supplies the integration network, the virtualisation base, the off-the-shelf Cloud services, the customer channels... that ultimately automate the virtual value chain.

The enterprise creation becomes a matter of integrating the partner services and the Cloud infrastructure that deliver the value chain the entrepreneur establishes. Everything is rented.

The cost of failure is much smaller as such.

The only function that remains in the physical enterprise is the management that selects, configures and coordinates the links of the virtual value chain. This function will also identify the enterprise.

The Digital transforms as such the way our enterprises are created and operate.

Companies in partnership, collaborating to deliver a product, act as the value chain links of an overall virtual enterprise composed of them, the many distributed enterprises.

The name of the game is cooperation. Without the Digital technology progress, that would not have been possible though.

The impact of Digital on the enterprise

https://it.toolbox.com/blogs/adriangrigoriu/the-impact-of-digital-on-the-enterprise-070715

July 07, 2015

The Digital would enable the enterprise and its stakeholders benefit in many ways.

The enterprise would be increasingly distributed, interconnected and automated. Many new small enterprises would be part of the enterprise virtual value chain in an interconnected economy.

It would be agile, faster to market as such, leaner and meaner.

The integration of data, the user experience and the quality of intelligence would be progressively better.

Customers would benefit from better and new types of products, all digitally enhanced.

All technologies, capabilities and products would be enhanced by Digital technology. That would pave the way to the Internet of Things (IoT), that is Things that co-operate to deliver a service.

The evolution to Digital is not an option but a "must". But while we are already doing it, we have to prepare for the increasingly accelerated rate of Digital progress.

The Digital evolution would affect the way we do business and the organisation of the enterprise.

We must prepare the enterprise to evolve towards a virtual enterprise, enabled by Digital technology, where various business processes and services are/maybe outsourced to partners in the Cloud world in various business models.

To cope, it is important to comprehend our own enterprise better, its structure and operation so that we can factor the Digital in a quick and safe manner.

We have to be good at evaluating the technologies that are about to change the enterprise.

We have to include the Digital in our Strategy and planning.

The Digital technology would create many new products and services. Think about them early.

The Digital would enable innovation and invention in many sectors.

Reflect on that.

What do we need to do in practice?

As always, a solution is to create a function in the enterprise that focuses on Digital.

What would the Digital Office do for the enterprise?

https://it.toolbox.com/blogs/adriangrigoriu/what-would-the-digital-office-do-for-the-enterprise-072115

July 21, 2015

Digital, perhaps, is the biggest factor of change in the enterprise or elsewhere today. To ensure our enterprise succeeds in a digital future, we have to understand first the technology impacts and trends.

Hence, it's a good practice to create a function in the enterprise that focuses on the digital issue.

The aim of this Function in the enterprise is to prepare the enterprise to evolve to Digital,

- analyse the evolving and new technologies potential impact on your business

- liaise with functions to understand business technology needs

- propose a digital roadmap for discussion and approval

- merge Digital evolution into the enterprise strategy

- architect technologies integration to functions without duplication or unnecessary variation or replacement

- produce the target Digital enterprise blueprint

- coordinate the digital transformation process

What the Digital Office has to do before even looking at Digital:

1. understand better and describe our own operation and technology capabilities.

2. prepare a technology obsolescence roadmap

2. architect our enterprise so that it can be easily configured out of services that can be filled in by best of breed, off-the-shelf applications available on-site, in the Cloud or elsewhere

The Digital Office should be, as such, in charge of the emerging digital technologies, the digital roadmap and perhaps enterprise architecture. The function would be operating at the top management level rather than IT.

Ironically, the digital revolution gradually removes the technology as an enterprise concern by moving it back to the Cloud.

Hence, the digital office function may have to discover first the existing business landscape and architect the business to be able integrate digital functionality as technology evolves.

There is always the risk though, that a massive electromagnetic wave reduces to digital technology to rubble in an instant, and with that your enterprise. We may have to consider this scenario.

What can we do to mitigate the Digital tsunami threat? Do services, SOA

https://it.toolbox.com/blogs/adriangrigoriu/what-can-we-do-to-mitigate-the-digital-tsunami-threat-021816

Feb. 18, 2016

Many argue that technology has been increasingly and successfully adopted in the enterprise. So what is new with the Digital fuss we make now?

The answer is yes, we did adopt many technologies so far but the issue is that the current technology change rapid pace overwhelms us now. And we can see little prospect of slackening.

Moreover, today we need so many months if not years to upgrade an application suite during which things could change dramatically in the digital arena.

What happens if a company like Apple makes a move in our space as it did in the music and mobile phones field? Do we surrender as others did?

The dark cloud that threatens our enterprise is the Digital technology progress pace and amount of change that gives us less and less time to breath. And it's getting faster by the day.

Also, we have to adopt more technologies at virtually the same time. We did not have this problem so acute until now. Sure, we did space them out, implemented them one by one rather than boil the ocean. But that is not longer possible.

On the other hand, we have to do business, our reason to be, rather than change the underlying technology all the time.

What can we do though? There are ways.

Take for instance enterprise SOA declared once dead. Services do hide their implementation. Hence technology does not matter. Well to a degree. Because newer technologies makes scaling easier and faster. Take for instance the virtualisation that enables scalability, redundancy, portability, OS independence...

Few have succeed with enterprise SOA though because, at the enterprise level, performed for the sake of it is a huge and costly transformation which could be hardly justified in itself, at least until now. Besides, each enterprise had to define and build our own SOA services. A reference business architecture that emphasises services is necessary to streamline the effort.

What can we do to mitigate the Digital tsunami threat? The Cloud (i)

https://it.toolbox.com/blogs/adriangrigoriu/what-can-we-do-to-mitigate-the-digital-tsunami-threat-i-022116

Feb. 21, 2016

But why not fight the technology threat with technology the way we fight poison with poison?

Enter the Cloud era where we do not own technology any longer. We leave the technology companies do the technology part. We just mind our own business. We just buy services from specialised service and Cloud companies. In fact, airlines have rented for a long time now the application of flight tickets and hotel room reservations.

Also, it is a bit anachronic today to build and operate own data centre when there are firms out there that do it better and cheaper because they have the top expertise and the economy of scale. They are building today extra compact and green data centres in containers that operates underwater for cooling.

The Cloud services are inherently SOA, services accessed through APIs. They come ready-made with auto-scaling, redundancy, reporting... capabilities. The combined Service and Cloud approach is optimum.

To sum up, the enterprise IT can gradually move to the Cloud by adopting its services, IaaS, SaaS... The technology, of little interest to the enterprise in itself, moves as such into the Cloud, hidden behind services.

Therefore, we are no longer concerned with the Digital technology in the enterprise. We no longer have to implement and integrate technology but business services. Savvy business people can do that.

But, since the transition to Services and Cloud may take time we have to mitigate the Digital in other ways as well.

The Digital threat mitigation begins with the preparation of our enterprise for the now continuous and increasingly rapid change.

Hence, we have to render the enterprise agile. But while sounds good, DevOps, it is mainly about own software development in the enterprise, which, in the Cloud era, makes less sense.

Still, the capability development, change and release management processes have to be adapted to this age of light speed change.

But can we change the enterprise when we have not even properly documented its structure and operation? Currently each of us have a different and only partial understanding of how our enterprise works. That obstructs communication, collaboration, development and so on.

To run in Digital race we must build an emerging technology function

https://it.toolbox.com/blogs/adriangrigoriu/to-run-in-the-digital-race-we-must-build-an-emerging-technologies-function-022416

Feb. 24, 2016

Setting you up to understand the technology landscape is key to determine what technologies would affect you the most. Because you cannot adopt them all. And to implement them in concert, while replacing and evolving the existing landscape at the same time, you need an Enterprise Architecture practice. Both will contribute to your enterprise evolution to Digital.

The emerging technology function and team, if newly created, has to start with the inventory and evaluation of the various technologies and establish their degree of relevance. Gartner's hype cycle is as good a starting point as any.

Watch also the capabilities and the roadmap of the next generation IT applications and infrastructure because most suppliers had done, like you, a technology landscape evaluation.

You first need to construct a new technology knowledge database, or at least a taxonomy that records definitions, descriptions, maturity, predicted impacts, dependencies, endorsements and proposed further actions for the participating enterprise stakeholders (specific departments, marketing, IT test, development and strategy teams) to take. It must be an enterprise wide effort otherwise the effort will fail.

There may be many issues like applications and technology overlapping in functionality. Take for instance a new applications suite which comes with a function you already have. Ideally we should look into components, services but, in practice, application suites come with the advantages of an integrated information architecture, ready-made enterprise buses, harmonised access control...

Also the Big Issue is that a technology alone may not realise much taken in isolation. You have to analyse other technologies it may request to function, the technology to be replaced and the cost of replacement and the legacy you have to integrate it with. Hence you have to evaluate the whole technology landscape before making up your mind. Otherwise you may end up with multiple, rather ad hoc, transformations. That is you need your EA in place by then.

Therefore, sketch scenarios of integrating the new technologies with the existing. There may be a few alternative scenarios.

Create target enterprise pictures for each scenario to illustrate how does the enterprise look when all technologies of interest are factored in. Start with the business blueprint. Think of new business models.

For each scenario evaluate roughly the resources needed, costs, end benefits, risks, transition period... that is, do the value proposition.

Take into account the risk of not implementing an option, that is the cost of the opportunity lost.

Get Ready for the Digital Future

https://it.toolbox.com/blogs/adriangrigoriu/ready-for-the-digital-future-012019

Feb.04, 2019

Peter Weill and Stephanie L. Woerner state in **Is Your Company Ready for a Digital Future?** on MITSloan Management review that *"there are four different pathways that businesses can take to become top performers in the digital economy. Leadership's role is to determine which pathway to pursue — and how aggressively to move... However, the goal isn't digital transformation but rather business transformation"*.

It is mostly true that a business does not engage in a Digital transformation for the sake of technology alone. Because the transformation costs a bundle, takes a long time and effort, it disrupts operation, requires new skills and re-organisation while it may fail to deliver. If the benefits do not outweigh the costs, the company may go broke. That being said, exceptions proves the rule. There are cases when we update the technology without really changing the business functionality. We do that because we have to when the technology reaches its limitations (speed, storage...), becomes obsolete in terms of language, version, no longer supported (Windows7, ...), or too expensive to support or further develop. My very blogging platform has been replaced with a new technology even if it has now less functionality and is slower than before.

Peter and Stephanie then say:"Becoming future-ready requires changing the enterprise on two dimensions — customer experience and operational efficiency".

The dimensions have less to do with the Digital future readiness but with the current enterprise performance. In fact, a company that exhibits both excellent Customer Experience and Operational efficiency may be still as unprepared for the Digital future as any enterprise, or even less so because the enterprise may employ over optimised, wired in and as such hard to change technologies.

Hence, the Digital transformation will still find the enterprise hard, slow and costly to change even if it is positioned well in the two dimensional quadrant. Good Customer Experience and Operational Efficiency do not guarantee the enterprise readiness for the Digital future but only a good performance in the present. And, even though the customer experience has been already thoroughly changed with .com, the online sales and digital marketing, it can be still poor if neglecting human factors which have little to do with technology.

Yet, Digital readiness has nothing to do with the Customer experience and Operational efficiency. In some cases it could even be the opposite; the processes optimised to bare bones may be hardly adaptable or modular because modularisation introduces overheads. But "customer experience" and "operational efficiency" are the usual workhorses in all business discussions. The two dimensions, Customer Experience and Operational Efficiency just enable the simple analysis of the performance of an enterprise, any enterprise for that matter.

It is also exaggerate to assume that the Traditional-Traditional enterprise in the 1st quadrant exhibits Silos and Complexity, because that would assume that all enterprises today are Silo-ed and Complex. Neither do good Customer Experience and Operational efficiency imply in any way Agility or Modularity.

In any case, Digital future ready can only mean that an enterprise is prepared for any Digital change the future may bring. And for that an enterprise must be the Agile. But how does an enterprise become Digital future ready, i.e. easy and fast to change?

The Digital automates business operation, digitalises our products, changes the way we work (remote access), commute (air taxies, fast Loop trains...), meet (online), interact (virtual reality), manufacture parts (3D printing), make decisions (AI and Big Data)...

To prepare yourself for the Digital transformation, you have to understand this:

1. The Digital transformation should be initiated as soon as the associated business case and the business models are proved

2. The Digital technology itself would facilitate the Digital Enterprise transformation. With the move of IT into the cloud, the Digital itself gives us solutions for the Digital Enterprise transformation. Due to the Digital technology we can outsource now entire functions to partners. The Cloud removes the worries about the Information Technology by removing it from own premises and outsourcing its installation and maintenance.

3. There would be less and less Digital technology in the future Digital enterprise Digital Enterprise would outsource most of its Technology to the Cloud.

4. The Digital Enterprise would be increasingly Virtual/Networked and Cloud based

Digital changes the organisation and relationship to partners; it enables a company turn Virtual by outsourcing value chain links and functions such as manufacturing, marketing... in fact all of them except Governance.

5. With the Digital, the way we do business, i.e. our business model may thoroughly change to new online, over the net and sharing models. Enterprises will increasingly employ the Sharing/Participating Models where the resources are owned and provided by the participating human resources at their locations. Take for instance Uber, AirB&B...

6. The Digital transformation is an on-going, never ending journey rather than an one off effort but it will take place faster and faster.

Keep in mind that executing well a digital transformation is a necessary but not sufficient condition to perform well in the digital economy, whatever that is, because there are so many ways to get it wrong. An example would be choosing the cheaper but less performant technology which does not integrate with your other technologies.

Still, while surveys like this inform us of how other enterprises approach the Digital readiness issue, the approaches of other enterprises may not be suitable for you. In fact, there may be as many ways as enterprises given your specific business models, mix of technologies and their state of obsolescence, your strategy and vision, etc. In any case, surveys alone do not distil the existing approaches generic methods applicable to all enterprises.

How to Get the Enterprise Ready for the Digital Transformation

https://it.toolbox.com/blogs/adriangrigoriu/how-to-get-the-enterprise-ready-for-the-digital-transformation-020519

Feb.05, 2019

The Digital technology pace of evolution is overwhelming. If your competitors succeed to employ them before you do, they will surely gain a competitive advantage. Besides, the digital evolution will have an increasingly brutal pace. It will feel more like a revolution. To cope, you may have to pre-transform your enterprise to be ready for the Digital transformation which is an ongoing rather than an one time development.

Simply put, to be ready for the Digital, the enterprise must be agile, prepared for change.

But what do you, the leaders as they like call you today, have to do about it?

Initiate an Enterprise wide Programme to:

1). Document your Enterprise Architecture (EA)

To enable the collaboration between stakeholders in the digital enterprise transformation so that everyone could have the same understanding of the enterprise and language, the same components to represent with same notations. Since EA provides the synoptic view of the enterprise (the Business, Technology and People organisation in integration) a stakeholder could navigate a process from one function to another and identify the implementing technology, in order to understand and improve operation, fix defects, analyse the impact of change and so on.

EA also enables the mapping of strategy and transformation workstreams to EA components.

2). Reduce the Architecture Debt

The Debt should be documented first on the current EA model and then reduced by employing architecture principles.

The elimination of debt would reduce the overlaps, duplication, repetition or unnecessary variation in processes, platforms and roles... and as such would reduce inefficiencies and costs, which may otherwise be inherited by the Digital enterprise in construction.

3). Virtualise the Enterprise

To cope with the increasing complexity and change, any enterprise is increasingly confronted with, the enterprise has to be gradually virtualised. Virtualisation introduces an abstraction layer that hides implementation and standardises access to its functionality. Hence, since the using entity sees only the abstraction tier, no matter the application design or its technology.

· A. Virtualise IT

Desktop Virtualisation, Server Virtualisation, Storage Virtualisation, Application Virtualisation, Network virtualisation (Network Function Virtualisation (NFV) (Portable Software instead of Hardware Nodes), Software Defined Network (SDN) an approach that opens up network management through APIs). See The Virtualization of the Enterprise

· B. Virtualise the User Interface

To enable a uniform UI, no matter the application type, implementation language, server OS or access device. This is realised today by employing HTML, HTTP, REST....

· C. Virtualise Business Flows

By modelling and controlling the service orchestration. The business expert directly creates, tailors, changes and configures a flow from a graphical interface. The technology matters no longer to the business user who just assembles a process out of lego like blocks from services in a catalogue and sets the business rules employing an orchestration tool. Moreover services may be leased from the Cloud rather than owned by the enterprise.

Hence, the business may directly model the process online and change , simulate and stage it out of services... without help from IT.

·D. Virtualise Information

By organising it in an MDM (Master Data Management) like tier, offering a gateway to the enterprise information that transfers and transforms the information as necessary, to present it to the user service.

4). Do model the future Enterprise around Services employing SOA tenets and technology like APIs, web services, microservices...

Existing complexity could be encased in components, accessed only over interfaces, so that complexity is hidden from external parties. The API paradigm bundles complexity within objects to make possible the separation of concerns and partitioning of the enterprise transformation on components in workstreams. Services allow no longer back doors to systems often used for quick fixes that become nightmares in the long run.

5). Do outsource services and technology... to the Cloud

In the beginning, outsource the Digital technology so that the increasing IT complexity can be outsourced to the Cloud where the technology is owned and managed by somebody else, more effective at that and benefiting also from economies of scale. See The Cloud Enterprise, The Digital enables us to outsource the Digital. Outsourcing the technology enables you to avoid the increasing demand for new skills and talented but expensive IT resources. Besides, the future enterprise would be able to focus on business rather than the fast changing Digital landscape.

Don't take the Digital full on, do outsource it to those in the know. Remember you are not in the business of IT. Let's leave that to the specialised companies whose business is the Digital technology. You should not bother about IT when your business is manufacturing or constructions.

Outsource Business Processes as BPO (Business Process Outsourcing). BPO outsources in fact an entire capability to partner firms that execute it. BPO is more than SaaS (Software as a Service) in that it outsources the process and people not only the technology.

In conclusion

You may consider all five points above as the first phase of the Digital Transformation. But do avoid executing this phase in parallel with your Digital transformation because it would compete resources and come too late anyway.

In the absence of this readiness phase your Digital transformation will stumble at every step, will suffer delays and your business will become unstable. That is because your Digital technologies will replace systems that are wired together in a hairball and exchange incompatible information formats.

Still, even if this phase is hard to justify profit-wise, here is what your management shall get:

- By designing the enterprise around EA, Services, Virtualisation and the Cloud and by reducing the enterprise architecture debt, your enterprise would be modular, able to deploy new Digital capabilities and scale them faster in response to market changes.

- You'll control your OPEX by paying for IT capability usage alone rather than for ownership, maintenance, upgrades, replacement and recycling.

- The Board would talk no longer about buying expensive Windows or Linux servers every two years or so. They would not have to understand any longer the difference between a SQL or Non-SQL databases.

- The enterprise would evolve towards a virtual (networked) enterprise built on a value chain of links which may be provided by 3rd parties.

The Preparation of the Enterprise for the Digital Transformation

https://it.toolbox.com/blogs/adriangrigoriu/the-preparation-of-the-enterprise-for-the-digital-transformation-100417

Oct. 04, 2017

It is good to prepare the enterprise for the incoming digital transformation. Because it may have a brutal pace.

Here are six proposed best practices for rendering the Enterprise ready for the Digital Transformation. Failing to apply them may delay accomplishment, fail the transformation or render it long and costly, full of miss-steps and rollbacks.

What you achieve through preparation is a clean, streamlined enterprise that works as planned, as is. Once documented, you may plan the transformation and proceed on the Digital path. Because it is long road rather than an one time development. But indeed, some of the preparations, once plotted, can be executed on the digital roadmap.

1). Model your full Enterprise Architecture

to document your enterprise so that every stakeholder can understand and use EA, minding own business in the transformation.

EA would provide the common language, components, representations, connections, dependencies between the parts of the enterprise and synchronization between transformation streams.

Because EA supplies the whole view of the enterprise, the Business, Technology and People organisation in integration, that is the business processes and the people and systems that executes them. You can navigate from one function to another to track a process, plot the transformation and analyse the impact of change. EA enables collaboration between stakeholders in the realisation of the digital enterprise transformation.

EA also enables you to discover your enterprise and act safely on the enterprise operation faults and change and synchronise development projects.

EA facilitates strategy mapping to enterprise objects and transformation workstreams.

2). Achieve the architectural debt reduction through EA.

Debt reduction can be observed and realised through action on architecture. The architecture principles must be enforced to reduce and keep the debt to a minimum.

The reduction of the architecture debt realises a drop in overlaps, duplication, repetition or unnecessary variation in processes, platforms and roles... and as such a decrease in inefficiencies and costs, which may otherwise be inherited by the new built Digital enterprise.

The Preparation of the Enterprise for the Digital Transformation (i)

https://it.toolbox.com/blogs/adriangrigoriu/the-preparation-of-the-enterprise-for-the-digital-transformation-i-100517

Oct. 05, 2017

3). To cope with the increasing complexity and change, any enterprise is confronted increasingly with, the enterprise, have to be gradually virtualised starting with the IT.

Virtualisation introduces an abstraction layer that hides the virtualised object implementation and standardises access to its functionality from no matter where. Hence, since the user works sees only the abstraction tier, one can realise a traditional physical server box in software or implement any user interface in HTML, no matter the application and its technology.

This looks like a Black Box approach. We are interested no more in what's under the hood but in the functionality exposed to the outside world. The technology matters no more, except for geeks, it is "egal" or "wurst" as a German would say.

A. Information Technology Virtualisation

- Desktop Virtualisation

- Server Virtualisation

- Storage Virtualisation

- Application Virtualisation

- Network virtualisation

- Network Function Virtualisation (NFV); instead of dealing with physical boxes one manages apps in containers and virtual servers that may be easily created, moved, replaced, cloned, re-started, configured, scaled, backed-up,....

- Software Defined Networks (SDN) an approach that opens up network management through APIs to humans and the intelligent configuration software of the network virtualisation centre.

B. User Interface Virtualisation

The same kind of GUI no matter the application, server OS, or access device. No more GUI libraries for each language and OS. One single GUI paradigm no matter who accesses what. The GUI virtualisation is enabled by technology as well, by the HTML language.

C. Business Flow Virtualisation

An enterprise flow ultimately consists in the business rules driven orchestration of a number of services connected to an enterprise bus.

The business expert creates, tailors, changes and configures a flow from a graphical interface. The services may call each other or may be activated by events they are subscribed to. This paradigm aligns well with the serverless Cloud.

The technology matters no longer to the business user who just makes the process out of lego like blogs, services listed in a catalogue, employing an orchestration tool. The services may be leased rather than be owned by the enterprise.

The business may directly model, without the need for IT, change the process, simulate and stage the process, all online.

   D. Information virtualisation.

Information is hidden by an MDM (Master Data Management) tier that transfers and transforms it as necessary to present it to the user. MDM offers a gateway to the enterprise information.

The Preparation of the Enterprise for the Digital Transformation (ii)

https://it.toolbox.com/blogs/adriangrigoriu/the-preparation-of-the-enterprise-for-the-digital-transformation-ii-100617

Oct.06, 2017

   4). Do model the target Enterprise around services (SOA, APIs, web services, even microservices... so that complexity is hidden from stakeholders inside services.

The SOA and APIs paradigm bundles complexity within objects - complexity invisible therefore to external parties - and as such makes possible the separation of concerns and partitioning of the enterprise transformation on services and workstreams. This approach breaks complexity in manageable pieces and thus eases change. Besides, there are no longer back doors for quick fixes that become your nightmare in the long run.

The services paradigm aligns easily with the EA capabilities approach.

   5). To defeat the growing Digital threat, do outsource the Digital technology. The threat comes from the fact that, without digital, the enterprise may lose out to nimbler competition or may fail the transformation altogether. The increasing IT complexity can be outsourced to the Cloud where the technology is owned and managed by somebody else, more effective at that.

Outsourcing the technology, in particular to the Cloud, enables us to outsource the incoming Digital that increases exponentially the need for new systems and fresh, talented but expensive IT resources. By outsourcing the technology, the future enterprise would be able to focus on business rather than the faster and faster changing Digital landscape. Don't fight the Digital. do outsource to those in the know.

   6). Do outsource business functions as BPO (Business process Outsourcing). BPO outsources an entire capability, that is the process, the people and technology that execute the capability to partner firms.

The enterprise evolves already towards a virtual (networked) enterprise built on a value chain of services provided by 3rd parties. See The Cloud Enterprise.

Once the analysis phase is over, you will most probably want to merge some of the the architecture debt requirements, projected end service/capabilities, digital solutions and business strategy in the target picture of the Enterprise in various phases of the enterprise transformation.

Any other approach may lead you either to a full preparation phase, harder to justify profit wise, or to parallel transformation tracks which sooner or later enter in conflict for resource usage, if not urgency and outcomes.

Digital Enables Us Today to outsource the Digital Problem (i)

https://it.toolbox.com/blogs/adriangrigoriu/digital-enables-us-today-to-outsource-the-digital-problem-i-100317

Oct. 03, 2017

The Shadow IT solution, which appeared as a response to the unresponsiveness of the IT department, added even more IT to the enterprise, introduced duplication, unnecessary variation and maintenance and, in the end, created new IT silos.

Yet, you are not in the business of IT. Let's leave that to the specialised companies whose business is the Digital technology.

We should not bother about IT when your business is manufacturing or constructions.

History proves the Cloud is right. Millennia ago, we used to make all things by ourselves. Yet, specialisation created in time the trades that provided those services for us. The associated guilds guaranteed their quality. We, ourselves, are cleaning no more today our homes. We build no more our houses. No more self fixing of the plumbing, painting the walls... We became so effective in our own work that we are able to make a profit from which we pay specialised firms to do this other work for us. Specialisation replaced our many chores. We should do the same with the IT in the enterprise.

By employing the Cloud, your enterprise would be able to deploy new and scale faster business capabilities in response to market change. And you'll pay for IT usage rather than for ownership, maintenance, upgrades, replacement and recycling.

The Board would talk no longer about buying expensive Windows or Linux servers that you have to replace and recycle in two years time. They would not have to understand the difference between a SQL or Non-SQL database or why SAP deployment takes months if not years.

The cloud is precious because it allows you to focus on your business rather than its IT, an alien preoccupation to your business people.

The Digital itself enabled the outsourcing of the IT to the Cloud.

Hence, rent out the IT that supports your business, rather than buy, own, maintain, evolve, scrap and recycle it. Because today, doing IT in the enterprise slows your enterprise down in the face of increasingly steep competition.

Nimble IT firms would provide better, more reliable, scalable, secure and cheaper services that you can in the enterprise.

How Can a Company Make Sure That the Digital Journey Succeeds?

https://it.toolbox.com/blogs/adriangrigoriu/how-can-a-company-make-sure-that-the-digital-journey-succeeds-041719

Apr. 17, 2019

The Digital road is long with no end in sight. In fact, we have already embarked on this road long ago. But the technology progress accelerates today at an unprecedented pace. Since it affects now the whole enterprise, technology becomes a key competitive differentiator able to make or break the enterprise.

To embark on a Digital journey a CEO must be aware that:

  1. All enterprises must take the digital enterprise path.

The enterprise is going to be digitalised nolens volens. It cannot really escape the technology progress. According to Ray Kurzweil, *"technological change is exponential, contrary to the common-sense "intuitive linear" view. So we won't experience 100 years of progress in the 21st century -- it will be more like 20,000 years of progress (at today's rate)... We're doubling the rate of progress every decade"*.

But, even though the digital future is inevitable, we can still make choices and actively control the digital evolution from as early as possible to get what we want, in accord with our vision.

  2. The technology capabilities would enable the Business to be in control of the enterprise rather than continue to tinker with technology like today.

The enterprise will be designed, architected from in-house parts and services from various Business Process and Cloud providers.

The capabilities would be purchased and configured on-line and mounted only for the required period

Technology expertise will be ultimately relegated to the service provider firms rather than to each and every enterprise. The paradox is that the progress of IT leads increasingly to the outsourcing of the very technology that enables it.

What makes the difference is not so much the technologies employed but the degree of integration into your enterprise operation and vision so that most suitable technologies offer your on time the maximum benefit at minimum cost.

3. The Digital is a continuous long term transformation driven by a Digital Roadmap and Strategy (see this), not an one off Digital Transformation.

The Strategy shows the direction while the Roadmap establishes the key technologies, business milestones of the continuous transformation. Enterprises that attempt to solve the Digital in one go fail. This is a key reason most enterprise transformations fail. Enterprises attempt to transform too much in one go and then discover that have to start anew. The must be aware that the transformation is perpetual and as such a Digital Strategy to guide the long term transformation and a Digital Roadmap to establish the first hurdles are necessary.

4. And, not least, most Enterprises have grown organic today.

The organic architecture makes the enterprise more difficult to understand, operate and change. Your Digital transformation is endangered by the hazards posed at change time by such an architecture. The enterprise needs a more structured architecture first.

The organic enterprise is harder to control and transform because its structure is not regular. Fact is that the enterprise today has grown into a hair ball with the functionality and interconnections added as they happened with local fixes and temporary solutions rather than planned and taking into consideration all implications and dependencies in the context of the whole.

Enterprises are as such more complex than necessary and less agile because any change may have unintended consequences which require fixing and testing and further delay the transformation.

In order to increase the chances of the Digital transformation, the enterprise must be detangled, its complexity reduced while its agility increased.

This architecture correction transformation will have to take place at the same time with your Digital transformation. because the funding would be very hard to justify otherwise.

To make sure that the transformation succeeds, **the CEO must first n**ominate a Transformation Leader who understands technology platforms and the workings of the enterprise.

A choice is the Enterprise Architect indeed, but one able to model the enterprise rather than one certified for the fake EA frameworks of today which would not help but delay and cost you a fortune, by delivering framework related rather than the outcomes required in the transformation.

The Transformation Leader must

1. assign the permanent core teams and organise the transformation programme

2. have the current Enterprise Architecture modelled

have the abstract target Enterprise Model designed and have a plan drafted to detangle, simplify, reduce architecture debt, modularise and employ APIs to render the enterprise agile to all future change. Alexander the Great cut the Gordiam knot. If you cannot detangle the enterprise simply cut the knot and redraw the connections.

3. have an emerging technologies report produced with the relevant technologies mapped to Enterprise Architecture components.

4. have the target **implementation** Enterprise Model devised by

- o have the target architecture designed – architecturally correct, modular, organised around independent blocks with interfaces, aka services.

- o assign sub-teams to map various technologies to the enterprise functions and design the solution architectures for each function for various technology combinations.

- o compare the resulting target implementation architectures with regard to achieving your goals: fixing the current problems, reducing the architecture debt, implementing the new technologies and strategic business directions.

- o Select the target implementation architecture, shaped of all solution architectures, that best suits your needs and funding and minimises risks.

- o To ease your task, both components and project workstreams must have well defined operational interfaces between them because they should be as   independent   as   possible. Teams should produce in further detail the solution architectures for each component in alignment with all others.

- o Do involve suppliers in the solution architecture design. Check designs against the key end to end flows of the enterprise. Iterate. Do join all solution architectures in the overall Enterprise Architecture. Use a tool to align components, notations, information etc...

5. produce the Enterprise Transformation Strategy and Roadmap

- o and the short term programme plan composed of the component workstream projects that implement the solution architectures agreed. Each workstream would transform the component from the current to the future state determined by the business strategy, architecture debt reduction... Do prioritise the workstreams. Note dependencies at planning.

- o select an implementation strategy : either implement a parallel customer platform you handover customers to (Costly).or replace components in place over weekends while the enterprise still operates during the week (Risky).

- o Establish milestones to assess risks and deliveries

6. execute the long term strategy piece meal, iteratively, with go/no-go milestones, having the benefit of the current Enterprise Model and the coherent solution architectures that converge to the target Enterprise Model. The roadmap is transformed into a plan with resources at least one year beforehand.

The Enterprise Must Be Rendered Agile Before the Digital Journey

https://it.toolbox.com/blogs/adriangrigoriu/the-enterprise-must-be-rendered-agile-before-embarking-on-the-digital-journey-041519

Apr. 15, 2019

The Digital technology makes giant steps today. Not only IT is rapidly changing, but all other technologies are increasingly digitalised and interconnected today, employing microprocessors, software, artificial intelligence, sensors and actuators that enable these technologies be digitally controlled. The digitalised technologies progressively enable the automation of the enterprise.

Anyway, it is clear that, from now on, the Digital rapid evolution requires the enterprise be able to change at a fast pace. Hence, we must render the enterprise agile before embarking in the never-ending increasingly faster Digital transformation.

Yet, since the Digital is more like an IT++ transformation, because Digital is more than IT, it has even more chances to fail than any IT Transformation which routinely fails at rate of 75%. Because enterprises get no clear picture of what Digital transformations are in practical terms, enterprises postpone them indefinitely. Besides, in the UK, the CEOs (see a post) are now made responsible - for now, their bonuses will be penalised they say - for the mal-operation of the banks and for the transformations that negatively affect their customers.

Hence, long live the legacy in the enterprise. But, even if enterprises postpone transformations, they cannot defer them forever. Enterprises looking at implementing the business vision and strategy alone, ignoring emerging technologies and the new capabilities and the business models they offer, have to soon face the competitive advantage gained by the enterprises that already deploy them. This is particularly true in the IT intensive financial industry under sustained attack now from the Fintech startups.

But how can your enterprise succeed in this Digital journey where big companies, big money and big contractors have failed in their IT transformations?

The most important step is the preparation of the enterprise so that it can be detangled, simplified and rendered agile for the everlasting Digital transformation. The preparation of the enterprise which would consist of:

1. Because enterprises today have not been designed or planned, the current enterprise has to be first documented in sufficient level of detail

The business needs to commission the Enterprise Model first to make sure everybody talks about the same components and processes, in the same language on the same blueprints; to ensure that every part is owned by a team and its blueprint is aligned to the overall enterprise blueprint.

Outcome: the Blueprint the current enterprise that enables you to understand and change   it.

2. The architecture debt must be reduced beforehand

Essentially, it is time for the enterprise to pay for the times when expediency won against thorough work , that is when its architecture debts have been created . All hastily done changes, implemented out of context, must be reviewed and their potential fixes documented because you would want to know about all problems you may encounter during your transformation. Document the actions that must be performed to reduce the architecture debt. Plan to pay your architecture debt.

Outcome: solutions architectures and target EA that remdey the debt.

3. The abstract target enterprise architecture must be modelled as independent functions with interfaces/APIs, so that the enterprise complexity is encapsulated while its agility increased in order to improve the chances of the digital transformation.

Document now the target high level picture of the enterprise that structures the enterprise according to architecture principles, planning to reduce the hair ball.

3.1. Plan to organise the enterprise in independent functions so that they can be looked at separately by independent teams, assured that the parts fit in the whole. The enterprise should be as such organised in blocks, in a lego like approach. A modular enterprise is agile, since the independent blocks can be changed or swapped with little impact on the whole. Yet, the enterprise functions aren't they constituting siloes yet again? No, because now siloes are created in the context of the whole.

3.2. Plan access interfaces (APIs) to functions so that connections go only through interfaces

Outcome: conceptual model of the target enterprise built around services, i.e. functions with interfaces.

4. Merge the Business and Digital Strategy witth the strategies to reduce debt and modularise the enterprise

Digital Strategy establishes the kind of automation of manufacturing, decision making... , interfaces all based on the capabilities of the new technology the business wishes to adopt in the future.

5. Model the target <u>implementation</u> enterprise architecture

The industry offers today ready-made, off-the-shelf business functions built in IT platforms which must be assembled in a coherent target enterprise. Past are the times when complex business applications could be built in-house.

5.1. Fit in the various IT platforms candidates for the enterprise realisation and compare the resulting outcomes from a cost-performance point of view

Unfortunately, most IT platforms are rather monolithic, non-standardised, overlapping and incompatible since each has with its own functional partitioning, data types.

5.2. Select the target platforms and the resulting implementation architecture

The selection of a digital platform is a trade off between the functionality it provides and its capability of being integrated in the overall enterprise, in particular with regard to data.

Unless strict security requirements are imposed or the functionality is core to the enterprise, plan to employ cloud platforms.

The enterprise does not need to own all its functionality. Service orientation is key to outsourcing since a service is essentially an independent block of functionality with access interfaces.

6. Devise the Enterprise Architecturally correct Business + Digital Roadmap and Strategy

The roadmap establishes what is going to implemented in what time frame and after what milestones.

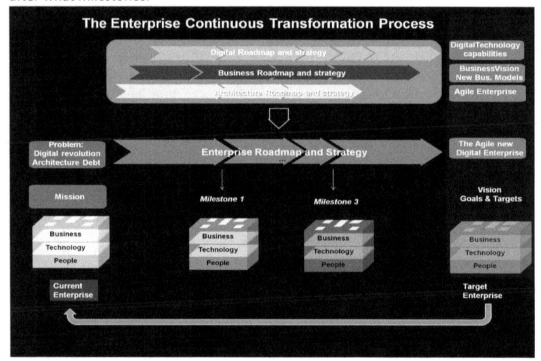

The Business Digital Strategy lays out what is the business goal, how decisions would be made, when would the roadmap be reviewed, etc.

Devise the target and transition architectures for each Roadmap milestone.

7. Iterate: repeat

The Enterprise Needs a Digital Strategy, Not a Digital Transformation

https://it.toolbox.com/blogs/adriangrigoriu/the-enterprise-needs-a-digital-strategy-not-a-digital-transformation-032019

March 20, 2019

Because technology has progressed so much in a short amount of time, the enterprise has to go through a Digital Transformation pundits say.

In fact, in many cases, to change the de facto situation, we should rather talk about a Digital Revolution because, since many enterprises preferred to hold onto their current technology until it turned legacy, the introduction of new technology means a leap over generations of technology which may be only realized by a Digital Revolution.

Why do we need emerging digital technologies in the first place?

1. IT turns obsolete today almost as soon as we create it.

Take, for instance, the servers lifetime or your mobile renewal rate which can hardly be measured in dog years nowadays because it is perhaps three to five times lesser than that. We have to deploy emerging technologies at an accelerating rate.

2. To reduce the technology debt accumulated in the enterprise

By postponing technology refreshes indefinitely, technology change accumulated in the enterprise. Many transformations would have to swap as such platforms separated by generations of technology. But, the bigger the technology debt, the worse the technology integration in the enterprise. Mainframes, client server, web paradigm, cloud are just a few of the technologies of the different generations having to work together in the enterprise.

The Technology Debt, newly defined here, is the difference between the newest technology on the market and the existing technology generation in the enterprise.

3. Enterprises, to stay competitive, must take advantage of the new Digital Technology processing capabilities

They have to increasingly faster deploy, serve more customers, and grow more reliable, fault tolerant, scalable, configurable, agile, customer friendly and be interconnected.

4. To prevent disruption brought about by the new business models enabled by emerging technologies today which were not possible yesterday.

The new business models may change the way a business operates and the way processes, employees and assets are managed and owned. Take the case of sharing in the transportation industry, which enabled Uber, Lyft, etc., where disruption was least expected.

5. The Digital Technology progress accelerates today past the normal pace of enterprise transformation.

Essentially, today the technology progresses faster than the enterprise can change.

In short, the enterprise has to adopt new technologies to respond to the increasingly faster changes of the world around. CDs, cassettes, and even petrol cars became a thing of the past already, all during our lifetime. There is an increasing pressure to implement the touted Digital Transformation because the rate of technology progress today surpasses the rate at which the enterprise can change. Yet, CEO's fear that in reality most transformations fail **(see** this**)** and as such postpone the digital change.

But Digital Transformations fail. That is because:

1. The organically grown organization is hard to change.

The enterprise needs to be detangled first to enable further change.

2. Enterprises have to overcome the silo thinking and organisation.

In a so complex world our thinking and work is increasingly silo-ed. We do understand well our piece, but we do not understand well the rest of the enterprise operation; too often we do not care or even know what happens to other parts of the enterprise. As such, change is operated in siloes rather than across them. Hence, siloes must be dealt with before any transformation.

3. The enterprise processes and the associated IT are not properly documented.

IT installations, additions, changes are seldom documented in a standardized integrated way or in one place. How can you change something you don't know?

4. IT itself grew unnecessary complex for the enterprise. And, since complex is harder to change (because there are more systems, more connections, more dependencies...) IT transformations have a greater chance to fail today.

5. New digital(-ised) technology platforms bring along different business processes which are often neglected in the transformation. Still, they demand new people skills, training, reorganization,...

6. Digital transformations has even more chances to fail than the IT transformations which fail at a 75% rate

Digital is more than IT. IT can be thought as the Digital Technology of an enterprise consisting in application (suites), enterprise class servers and networks. Digital, though, is about the capabilities introduced in many other technologies and products today in the form of microprocessors, firmware, sensors and actuators embedded in every little thing (such as phones, cars, toys, medical equipment, rockets, production bands, mining equipment...) enabling them to collect data, process locally, make decisions and communicate between them. Hence, not only IT platforms, but most other technologies must be digitized so that they can be digitally controlled and automated.

7. Digital is a too large one off transformation and as such risky from start

But the larger the transformation, the greater the risk of failure. Hence it must be implemented piece meal in time as a Digital Roadmap and Strategy

Any management would surely ask: "After executing this digital transformation would we be able to resume business as usual?" The answer is obviously "no" because, by the time we finish this digital transformation, we'd need yet another digital transformation. The technology continued to progress rendering again our enterprise, obsolete and noncompetitive. Since there is no end in sight, the Digital adoption cannot be accomplished in a single transformation, but in a rather step by step adoption of the technologies that can return business advantages. But then, rather than putting our enterprise through a never ending chain of digital transformations, should we not rather think of a business as usual process that continuously adopts emerging technologies at the right time?

Hence, rather than embarking in a Digital Transformation (DT) the enterprise should rather proceed with a Digital Strategy (DS). Any CEO would embark on a Digital Strategic path rather than on an one-off large Digital Transformation which presents so many risks. A Digital Strategy is a long term plan of action designed to monetize the advantages of the appropriate emerging technologies deployed in correlation and integration.

As opposed to a Digital Transformation or an uncorrelated sequence of them, each planned and executed separately, one after another, a Digital Strategy is a plan that stipulates upfront the end architecture and all foreseeable actions toward the digital business vision, plan updated when necessary as the time goes by.

Our Digital Strategy is the plan that covers all the transformations of the enterprise for the foreseeable future. It does not consist in a huge one off transformation, but in a coherent long-term plan to implement the digital vision in small transformations that build toward a target enterprise model. The plan has milestones where we always revisit the Digital Strategy.

The Digital Strategy is the Road Ahead as Bill Gates said.

To Soften the Impact of Digital Hide Technology in Services (i)

https://it.toolbox.com/blogs/adriangrigoriu/the-digital-transformation-begins-with-the-realisation-of-the-architecturally-correct-debt-free-enterprise-i-040218

April 02, 2019

The Digital Transformation (DT) is not an one off effort, but the first step in an on-going transformation since technologies will never cease evolving and changing and increasingly faster at that. In fact, there is no single digital transformation, but a never ending series.

This first step though, the step we call today Digital Transformation, should not be about implementing a technologies, but about the realization of an enterprise agile to digital change. The rest of the series of transformations would be then rather business as usual. Without agility, subsequent transformations would have a large chance to fail because change is hard to operate in an undocumented spaghetti like architecture with lots of duplication in processes and platforms, unnecessary technology diversity and interconnections and dependencies all over the place. Hence the first Digital Transformation has to document the enterprise, streamline and reduce its complexity.

What would be though the strategy for Digital Transformation success in a world increasingly driven by technology?

Rather than facing a future where the enterprise has to change every time a technology changes, why not remove the technology from the enterprise as much as possible? Were technology hidden behind interfaces, the enterprise would not have to see and manage its complexity. The principle is: a technology out of sight is out of mind.

Furthermore, if technology is embedded in business services behind interfaces, one can delegate the technology management to the internal or external autonomous business service suppliers. Then, rather than attempting to master and manage all technology in the enterprise, which is surely an enormous task in the digital future, one could outsource the technology to specialist business service providers. Technology would be dealt with by the specialist service providers then rather than in the enterprise. Let the kind of Amazon, Microsoft, SAP, Oracle deal with their own technology.

The enterprise can as such regain its focus on business. A service based enterprise is an enterprise which processes mainly consist in the orchestration of autonomous business services. The enterprise transformation would not demand as such exhaustive digital talent, but only integration of business services with a minimum of technology understanding.

DT begins with architecturally correct, debt free, service based enterprise (ii)

https://it.toolbox.com/blogs/adriangrigoriu/the-digital-transformation-begins-with-the-realisation-of-the-architecturally-correct-debt-free-service-based-enterprise-i-040418

April 04, 2018

In the real world, technology will co-exist in the enterprise with the services provided by outsourcers and the Cloud for a long while. There is no pure service based enterprise. The Digital Transformation today has to begin as such with the realization of the architecturally correct and debt free enterprise. Without that, change would be applied to an untamed enterprise with unpredictable consequences.

The first milestones in the Digital Transformation should be:

1. The upfront establishment of

(a) an Emerging Technologies (ET) team that surveys technologies, evaluates them, analyses their place in the enterprise and delivers the ET database and process, reports, alerts, presentations, testing and prototypes and ultimately a pure technology road-map,... ET would also evaluate the relevant technologies employed by business service providers.

(b) an Enterprise Architecture practice (team, method, standards...) that shall provide the enterprise models that document the current enterprise and project the future states so that changes could be analysed, aligned and harmonized on enterprise models in context and impacts could be evaluated by stakeholders in concert. The EA team would evaluate the technology and architectural debt of the enterprise. That target architectures in various phases would consist of a mixture of IT, outsourced applications and managed, Cloud and BPO (Business Process Outsourcing) services.

2. The implementation of the architecturally correct, debt free enterprise states to reduce overlaps and unnecessary duplication or variation while promoting standards that ease harmonization and future decision making.

3. The design and realization of the service based enterprise nimble to change. That is because services exhibit APIs that hide the implementation technology which can be provided as such by interchangeable technologies and parties, like standard parts in the car industry. By hiding the realization technology, we can change it later with ease and can outsource to manage it no longer.

4. The implementation of the technologies prioritized.

The Far Reaching Impacts of Digital Technology So Far (iii)

https://it.toolbox.com/blogs/adriangrigoriu/the-far-reaching-impacts-of-digital-technology-so-far-iii-040218

April 02, 2018

Nikki Bair writes for Forbes about What Digital Transformation Actually Means For Retail.

As the technology evolves, the role of humans moves up in the value chain. Man won't have to dig ditches or plough the land any longer but to drive a machine that does that, remotely at that. The pilot does not drive any longer a large airplane, the computer does. AI does the decision making, facts matching and customer advice. And so on.

The retail industry is revolutionised today by the growing online sales, marketing on social media, VR in shops, drone deliveries...

Online customer reach, remote working, distributed enterprises, outsourced data centres... are now a reality because of the increasingly nimble, fast, reliable and ubiquitous networks. The new digitally enhanced products and technologies are now the norm. Cars have now hundreds of digital chips inside.

Digital technology impacts on the business:

.- new business organisations such as virtual/networked enterprises based on services provided by partners. An airline, for instance, already outsources today the bookings and reservations, catering, cleaning, luggage transportation, airplane maintenance functions...

.- IT-less enterprise with IT outsourced to remote data centres and the Cloud.

.- new business models such as Sharing

.- remote workforce

.- business processes adjusted directly by business experts from orchestration consoles

.- self-adapting, self-repairing (with IoT sensor input), automated business flows

.- new, self-driving transportation systems

.- AI driven customer advice (bots) and decision making

.- real time and localised Business Intelligence driven marketing and sales

.- social media for communications with customers

.- blockchain based, undeniable contracts and transactions

.- Virtual Reality assisted shopping, presentations, training, simulations

The Digital Transformation is Just the Preparation Step in a Long Journey

https://it.toolbox.com/blogs/adriangrigoriu/what-digital-transformation-really-means-for-us-040218

April 02, 2018

We keep talking about the Digital Transformation today even though few of us do have a clear picture of what it means for the enterprise.

Nikki Bair writes for Forbes about What Digital Transformation Actually Means For Retail.

"Digital transformation. At its highest level, it means using digital technologies to create game-changing business innovations that disrupt existing industries or create whole new ones. That's a pretty simple definition, but it quickly gets very difficult to drive that down to specifics".

Yet, Digital Transformation (DT) is not really about game-changing business innovations even though, sometimes, it may lead to that. In fact, we may have to change technology only because is more cost effective rather than innovative.

Yet, the digital transformation is no different from any other transformation. It has been happening for a long time now, in fact, since the advent of computers and later, the integrated chips. It is just that the tremendous pace of technology progress drives business change today at a rate at which businesses could barely cope with, threatening as such their existence in the increasingly competitive landscape.

"We won't experience 100 years of progress in the 21st century — it will be more like 20,000 years of progress" according to Kurzweil's Law of Accelerating Returns.

Proving the Moore's Law, a top mobile phone today has more processing power than a mainframe or space station of the past. The network speed grew exponentially too making possible the Cloud, that is, accessing your outsourced IT over the net, which in turn enabled profound business model changes, such as in the Sharing industry based on mobile terminals, applications and networks.

But, the first step in the enterprise digital transformation is for the enterprise to become nimble enough to cope with the accelerating Digital evolution or, more likely given its exponential curve, the Digital revolution. To render the enterprise agile to change, one has to model the enterprise, pay the architecture debt and organise it around services.

The Digital Tranformation Path chosen on the combined Impact of technologies on the Big Picture

https://it.toolbox.com/blogs/adriangrigoriu/how-can-companies-succeed-on-the-digital-path-to-the-future-051420

May 16, 2020

A problem for the digital transformation today is that Board of Directors do not understand technology. But, should the Board of Directors be selected on technology acumen too?

That companies seldom have technology savvy leaders we already know because the technology background has been, more often than not, looked down upon. Technology was considered, until recently, only a costly implement. Well, the Board members were not chosen on the technology acumen criteria anyway. But, the truth is that it is hard enough for technologists, consultants and analysts to keep up with the digital technology progress, nevermind the business directors.

Nevertheless, the problem the executive lot is confronted with today is not only that without the latest technology their business can hardly survive the competition race, but also that the digital evolution is increasingly outpacing the current business rate of change. That is, we are going through a digital revolution rather than an evolution. Some suggest that technologists or CIOs should sit on the company boards. But, to start with, the board meetings are for making business rather than technology decisions.

Anyway, since digital innovation and transformation come rather in conflict with the IT mission to keep the business lights on, which in practice means the fewer changes the better, CIOs have an inherent conflict of interest and, as such, they should be the last people considered to make such technology decisions or sit on the board. The CIO's main task and skills are to make sure that the IT operates five nines rather than plotting the digital future of the enterprise.

Yet neither the Strategy Directors, CMOs, nor the technologists can decide on the technologies adopted in the digital transformation. Strategy Directors do understand the business needs enough to establish the strategic directions, but they would not be able to pinpoint the technologies which realize the best the direction until the technology impacts are translated into business impacts. The

CMO's scope is products, sales and marketing strategies, rather than the technology of operation of the enterprise. Technologists have the know-how, but not the big picture of how well technologies serve the enterprise. And so on.

In any case, what the executive lot has to make sure is that the Digital Transformation path is chosen on the combined impact of the new technologies on the big picture of the enterprise rather than on the merits of technologies taken in isolation. That is because the digital impact is not so much in IT, but on the future products, business models, processes and the enterprise organization itself.

Think of the new enterprise business models imposed by technology progress such as:

1) The sharing business model or in other words enterprises such as Uber, AirBnB, consisting of participating resources supplied by many rather independent participants, usually geographically dispersed so that they can provide local services. The digital technology enables an enterprise to coordinate the geographically spread participant labor and the resources into the virtual enterprise.

2) The outsourcing of IT to the Cloud

3) The outsourcing of an entire business process to suppliers

Nevermind the new remote work business model pioneered during this crisis, but which is set to stay for the benefit of all parties and in particular, the environment.

Hence, the up and coming **Cloud Enterprise** is a virtual enterprise which Value Chain consists mainly of services outsourced to a Cloud of IT, Business Services and remote Labor & Resources suppliers.

The point, so far, is that all the above is made possible by the digital technology today. In this context Enterprise Architecture and Security become crucial. Because, how can you outsource a service if you don't know its dependencies on other services or if you cannot protect the remote interactions?

So, what the board and the executive lot need to understand and agree upon is not the technologies themselves, but the projected enterprise big pictures realized by technologies in various end architectures. Drawing this big picture, architecture is not a job though for the Board, Strategy Director, CIO, CMO (Chief Marketing Officer) or technologists.

The digital, rather than becoming a top management expertise, should be the task for the new Emerging Technologies and Enterprise Architecture functions.

A team of technologists should produce a knowledge database with the emerging technologies relevant to the enterprise. A technology record would consist of descriptions, sources. position in the hype cycle, associated costs, risks... value propositions and recommendations. The better the technologies records the better the decision making.

The Chief Digital Officer will lead the new emerging technologies function. The role of the Digital Chief Officer is to create and manage an Emerging Technologies knowledgeable in order to:

.- Analyse all technologies and sift them

.- Categorize technologies on impacts on the enterprise automation, communication and collaboration, decision making, data and content management, products...

.- Produce value propositions for each technology

.- Promote technologies on the path of acceptance

.- Organize trials with go/no-go stages of realization

Yet, even with the new Chief Digital Officer and the emerging technologies function, the enterprise is no wiser with regard to the digital transformation. That is because to be evaluated in context, the technologies must be first projected onto various target architectures for the enterprise taking into account not only all the technology interactions, dependencies, redundancies and roadmaps, but also the future end to end business flows and organization.

Hence, the Enterprise Architect, who must chose, map and combine all new technologies on the future enterprise picture in various scenarios, becomes the key player in the digital transformation.

The role of the Enterprise Architect in the digital transformation is not only to map and integrate the technologies in the enterprise big picture in various scenarios agreed with stakeholders, but to ultimately produce the report for the executive lot and board examining choices, exhibiting business cases and business models and making recommendations.

Yet, as a note, the Enterprise Architect is not the usual enterprise wide IT Authority of today as often assumed, but the Modeller of the Enterprise.

Yet, while the Digital Technologies will change the future, the reality is that the enterprise needs to focus on its business rather than on the ever changing digital technologies landscape.

That is because not every company can afford the investment in technology and its expensive eco system of specialists, training that had to be maintained.

Thus, the enterprise should become as technology agnostic as possible. But, the digital enables the technology agnostic approach as well.

Here are the principles of digital transformation that insulate the enterprise from technology change:

1) Encapsulate technology behind interfaces in SOA like services that hide the technology

That is because complexity, in order to be conquered, must be divided and encapsulated in modules which can be dealt with in separation by different parties.

2) Outsource the most challenging technology services to specialist/cloud

companies

EA As Reference, Governance and Story for Enterprise Transformation

The Digital Transformation Guide for the Executive Lot

https://it.toolbox.com/blogs/adriangrigoriu/ea-as-reference-governance-and-story-for-enterprise-transformation-082319

Aug. 25, 2019

EA governance for the enterprise transformation

The EA group has to create a governance framework that would be employed in the consistent design of EA artefacts, solution architectures and EA decision making process.

All stakeholders have to conform with the EA governance. For instance, stakeholders should check the EA before any investment in their field to determine the components affected, the platforms recommended and similar technologies already available so that the investment attains is objectives without creating duplication or overlay in the process.

Because architectural debt is created if "projects make decisions in isolation.

The governance should act through established and widely approved principles, control checkpoints in processes and project phases, roadmaps, strategies and decision making policies that establish who makes what decisions on which parts... The governance should be agreed beforehand rather than being elaborated on the run, as it happens today. One has to make sure though that the governance has input and meets the approval of all concerned parts. Governance should be approved by a more encompassing and different body from EA so that project architects and many other stakeholders may have a say.

Then, projects and activities should all submit to the governing rules and body, which body may not necessarily be the EA group but may have participation from. The Governance should be constantly reviewed and updated.

Governance reduces chaos. Governance avoids friction. Governance enforces integration, consistency and predictable results.

EA as reference for the transformation

How do you design the target architecture if you do not discover and document first the architecture of what is out there? How could you expand a building without taking into account its current structure? You may end up transforming a barn in a concert hall.

In the absence of the current architecture, the enterprise may end up being re-designed from scratch at each cycle.

How could you plan a proper enterprise transformation if you do not know the current organisation and processes, the current systems and technologies, the as-is capabilities to act on their strengths and weaknesses?

How could you perform the gap analysis and establish the roadmap to the end state?

What would happen with the current platforms, skills and investments if you replace them when you ignore them starting from scratch?

How would the enterprise continue to deliver its products and pay your salary during such a transformation that may end up making you redundant?

The EA blueprint is about the current enterprise state. It enables the understanding, maintenance, fixing, improvement and transformation of the enterprise.

The enterprise evolves incrementally employing the existing processes and platforms rather than in revolutionary cycles. Even revolutions re-use existing structures.

Besides, a target enterprise that fails to consider the current operation and technologies would make your management cringe, to put it nicely. The transformation cost and risks would be insurmountable. Abandoning assets half way through their life cycle, unamortised yet, would waste investments. What would the shareholders and the investors say?

Too often though strategic transformations start, unfortunately without the architecture of the current enterprise. Too often the current EA is just embedded in people's minds. That increase the risks and costs of any transformation because nobody has the entire picture to make sure the transformation streams work towards that single goal. The current EA would make the transformation faster, cheaper, more effective, predictable and less riskier. The current enterprise architecture is a reference for the enterprise transformation because we refer to and transform what we have rather than building the enterprise from scratch.

EA as a story for transformation

So, where is the "story" idea coming from? To me the question is, are we turning our backs to "A picture says a thousand words"?

After all, EA is an architecture and the blueprint of the enterprise. At least, the words in the naming lead us to the logical conclusion that EA is a picture. And a building architecture is expressed in blueprints rather than stories, as we all know.

The story approach looks like springing from the popular tradition of employing plastic imagery, metaphors and comparisons to explain things in simple terms to people who have little patience, time and knowledge of the domain. And, at times, we may be all appreciating a well told simple story rather than the technical explanations.

It is also true that in recent times, even the professional literature is full of stories written in a colourful language rather than worded in the precise language of the profession.

A story may help stakeholders visualise how the enterprise will work after development. A story may come as a presentation to gain approval from the relevant stakeholders. The story is not used though to develop EA but to narrate the "change" for people to understand and subsequently approve it.

Anyway, it is not the EA architect that dictates the future state of the enterprise but the management, its vision and business strategy. Is it likely then that the strategy team puts together the story anyway.

What an EA architect has to accomplish then is to translate the story into use cases and target EA the that illustrate the impacts on processes, organisation, components and technologies of the enterprise.

The EA architect should devise the architecture that illustrates "how the new world would work" and the roadmap to show "what change would happen".

Nevertheless, should such a story be necessary, the teller function should be perhaps played by strategy and marketing teams. It is the marketing that usually illustrates how the "customer is made happy" for example.

Are we, the EA architects, in a position of command to tell stories and have the people listen? I doubt it. Would the management even expect the EA architect come with tales instead of pictures and roadmaps?

Ultimately, it is true that we have to "sell" the EA results as best as we can, by telling stories, if necessary. But that's not part of the EA development or utilisation process. Anyway, the architects have to be fluent in explaining the impacts of EA, stories or not. They should be indeed good communicators.

To conclude, stories may help certain audiences understand change by employing common language and light narrative. But stories are not how EA is done or represented though.

HBR AND FORBES ON WHY DIGITAL TRANFORMATIONS FAIL

The Digital Transformation fails because..., according to HBR (i)

https://it.toolbox.com/blogs/adriangrigoriu/the-digital-transformation-faila-because-according-to-hbr-i-040618

April 06, 2018

Why So Many High-Profile Digital Transformations Fail Thomas H. Davenport and George Westerman write for HBR:

"...Ford invested heavily in digital initiatives only to see its stock price lag... These companies spent millions to develop digital products, infrastructures, and brand accompaniments, and got tremendous media and investor attention, only to encounter significant performance challenges, and often shareholder dissent...".

Today, even academic and business consulting firms like HBR, Boston Consulting, McKinsey, Forbes, ... which kept for so long their distance from IT, are all into Digital, telling us incessantly, if not the technologies, what we have to do to save our enterprise under the assault of technology. They are even into Enterprise Architecture (EA) today, which was so IT, that they wouldn't touch it with a pole. Gartner even kindly helps us sleep at night by providing all the right EA answers.

Yet, not noticed enough at this time, the IT continues to slide out of the enterprise into the Cloud. The more Cloud there is, the less Digital in the enterprise. Even if Digital continues to change the enterprise, it does so through new and enhanced business functionality, realised indeed by an ever innovative IT that we see no more because it is moving into the Cloud. Yet, we are on a digital transformation path where the Cloud penetration is at about 20%.

In this context, without a thorough effort to re-evaluate your enterprise vision with a view to emerging technologies you may miss developments that may render your enterprise more cost effective or you may miss the digital technologies that enhance your products, without which they may become obsolete overnight. Your car becomes electronical and computerised, while your cooking pot embeds AI...

But since the Digital Transformation (DT) is likely to go on forever, the DT we are talking about now is in fact the first step in a series of digital transformations, which should realise an enterprise that is ready for the digital fast lane. The DT success comes now, not so much from the transformation itself, but from the proper preparation and planning of the enterprise for the foreseeable future.

Once your enterprise turns agile to change and the Digital roadmap and planning are set and harmonised with your business long term goals, the Digital transformation becomes an organic part of your business Strategic Transformation. New iterations of the Digital Transformation will follow consisting in change preparation, planning and execution.

The Digital Transformation should begin with the analysis of digital technologies in order assess the multiple impacts on the enterprise in order to be able to determine a harmonised roadmap toward a target enterprise picture that can deliver your business vision. Your strategists have to work now with technology gurus and Cloud partners since most business changes today are induced by technology whose renewal cycles get shorter and shorter.

Why Digital Transformations Fail, According to Forbes

https://it.toolbox.com/blogs/adriangrigoriu/why-digital-transformations-fail-according-to-forbes-040618

April 06, 2018

Steven Zobell, Chief Product and Technology Officer for Workfront, writing for Forbes explains: Why Digital Transformations Fail: Closing The $900 Billion Hole In Enterprise Strategy

"This year enterprises are expected to 1.3 trillion (USD) in digital transformation initiatives to apply digital capabilities to improve inefficiencies, increase customer value and create new monetization opportunities. Tragically, research tells us that 70% of these initiatives will not reach their stated goals. That equates to over $900 billion worth of spend that will miss the mark".

Why does this happen? Steven comes with the answers:

"1. Teamwork is forgotten in business transformations... "

Because of a work ecosystem that is largely analogue and silo-ed.

Too much of the workday is swallowed up by email, administrative tasks and meetings. Substantial time is lost in the frustrating "shadow work" ...

"2. There is no system of record for work"

Enterprises lack an operational system of record that acts as the authoritative source of truth for the organization's work investments, progress and results.

What to do? Steven says:

"1. Understand the modern assembly line:" We still treat employees as artisanal craft workers — silo-ed individuals, manual handoffs, old tools — instead of

integrating them into an enterprise team with platforms that provide visibility across the entire assembly line and automate individual and cross-functional work.

"2. Shine a light on shadow work"

3. *Consolidate sources of truth:* *We spend a quarter of our* time *looking for information.*

"Digital Transformation Is About People we must rethink how our teams work together ...".

The Digital Transformation (DT), as the names says, is about Digital first. People do obviously come into it because they are both affecting and affected by Digital.

To start with, the Digital Transformation fails but, since 70% of all IT projects fail anyhow, the situation is bad but no worse than normal.

The article, starting from digital transformation, slides almost immediately into the problems as usual in a business. Not that we should not try to resolve them.

The advice sounds though like if we have a problem, the solution is to solve that problem. I feel that, but I think we should be more specific. W hat has all the above to do with the Digital Transformation, the digital part specifically? I can see that a few legacy issues, as old as the enterprise, were underlined. But, I am sure that Forbes can do more about identifying the problems specific to the Digital Transformation.

Why Digital Transformations Fail, According to Forbes (i)

https://it.toolbox.com/blogs/adriangrigoriu/why-digital-transformations-fail-according-to-forbes-i-040618

April 06, 2018

Steven Zobell, Chief Product and Technology Officer for Workfront, writing for Forbes explains: Why Digital Transformations Fail: Closing The $900 Billion Hole In Enterprise Strategy.

The article, starting from digital transformation, slides almost immediately into the problems as usual in any business. Not that we should not try to resolve them.

Yet, the problems, teamwork and systems of record, are well known and discussed extensively in the business literature. They do obstruct the digital transformation, but no more than they do to any other work or transformation in the enterprise.

Steven Zobell advises us thus to increase teamwork by integrating it in the assembly line, reduce shadow work (email...) and establish a system to record the on-going projects, a single source of truths that is, and to enable work visibility in the enterprise on end to end process basis.

Teamwork is such an old problem. How is it supposed to work though, when top performers have to ever donate their results to a team they are not even the manager of? Perhaps, the good old forgotten meritocracy, that rewards work, talent, sweat... has to be put in place first. The company culture may have something to do with it too.

"Understand the modern assembly line" hints Zobell though towards *"platforms"* that provide visibility for integration of work in end to end flows. That can be achieved, in today's terms, by employing BPM (Process modelling, 6/Lean Sigma...) as part of an Enterprise Architecture effort rather than talking about "assembly line", rather specific to the manufacturing industry.

As for Shadow work, it is perhaps 90% of work in 90% of the enterprises. We all spend most of our time in phone calls, emails, meetings, weekly reports... That has something to do with performance management and company culture and motivation as well.

"Consolidate sources of truth" sounds like a recommendation to rationalize the information about the enterprise. That sounds both like a plead for a proper Information Architecture, and a sound Enterprise Architecture planning effort.

The Digital is a transformation all enterprises have to go through. It does not guarantee though the success of your enterprise. It is nevertheless a condition for your enterprise survival. But to achieve success we should identify those digital specific issues. Hence, it is good to let space to leaders to vent their problems but Forbes could also publish those who can say or do something about them, in particular for the digital case, chronic now.

THE CIO, CDO ROLES IN THE DIGITAL TRANSFORMATION

While the Chief Marketing Technologist role is new, the work is old

https://it.toolbox.com/blogs/adriangrigoriu/while-the-chief-marketing-technologist-role-is-new-the-work-is-old-070114

July 01, 2014

This HBR article looks into "The rise of the Chief Marketing Technologist"

 Marketing has always worked with R&D, product development, Emerging Technologies (ET) and technology strategy functions to put together its strategy with regard to new products and markets.

That means that this kind of work has always been done with or without a Chief Marketing Technology or Technologist in place.

Yet, how many companies still have R&D and emerging technologies functions today? The marketing technology function appears to fill such a gap.

The marketing technology unit may better fit though into the technology strategy function or the like depending on the current organisation design. That is at least because technology and marketing people and skills are not the best match in the world.

In the end, the Marketing Technology outcome has to be still fed into the Strategy function for subsequent coordinated implementation in the context of the enterprise wide strategy.

Selecting technology for marketing use is a different matter altogether because not every function can choose its technology ignoring all other. It is rather a matter for architects to act upon. But it depends to a degree, on the Cloud adoption strategy and the current centralised or distributed organisation of IT.

The Digital Officer role is the conceptual Enterprise Architect

https://it.toolbox.com/blogs/adriangrigoriu/the-digital-officer-role-proposed-by-

Dec. 02, 2014

The ongoing "digital enterprise" transformation is nothing specific or new. It is just the ever faster accumulation of digital developments in the enterprise.

The on-line digital services and retail, the many social networking communication channels the new electronic payments and money, the mobile access to the enterprise, the automation of processes, the increasingly affordable big data intelligence, the computing cloud transformation, the virtualisation of the data centre and networking... all concur to change the enterprise at a rapid pace.

As an observation, while the Cloud is a technology development at its root, its outcome is to remove the technology from the enterprise, diminishing the need for skills to manage the enterprise own IT servers and applications.

But this digital change must be properly understood and controlled so that best solutions be implemented on time and at minimum cost.

The major issue is that, the enterprises that cannot keep pace with the digital evolution are at a major competitive disadvantage.

To alleviate that, a new digital officer role if often proposed today in the enterprise. This officer would understand the digital landscape and ensure that the enterprise keeps pace with technology evolution at all times.

To take advantage of technology, the digital officer should understand both the technology landscape and the overall enterprise operation. He should integrate and map the latest technologies on enterprise functions, processes, systems... and propose a roadmap of digital evolution.

Since the digital officer needs to understand the big picture of the enterprise, analyse impacts and plan the digital transformation, the projected digital officer role looks very similar to the conceptual Enterprise Architect of today which acts at the enterprise rather than IT level where most EA architects work today.

That is, the digital officer in business terms and the Enterprise Architect in IT speak are pretty much the same role. While the digital officer naming emphasises the domain, the enterprise architect denomination expresses perhaps how it should be done.

The IT function may still keep its IT enterprise architects though.

To convey consistency, predictability, credibility and consistency the digital officer needs an enterprise wide framework to understand not only the business structure and operation but also the technology impacts on them.

The CMO Versus CIO Issue

https://it.toolbox.com/blogs/adriangrigoriu/the-cmo-versus-cio-issue-120514

Dec. 05, 2014

Quite a few articles have recently discussed the relationship between the CIO and the CMO.

When will this madness stop? writes that "an increasing number of CMOs are being tempted to bypass their IT function and deal directly with IT suppliers" while

All that talk about CIO-CMO collaboration? Good luck with that

states that "more IT spending is going *around* rather than *through* IT departments".

Why is this happening? Is there something the CIO or us should worry about?

Unless the products and services are digital/IT, I see few reasons the CMO should either have a special relationship or should appropriate tasks or budget from the CIO.

On the other hand, as long as it provides a customer interaction channel or a market analysis tool, the technology is of importance to the CMO. But not otherwise.

The CMO role has a vested interest in the social engagement technology because it is employed for advertisement, polling and communications with customers. After all, that's what marketing does.

But the CMO and marketing should not be involved in any other technology decisions and sourcing of services because they have no competence, skills or even concerns in that respect.

The task of the CIO and IT should be to manage and renew IT and support staff.

With the advent of the cloud, business departments, not only marketing, may directly lease services, and implicitly technology, from cloud suppliers.

Because departments buy a business service rather than a technology and as such the expense should not really be in the IT budget or care.

Hence, it is neither the marketing and the CMO nor the IT and the CIO that choose a cloud service but the business department in case.

Still, no matter who procures the service and spends the budget, it is not a wise decision to do it without the advice of the CIO or better, the enterprise architect. At least because it may break for instance the information architecture and may add unnecessary diversity to the vendors landscape and as such to the enterprise skills base.

The owner of Enterprise Architecture

https://it.toolbox.com/blogs/adriangrigoriu/the-owner-of-enterprise-architecture-052315

May 23, 2015

Can anybody really own a part of the enterprise? What does ownership really mean? The business employs the term because there is a need for some body to be in charge of all issues related to an activity or aspect of the enterprise.

In this definition here, the owner is the group or role who is managing the activity, the EA, on behalf of the enterprise and is in charge of and in particular, accountable for its proper operation and development. All enquiries, issues, requests, complaints... should be addressed to the owner.

But, since we often prefer to lead by committee today, the accountability for decisions is diluted. It's not often that you hold accountable a board today. But the owner is still the one managing the activity, the practice.

The owner is not the sponsor of a development though even if the sponsor may have a stake.

The owner is not the CFO because the CFO is neither responsible nor in charge of that aspect. Do you address an EA request to the CFO?

To begin with, EA describes the enterprise, the current and future states.

As such, the Enterprise Architect and team own the EA blueprint, the graphical description of the enterprise, and the activity of discovery, modelling and organisation of the artefacts, related information and their storage and communications.

But stakeholders still own their own blueprints, which are part of EA. In fact, they are the ones authorised to maintain the information and execute changes. The Enterprise Architect though and the Architecture Review Board have to check compliance to architecture principles and guidelines. Top management owns the future picture of the enterprise, the overall vision and strategy even if, ultimately, each key stakeholder has devised, contributed and harmonised with the whole, the vision for own part. The architect translates it in practice.

With regard to who owns the activities that change the enterprise and implement the strategy and vision, there is too often no single strategic transformation owner. Quite often there are a few programs taking place at the same time, overseen by Programs, Change Management and the Investment Board.

But usually, there is no EA either, that is, an EA that covers more than IT and which would enable such a unified strategic program.

If there is an EA, the Enterprise Architect, even if not the owner, should assess developments for compliance to the architecture roadmap, principles and standards to make sure as such that major enterprise developments comply with EA and may not introduce duplication, unnecessary complexity, additional projects, non conforming technologies etc.

The Digital and the CIO

https://it.toolbox.com/blogs/adriangrigoriu/the-digital-and-the-cio-100717

Oct. 07, 2017

How the Meaning of Digital Transformation Has Evolved HBR's Tom Puthiyamadam states:

"Think back to 2007... Apple released the first iPhone... ride- or hotel-sharing companies didn't exist yet and the first generation of social media platforms were just hitting the mainstream... companies were mainly focused on data mining, search technology, and virtual collaboration.

Today, executives are directing their energy toward artificial intelligence, machine learning, and the Internet of Things...

... the companies that give CIOs a seat at the table, make IT a part of their strategy, and realize that the fate of their IT investments and business goals are intertwined will be most ready to face the challenges of tomorrow — and the next decade".

I agree up to the point at which I disagree that IT has to sit at the table, now more than before that is, because Digital innovation and transformation come rather in conflict of duty with the IT key task to keep the IT lights on.

Executives can hardly keep abreast with all the technology buzz today. Specialists can hardly cope with the progress and its diversity, never mind the impacts on the enterprise.

Anyway, companies should employ leased services rather than invest directly in new technologies which have always a way to fail to achieve the business goals they are supposed to. The role of the CIO should diminish as such.

Because the main Digital impact on the enterprise is not so much in IT but on the new business models and the organisation that it enables.

Think of the sharing or I would call it participating enterprise or industry. Uber, AirBnB..., resources (technology and human) are supplied by many rather independent participants, usually geographically dispersed to provide the local service.

The Digital technology enabled the enterprise incorporate the geographically spread participant labour and their own resources.

Also, the outsourcing of IT to the Cloud enables the virtual enterprise, the enterprise which outsources value chain processes to a cloud of 3rd parties.

Many companies have already outsourced their manufacturing, marketing, sales... and even strategy specification. For some knowledge intensive enterprises, the only remaining capability is the technology and aesthetic/industrial Design of the product.

The enterprise may own only the capabilities thought core, while the rest of functions are entirely outsourced to best of breed partners. But when core capabilities are outsourced too, the company itself may consist only of its governance function which identifies it.

The virtual company today integrates, coordinates and controls a value chain consisting of both outsourced and own functions and technology.

But the CIO's main task and skills is in keeping the IT lights on rather than plotting the Digital future of the Enterprise and determine its new business models or its outsourced functions.

The CIO evolves Towards the Chief Enterprise Architect Role (iii)

https://it.toolbox.com/blogs/adriangrigoriu/the-cio-evolves-towards-the-chief-enterprise-architect-cea-role-iii-061417

June 14, 2017

What is important to the enterprise new Cloud business model, is the fact that the business, rather than IT, contracts directly with the service providers and ultimately controls the cloud service.

The IT department is little involved because the service itself is a business matter for as long as the enterprise does not own, manage or maintain the infrastructure but only its outcome, the business service.

In effect, the IT role in this case is just to ensure integration with rest of the landscape.

The title of CIO is somehow misleading in the first place since the CIO does not really mean Chief Information Officer but Chief Information Technology Officer (that is CITO) which is different because it manages the technology that manages information rather than the information itself. For Information there is usually a different executive role in the enterprise that controls the access and protection of the business documents and data.

But, as the enterprise IT moved at a fast pace to the Cloud, there is less and less IT left to manage in the enterprise. The IT team no longer develops, installs, maintains or upgrades the technology because it is owned and hosted by the Cloud rather than in-house.

Hence, the role of the CIO, in charge of IT, has to change accordingly.

The CEA, Chief Enterprise Architect role gradually replaces the CIO, now that technology is going to the Cloud.

The CEA has the mission to integrate and harmonise the various cloud services, such as IaaS, SaaS, PaaS, with the in-house IT and the business processes outsourced to other 3rd party suppliers.

Thus, the integration of IT cloud services, in-house IT and outsourced business processes is the job of the Chief Enterprise Architect.

Interestingly enough, the CEA is not necessarily evolving from the CIO role because, while the CIO looks at keeping the technology in working condition, the CEA looks at business and technology integration. The roles may co-exist for a while.

During a transition period though, the technology will live in both in-house and up in the Cloud. Hence, we'd need both roles for the foreseeable future.

For a start-up though the CEA role to integrate the various outsourced services is a must today.

The CIO vs Enterprise Architect (EA) and Chief Digital Officer (CDO) (v)

https://it.toolbox.com/blogs/adriangrigoriu/the-cio-vs-the-chief-enterprise-architect-cea-and-chief-digital-officer-cdo-v-063017

June 30, 2017

The CIO role may fade in time as the technology moves into the Cloud, out of the enterprise. That is, because there would be little technology to manage in the enterprise.

Yet, the CIO can hardly take over the Chief Digital Officer (CDO) or the CEA (Chief Enterprise Architect) roles because they cover different domains and require unlike skill sets.

The CIO deals in IT development and maintenance and is good at organisation and command.

The CDO and is a technologist and visionary. The position, which is now establishing itself into the enterprise, looks into future enterprise technologies. Yet, while this role is key now, the truth is that its scope is increasingly decreasing as the technology moves into the Cloud.

The CEA role must possess architecture talents, a structured thinking and a wide knowledge of business operation and current technologies.

Its purpose is to develop and maintain the enterprise model which will establish a common understanding, vocabulary and blueprint for all stakeholders. The EA model enables complexity control and rapid change.

A CEA makes sure that the enterprise transformation is driven by its models so that no new unnecessary complexity is introduced, the enterprise remains agile and is able to execute its strategy.

The CIO can hardly play the CEA or CDO roles because structure and people skills would not help in understanding either the structure of the enterprise or the impact of future technology on the enterprise.

But the CIO may still play a CTO like role in IT companies, i.e. companies that deliver IT products or services or for which the production technology is IT. For instance a company that delivers online services. In essence, the business of these enterprises is IT.

Since the CEA role has to have a good knowledge of technology which today is a major factor in determining the enterprise architecture, it is well positioned to play the CDO role.

The CEA has to understand, decide on the usage and harmonise the impact of new technologies in the enterprise.

The CDO may best work as a part of the EA function.

The CEA works with Marketing to analyse the capabilities required for new products. And also with Strategy and Programme Management to establish the impact of strategy on the enterprise landscape and properly establish and execute the transformation portfolio.

CEOs have to think today about deploying the CEA role, in parallel with the IT and the CIO role, at the right level of authority, as the Cloud adoption quickly grows and the Digital explodes. The current IT oriented EA is failing to fulfil the EA promise.

The CIO in the Cloud Era

https://it.toolbox.com/blogs/adriangrigoriu/the-cio-in-the-cloud-era-061217

June 12, 2017

There are plenty of articles floating around about the role of the CIO today. Clearly, something is on people's mind. What is the problem though? The questions appear to be about the CIO's relationship to CMO (Marketing) and CFO (Finance) chief officers and about the future of the role, taking into account the Digital and Cloud rapid evolution.

The Cloud, for ease of understanding, is a business model where IT, rather than being owned and hosted in-house, is outsourced externally to specialist multi-tenant providers. IT services such as processing, storage and business applications... are increasingly leased now from cloud third parties.

As a result, the Cloud renders rather unnecessary the in-house IT equipment facilities and the IT force that installs, upgrades and maintains the IT infrastructure.

A Cloud service maybe quickly tested, installed and scaled over the net. For events, the service can be dramatically scaled up and subsequently down to adjust to demand without over provisioning which requires a tall initial investment that remains typically unused for the most of the time.

Moreover, with the advent of serverless or Functions as a Service (FaaS), the enterprise bothers no more to provision the infrastructure (virtual servers, storage...) for an application which just runs when awaken by an event, self-provisioning and scaling itself.

That not only reduces the effort and need for skills but also the cost of resources which are provisioned in a Just-In-Time model rather than permanently.

When not successful, a cloud service could be quickly closed down without loss since there is no initial investment in IT. The enterprise paid for its usage alone rather than owning the infrastructure.

Business can also quickly proceed with development, prototyping and trials in the Cloud avoiding the paralysis through analysis they suffer from when having to commit upfront highly risky investments.

The Cloud also provides on demand various degrees of security, backup, redundancy and failover on a pre-paid basis.

THE UK GOVERNMENT DIGITAL INITIATIVE

The UK Government Digital Initiative

https://it.toolbox.com/blogs/adriangrigoriu/the-uk-government-digital-initiative-032216

March 22, 2016

Government Digital Service

is a unit of the UK Government's Cabinet Office tasked with transforming the provision of government digital services.[1] It was formed in April 2011 to implement the 'Digital by Default' strategy proposed by a report produced for the Cabinet Office in 2010 called 'Directgov 2010 and beyond: revolution not evolution'. It is overseen by the Public Expenditure Executive (Efficiency & Reform)".

" The GDS is intended to "drive service delivery to digital across government and provide support, advice and technical expertise for departments as they develop new digital delivery models". This strategy is focussed on the application of *Agile software development* and *Lean software development* methodologies, supplied primarily via *small and medium enterprises* rather than large suppliers.

The GDS has a 'Digital Advisory Board' consisting of high profile external experts, which meets bi-annually and advises the GDS on strategy. As of 2013... GDS had over 200 staff; by 2015 that number had risen to approximately 500".

GOV.UK

"*is a United Kingdom public sector information website, created by the Government Digital Service to provide a single point of access to HM Government services... replacing DirectGov and Business Link*" "*The website was planned to replace the individual websites of hundreds of government departments and public bodies by 2014. By 1 May 2013, all 24 ministerial departments and 28 other organisations had their URLs redirecting to Gov.uk*".

G-Cloud

"is an initiative targeted at easing procurement by public-sector bodies in departments of the United Kingdom Government of commodity information technology services that use cloud computing. It consists of:

"- A series of framework agreements with suppliers, from which public sector organisations can buy services without needing to run a full tender or competition procurement process

- An online store – the "Digital Marketplace" (previously "CloudStore") that allows public sector bodies to search for services that are covered by the G-Cloud frameworks

The service began in 2012, and had several calls for contracts. By May 2013 there were over 700 suppliers."

The GaaP, Government as a Platform

https://it.toolbox.com/blogs/adriangrigoriu/the-gaap-government-as-a-platform-032416

March 24, 2016

"*Everyone in Government*... promotes the concept of Government as a Platform (GaaP). A recent video issued by (Government Digital Service) GDS gives a high level view of GaaP and states:

We think there is a simpler, easier way (than the independent service silos developed in the past that led to duplication). "It's an idea called Government as a Platform. It breaks things down into smaller parts like building blocks. Each block does one job. It's easy to connect blocks together and easy to scale them up when demand increases. If some part of the service breaks we can fix it or upgrade it easily" which "in some senses reiterates the Service Oriented Architecture (SOA) concept at a whole-of-government level".

Government as a Platform

"is a new vision for digital government; a common core infrastructure of shared digital systems, technology and processes on which it's easy to build brilliant, user-centric government services...

Government as a Platform is a phrase coined by *Tim O'Reilly in a 2010 paper*".

Essentially, the Government as a Platform aims to deliver IT services, that are to be shared by government departments. Currently these services are built in different ways in each department. By re-using and reducing duplication, Government as a Platform will save cost and provide a unified citizen experience.

It consists of:

- "*GOV.UK*, the single domain, is a platform for publishing. It's used by hundreds of departments and agencies, and replacing DirectGov and Business Link"

- "*GOV.UK Verify* – *a platform for identity. A new way for citizens to prove who they are when they use government services"*

Also common capabilities such as payment, case management, analytics, performance, email, appointments and hosting are explored. But there could be some more.

From a citizen point of view, imagine you can identify yourself only once and log to have access to all your information, taxes... that all government departments have access to the same information stored in a common repository, taking advantage of a common information architecture, that workflows move automatically your request from one department to another without you moving their papers around...

A question that arises though is how would the government departments and agencies pay for the GaaP services, which may be supplied by a 3rd party. A simple answer would be, per usage.

GaaP as a Service Delivery Platform (SDP)

https://it.toolbox.com/blogs/adriangrigoriu/gaap-as-a-service-delivery-platform-sdp-032916

March 29, 2016

It is worth mentioning perhaps that the Service Delivery Platform (SDP), which has captured the telecom and digital media industries attention for a long while, was designed too to supply common services for the products and operating companies of a media company group, like GaaP does, in principle, for the UK government agencies.

The SDP Architecture had to define all services that could be shared by various products and operating companies. The SDP did not cover though the enterprise support and development capabilities as GaaP might have to.

SDP had to

- offer an unified (roaming) experience to customers and suppliers, i.e. a common look and feel for all services and increase as such customer's familiarity with the products and adoption anywhere on the footprint of the enterprise group

- reduce duplication and overlap between products and group operating companies and save as such operational, support and development costs

- offer a gateway functionality to partners to deploy applications which employ network services (calls, location, messages...) in order to offer customers enriched applications

The key SDP shared services were found to be:

- the products presentation, discovery and delivery service (portal for rendering and transcoding, product catalogue)

- user/customer access management: identification, session management, subscription, personalization...

- common content management for such content as games, music... providers

- rating (real time too), discounting and billing service

- a standard product hosting infrastructure for all telco products

- the orchestration and integration middleware between all common services and products

- the control gateway for partner access to digital media services such as Presence, Location, Customer data...

- common operational support for the SDP services

Considered also are:

- standard product enablers like DRM, Device Management, Messaging, Location Presence...

- telco provided applications such as IPTV, Personal Assistants

The platform had to be implemented by

- agreeing the same SDP architecture in each operating company

- implementing the recommended technology platforms for the architecture in each operating company

GaaP implementation

https://it.toolbox.com/blogs/adriangrigoriu/gaap-implementation-040216

Apr. 02, 2016

A radical Service Delivery Platform (SDP) implementation solution is to instantiate, based on the SDP architecture, a central platform to serve all parties in a single geographical location taking advantage of the high speed broadband connections today.

But how does one realise such as shared platform for the government?

Without the current overall enterprise architecture, covering all products and agencies, neither the SDP, nor the GaaP can be properly defined and evolved.

A difference though between SDP and GaaP, is that GaaP may also cover the enterprise support and development functions, not only the citizen products.

One has to start indeed by documenting the current architecture of the various customer services, departments and agencies involved.

Then one has to analyse the resulting architectures, identify the common functionality and define the new services around it and the overall GaaP architecture.

There are indeed a few obvious services which the GDS has already defined and implemented such as identification...

At this stage, in designing the services, the implementation has to be considered though, since many services may be already implemented by existing technologies and suppliers on the market.

Then, the target architectures for each department had to be modelled taking into account the new services and the GaaP common platform.

In the implementation phase

- a programme would deliver GaaP in iterations, service by service.

- at the same time each department would implement its target architecture in a separate program taking into account the common services and the GaaP architecture and technology

An architecture development process would help manage the transformation.

It is important though that before the transformation, an architecture framework is defined: That will enable a common terminology, architecture principles, modelling and technology standards such as G-cloud), process checkpoints, roadmaps...

The GDS has already established common development principles and standards, discussed in the next posts, that will help govern the GaaP programmes.

The Government Digital Service principles

https://it.toolbox.com/blogs/adriangrigoriu/the-government-digital-service-principles-041816

Apr. 18, 2016

The first 7 UK GDS digital principles

(GDS = Government Digital Service) Principles:

  "Putting the public first, in delivering digital public services"

The public is the customer of the GDS.

for what it matters, everybody says the customer must come first but few put that into practice. True, without customers an enterprise has no purpose. But so overstated...

Still, there must be a balanced approach because the enterprise survival depends on other key stakeholders. For instance, beside the customer, the enterprise itself is as important a stakeholder because, if neglected, the whole enterprise fades away. It must be invested in, maintained, updated, developed, digitised... It must be cared for.

  "Digital by default"

The new services, products and technologies are increasingly digitally enhanced. The enterprise is increasingly automated, the sales and marketing are done on line, the interaction with partners and suppliers is electronic (B2B), communications are digital and so on.

Digital is what changes the face of the enterprise today. The principle states the obvious though.

"Putting users first"

Users should come first because they are the public, unless otherwise stated. Since that is already said in the first principle, the question is what is then a user as opposed to public? The user of the technology? Definitions are in order here.

Assuming though that the user is the public customer, the government does sometimes ignore its own customers, as we have all experienced. Because the government makes the rules, the citizen has not much choice.

Anyway, this is easy to enunciate but hard to achieve in practice because the government, or rather the state administration, is paid indirectly from taxes, no matter what quality of service. Performance KPIs, often employed, do not guarantee quality of service (QoS). They are too often becoming a purpose in themselves masking a still poor QoS.

"Learning from the journey"

In life, if we want to prosper, we have to do that. Quite a common a commandment. But perhaps not so in governments since the experience delivered to the public does not really affect the administration welfare. There must be, perhaps, an effective process of doing so, no matter the specific people and departments involved.

Since these principles sound rather general, a question that arises at this point in time, is if they are more like an aspirational behaviour, or mentality for the public service designers.

The Government Digital Service principles (i)

https://it.toolbox.com/blogs/adriangrigoriu/the-government-digital-service-principles-i-042016

April 20, 2016

The first 7 UK GDS digital principles

GDS = Government Digital Service

"Building a network of trust"

Applied to an enterprise development, it may suggest that not all colleagues but only a selected lot are to be trusted.

But trust cannot be relied upon in a business relationship. No key development should depend on trust alone. Trusting a party to deliver is like taking one's word for it. It is a serious risk as such. While trust is invested by a person in another person, it makes little sense between roles that have defined formal responsibilities. Anyway, trust loses its object when an individual moves on, changes roles, becomes unavailable...

Signed contracts, with performance and penalty clauses, should be in place between parties though.

Networks do work for personal benefits though because they support and benefit own members. often to the inconvenience of the rest though. A network of trust is often based on mutual interest where unwritten obligations bind the parties.

 "Moving barriers aside"

This is, perhaps, about barriers between parties and/or people.

Barriers are set by a variety of interests and attitudes. They may be created inadvertently by imposing single points of contact or by failing to inform the people with a valid concern for example.

Anyway, the point sounds more like a political goal rather than a principle. How would one achieve that though? In practice, often enough through the unity of purpose.

Organization and governance would also play a role an important indeed. A good organization would reduce the silo effect that raises tall barriers. A proper governance policy would make sure that the information would cross boundaries to reach all parties and decision makers.

In essence, the point appears to demand openness and transparency that enable the boundaryless information flow that TOGAF insists so upon.

This "principle" requires more elaboration though.

The Government Digital Service principles (ii)

https://it.toolbox.com/blogs/adriangrigoriu/the-government-digital-service-principles-ii-042216

April 22, 2016

The first 7 UK GDS digital principles

GDS = Government Digital Service

 "Creating an environment for technology leaders to flourish"

True, this may not always be the case for the government. Still, the government is not in the business of IT but of providing public services eventually supported by technology. Hence, the accent should be on rewarding performers of all kind rather than the technologists alone. After all, the technology can be all outsourced to the Cloud in the end.

Moreover, in a good work environment, everyone should flourish, not only the (technology) leaders.

This goal though may be achieved by removing the career *barriers* for the technology savvies while opening the *networks of trust to them.* which may constitute a barrier to promotion, as in the points above.

Were meritocracy is observed though, this outcome would be implicit. There would be fewer barriers and less need for networks of trust. Perhaps, a new GDS guideline should plainly support a meritocratic culture. But then one needs to explain how to achieve that.

"Don't do everything yourself (you can't)"

Obviously, you can't. Simply say so, i.e. say No or Yes but with additional human resources. And, if in a position of authority, do delegate the team and do organize, coordinate and supervise the work to make sure that the results deliver the system in budget and time.

Abolish barriers and empower people to act and make decisions independently. Choose the people you can trust to deliver.

That's, in fact, the good old delegation and empowerment practice not an advice to turn lazy.

This practice is often sidestepped because for some, delegation is achieved by handing off powers which does not bode well for the delegators because of the office politics. At times, to prevent that, people forego their annual leave taking it piecemeal.

This principle is plain and self explaining. But sometimes the obvious must be stated just to make sure it is... obvious.

The Government Digital Service principles should become culture

https://it.toolbox.com/blogs/adriangrigoriu/the-government-digital-service-principles-should-become-part-of-the-culture-042416

April 24, 2016

The first 7 UK GDS digital principles

GDS = Government Digital Service

But how do you translate the GDS "principles" in practice though?

Are they to be stuck on the lobby wall or on a portal banner for wide communications? Must them be learned by heart as a check list to remember in the everyday practice?

These principles sound more like best practices that the GDS owners and designers should keep in mind and apply in their work and relationships. How do you enforce these good practices though? Is there a need for a principles regulation body, a code of penalties and a "principles" police to penalise the non compliant?

How does one enforce the "Values" of an enterprise for that matter?

In reality, there is seldom a mechanism to do that. What that means is that the Values we often see bannered on the enterprise sites prescribe an aspirational ideal world seldom realised in practice.

To start with, the GDS principles should be reflected in the organisation design and the governance practice.

Every decision board should take them and their derivatives into consideration.

The principles should also be included in process milestones, governance policies, best practices... so that any decision making and major action shall consider them.

If every process, policy, rule... in the enterprise complies with them, then every action and decision in the enterprise would implicitly consider them. Hence, the specific enterprise development, the GDS, would inherently comply.

Not last, to make a difference, the GDS principles or practices should form, together with other principles and Values, the high code of values and rules that guides the effective and ethical operation of the enterprise: the Constitution of the Enterprise.

Ultimately, the principles should be, in time, reflected in the organization culture.

As it happens though, the whole lot of principles, sounds more like the set of seven commandments of the UK government. In practice, the principles are applied as much as the bible commandments are in real life. At least, the church apparatus has a way to promote the commandments.

Government as a platform, foundations

https://it.toolbox.com/blogs/adriangrigoriu/government-as-a-platform-foundations-042716

April 27, 2016

The *"Government as a Platform will provide a suite of common tools and components (eg GOV.UK Pay and GOV.UK Notify), that will make it easier for the digital teams in government to build services"*.

From "Foundations for Government as a Platform"

"This blog is about our work with departments and agencies to build platforms and *service design patterns* to make it easy for service teams across government to design, assemble and build services."

Foundations:

"Meet a common need"

The key word is Common. The government platform should provide services which can be employed at the same time by any and all government departments.

"Be independent"

The service should not be dependent on a single department specs. In fact the service should be abstracted so that it will constitute the common part that is used by all departments. The specific parts which should be implemented in departments are a condition of integration in each department.

"Make it easy for the user"

It's not quite clear who the user is though: the public or the government departments? Perhaps some definitions on the side are in order. But the common services should be user friendly, obviously. This criterion is valid for any product on the market. It's rather not worth mentioning.

"Be easy to integrate"

This is the main characteristic of any GaaP service. It means standard APIs and Protocols as much as possible. The overall UX design and customer interaction process must be done end to end so that even the delays are acceptable. The broadband network has to be properly provisioned, perhaps leased. A Cloud integrator can support the job if Cloud solutions are chosen.

"Be ready to grow"

Any business grows. This is yet again a requirement that is pretty obvious. One of those well known non-functional requirements, as we used to call them. To dynamically and quickly scale though at short notice, a Cloud provider should be chosen.

"Be easy to adopt"

Comes into the same category as the easy integrate requirements. It is about the transition of the service to the service management teams.

Government as a platform, foundations (i)

https://it.toolbox.com/blogs/adriangrigoriu/government-as-a-platform-foundations-i-043016

April 30, 2016

"Support service separation"

Services should not depend on each other so that they can be easily stopped, fixed or changed without affecting other services. They should conform to same standards, as for instance, they should employ same data schemes for information integration sharing across services and deduplication. This demands a common design time effort across all services and departments.

"Avoid being tied down to one supplier"

A good old principle. The idea is that suppliers should not lightly fail, and if they do, there should be substitutes capable of taking over the service. That means also that the G-cloud must offer alternative providers.

In the first place, the supplier firm should be viable in the long term. But, just in case, there should be at least two suppliers able to provide the service.

Since the GaaP services serve more government departments, the Cloud paradigm is well suited for the purpose. There is no point anyway in the government developing and owning IT infrastructure and application platforms that can be rented from a host of reliable providers selected from the G-cloud.

The G-Cloud is a catalogue and purchasing framework that allows UK public sector organisations to procure Infrastructure as a Service (IaaS), Software as a Service (SaaS), Platform as a Service (PaaS) and other Cloud services such as Integration as a platform from approved suppliers.

"Commit to maintaining the product"

This is an issue with any supplier. The supplier should be indeed signed on to maintain, develop and upgrade the service for the foreseeable future.

It is in the same spirit with the principles above aimed to ensure a reliable, delivering and enduring service from suppliers.

Yet, even if suppliers have such a major role to play, the government remains responsible for the integration of the supplier services in a single harmonious customer experience for the public. That is, the government (in fact the public body responsible for the GDS, GaaP, G-cloud...) is in charge of the cross service overall architecture, integration, unified services support, common UX design, principles and roadmap of evolution.

Government as a platform, foundations (ii)

https://it.toolbox.com/blogs/adriangrigoriu/government-as-a-platform-foundations-ii-043016

April 30, 2016

"Meet technical and design standards"

The design should follow the same standards for all GaaP services. The public services and suppliers should collaborate to devise and apply them. The technical and design standards should add to this already existing series of GDS principles.

Key standards should be established in the shared Information/data field, services APIs and protocols, GUI and UX design...

That would ensure that services reuse the same data, protocols, familiar GUI and in general offer the same look and feel that would make life easier for the public user and, in fact, for all parties at design and utilisation times. A customer, once identified, may access any public site without having to re-introduce personal data, re-log in etc.

The User Interface (UI) and eXperience (UX) design are essential at this stage because they must be done end to end over various platforms supplied by different parties.

"Be open about performance"

and

"Be open about cost"

These requirements also address the service designers and suppliers, requiring them to be open about the total cost of the service and performance. But these should be also clauses in contract because relying on principles and trust is not ideal.

In addition, it is cost wise important that suppliers sign on to do the changes and further develop the service without major additional costs as it often happens. This is a major issue at outsourcing. While the maintenance cost is reasonable, changes and development cost an arm and a leg.

Scalability is also an issue. But the cloud can scale capacity, network on demand or even automatically.

These supplier related principles set a healthy foundation for working with the providers. Long term strategic partnerships with key suppliers would be beneficial. They also offer insurance to suppliers so that they can plan long term.

And for the future, the GaaP cloud services may be extended to include the BPO (Business Process Outsourcing) paradigm that provides, not only the technology, but the end to end processes and the human resources that man them.

The Ten Commandments of the Government Digital Service

https://it.toolbox.com/blogs/adriangrigoriu/the-ten-commandments-of-the-government-digital-service-050416

May 04, 2016

"*Listed below* are the Government as Platform design principles and examples of how we've used them so far."

 This set addresses the design folk.

"Start with (user) needs"

While the user is important, as we all know, a key reason the GaaP (Government as a Platform) is underway is to reduce the taxpayers' cost by realising synergies between departments, reducing duplication/overlaps/ variation and expensive technology skills, to integrate information between departments *and* take advantage of the outsourcing business model offered by the latest Cloud technology in which entire application services are outsourced. All these concerns should be considered as requirements from start.

"Do less"

Perhaps the principle here is "*Re-use*". Or the idea is more like "Do once, reuse many" times.

"Do less" *without* explanation can denote too many other things, as in "Do less and less" which is not so unusual.

"Design with data"

Analyse user behaviour and design accordingly. That's sounds more like the 1st principle, "Start from user needs" or like "Start from requirements". But it also means "Justify each action and decision making with cold data".

"Do the hard work to make it simple"

KISS (Keep It Simple...) is The principle for some time now. But to KISS it, one needs to go through the whole cycle of understanding, true.

Simple is the result of a long and hard process of learning. First it means an accumulation of facts and detail that renders everything apparently complex. Then simplification comes gradually with structuring as understanding makes progress.

"Iterate. Then reiterate again"

As opposed to the one big delivery, typical of a cascade process, which is risky, takes long and may not consider interim changes and requirements... do deliver in small bits.

For that though, you need a full architecture upfront so that you can partition the work in independent outcomes from start.

It is an Agile like principle.

"This is for everyone"

This is about accessibility, more or less and the focus on customer rather than on a fancy design. That is access for all people no matter the computing skills.

This should be an outcome of a proper User Experience (UX) design. You have to consider personas with disabilities.

Ultimately, suitable access channels may have to be provided for each type of public user.

The Ten Commandments of the Government Digital Service (i)

https://it.toolbox.com/blogs/adriangrigoriu/the-ten-commandments-of-the-government-digital-service-i-050516

May 05, 2016

"*Listed below* are the Government as Platform design principles and examples of how we've used them so far."

This set addresses the design folk.

"Understand context"

That's simple to say but hard to interpret. Indeed everything happens in a context that, in fact, determines the outcome. The principle appears to require a deep understanding of the context in which a service is used. Like the emergency number 112 for instance, where any unnecessary word left in the prompt delays intervention.

"Build digital services, not websites"

That asks the designer to be practical rather than fancy which goes sometimes against the grain. This seems to overlap a bit the other principles. In practise, the design should avoid any unnecessary technology, information and decoration which don't add value to the specific outcome.

This is about a full User Interaction (UX) design rather than simple UI design.

"Be consistent, not uniform"

Essentially, the public services should have the same Look and Feel. But the designers should not sacrifice functionality or one of the principles above, solely to apply or reuse a pattern,

"Make things open: it makes things better"

The principle calls for open and share the design with the community for everybody to benefit from worldwide contributions.

In practice though, this demands the creation of an Open Digital Government Services environment and organization that enables sharing and contributions.

Therefore, the above 10 service design principles, or commandments if you like, stress the customers' requirements, reuse, agile iterations, KISS, accessibility. multichannel, UX philosophy, patterns, open source... which are all desirable best practices.

There seem to be a disjoint view though of the various sets of principles, commented here and in the previous posts, such as digital principles, design principles or those addressing the services and suppliers... It would be good to specify the audience and context of use for each set, to minimise, harmonise and place them on a single top level site.

Many questions still arise though. Why are the egoverment's principles so spread on different sites? Have the principles ever been harmonised to eliminate duplications...?

Are all these principles useful, are they live now?

Has there been any feedback and follow up to improve them?

Are foundations same as principles?

THE ENTERPRISE EVOLUTION TO THE CLOUD

The Transition to Shadow IT and the Cloud (ii)

https://it.toolbox.com/blogs/adriangrigoriu/the-transition-to-shadow-it-and-the-cloud-ii-061317

June 13, 2017

The revolution started with the shadow IT. Business felt satiated with the perpetual IT excuses and delays of the type "can't", "not now", "we are so busy...", "it costs", "we have to hire skills "...

The IT motivations seldom cut it with the business even when the reasons were real.

It is just that the priorities of IT and business clash, in particular when the IT is too slow to respond to the increasing market pressure. Besides, the IT takes a too large chunk of the budget only to keep the lights on. These all generate a lot of anxiety in the business.

So, the business units built their own shadow IT with priorities aligned to their business. Some organisations legitimated this approach by building a distributed IT department, made of "Shadow ITs" in each unit and a central organisation that was only responsible for correlating, harmonising and standardising developments.

But who ultimately took the investment decisions? It had to be the CMO (Chief Marketing Officer) for new products and services or the CFO (Chief Financial Officer) for new capabilities for instance. The CIO was still busy keeping the IT lights on.

But Shadow IT cannot compete in terms of manpower and skills with central IT. So, they chose to outsource technology solutions rather than implement them in-house. Because business does not care about the technology behind a service or not much in any case. They indeed want the technology asap, flexible, agile and last longer. But it should be totally invisible to them, if possible.

With the fast Cloud evolution, the need for Shadow IT diminished. Savvy business people could now configure themselves the services.

Businesses happily adopted the Cloud to deal directly with the service suppliers. That saves them hearing the constant demand for money to keep the IT lights on and the perpetual explanations about why the IT cannot do this or that.

The knowledge about business, rather than IT, is key now.

Some say that there still are Cloud security issues but compare that to the IT security you have in place today. Besides we had to live with Windows in the enterprise for a long time now even if it looks like a gateway to the evils of the world. Such as ransomware. You may find though that the Cloud is better at security than you are because it has to ensure security for each and every customer and between them. Because they can afford to invest in skills and technology. The national regulation constraints with regard to data location have been solved by the creation of geographical regions.

The IT Issue and the Cloud Solution (i)

https://it.toolbox.com/blogs/adriangrigoriu/the-it-issue-and-the-cloud-solution-i-061317

June 13, 2017

Yet, business is not too happy with the IT department. I cannot imagine why, you may say. Well, IT costs a big deal in comparison with rest of a business. Consider the numbing cost of servers, applications, licenses, maintenance, contractors, consultancies, training...

Quite often, an IT application or server upgrade costs more than the product itself. By analogy, major upgrades may cost as much as paint cartridges do in relation to cheap printers.

Moreover, the upgrades (servers, applications...) have to be done at an alarmingly decreasing interval, upgrades that disrupt too the business operation. Think of your Windows. Oh, please... not another update. Your servers and applications become obsolete faster than your mobile almost every two years or so nowadays.

The IT department has a life of its own, like an enterprise inside the enterprise. That is because IT skills are different from those of the business people and as such the dialog between the two is often marred by different jargons, interests, promotion ladders and cultures. Take for instance the IT which always wishes to adopt the latest technologies while the business is content to continue with the 50 years old mainframes for as long as they do the work.

Then, why do we have to have IT in the enterprise at all, in each and every enterprise? In the beginning we didn't. Then we did. Then we did not because we could outsource the IT infrastructure to a data centre and its maintenance to 3rd parties. But it costed a hand and a foot and we lost control in emergencies when a malfunction would have to put first together a conclave of experts from all companies in the chain.

Why not renting these IT capabilities and their management? The answer is that yes, with the cloud advent we can do that.

Because the Cloud offers now flexible Processing, Storage, Containers, development Platforms, Functions, Networking and instantly up and running IT applications from no matter where in the world, reliably, cheap and on a paid per usage business model.

The Cloud was indeed enabled by the progress in digital technology such as virtualisation of processing and storage, software defined networks, software controlled data centres, web interfaces for people (HTML) and technology (API economy), architecture styles such as SOA and micro-services...

The rise and fall of the IT in the enterprise

https://it.toolbox.com/blogs/adriangrigoriu/the-rise-and-fall-of-the-it-in-the-enterprise-012017

Jan. 20, 2017

In the last fifty years the IT in the enterprise grew from punched cards to in-house mainframes and then to many air conditioned and secured floors of racks of servers and switches.

Then, the IT overflowed into at least two data centres, one of which for disaster recovery, usually outsourced because their maintenance fell completely outside the competence of the enterprise.

We went on buying our own servers, storage, applications and suites. We bought our email system, office software, databases, IT support, call centre suite, access and authorisation and web servers, the enterprise portal, intranet, social media and file, document and content management systems...

We bought off-the shelf enterprise support suits such as ERPs and CRMs. We bought our own BI and data warehouse.

Then we purchased enterprise buses to integrate them all and the security, redundant systems, back up and disaster recovery to protect our systems from intrusion and failure.

With the business growth we needed more load balancing and content front ends and more backup and disaster recovery. We had to install even more security to protect our business, our data and customers' privacy.

And every system came with its own servers or appliances.

We procured, installed and maintained PCs and mobiles for everyone. Then we had to upgrade them every few years.

We started writing software to create our own applications.

As such we created our own development environment and its associated infrastructure for testing and staging. These systems, scaled down copies after the operational systems, had to be also customised, maintained, upgraded...

The IT in the enterprise grew and grew. Our enterprises turned into IT intensive companies.

Today, we have to keep the IT lights on. This is the key task of IT. We monitor, maintain and manage the IT every single day and night. Five nines is the standard of availability today because even short disruptions cost the business dearly.

The rise of the enterprise IT problem (i)

https://it.toolbox.com/blogs/adriangrigoriu/the-rise-of-the-enterprise-it-problem-i-012117

Jan. 21, 2017

It took years to install, customise and use the ERPs and CRM suites properly. Still, by then the technology was already slow and obsolete. The suites were hard and costly to integrate, update, upgrade, change or swap.

But we keep paying costly proprietary application licences and upgrades because our hands are tied by suppliers. They know we cannot do without them.

Years on, the BI and warehouse are still to return value, lying there mostly unused.

Never mind the various specialist applications the departments use, that cost, demand their own licences and servers and yet are rarely inventoried by IT and considered in the total cost of IT.

Since every application came with its own servers the utilisation rate of most servers was very low.

But, between two to four years, we have to replace the PCs, servers and upgrade the applications. That is expensive and risky because of potential business disruptions.

Meanwhile, the IT electricity consumption has become a huge problem because of the cost and environmental impact.

The applications we developed fade away because languages and skills turn obsolete, developers leave and the applications structure is lost in the mists of time. Applications can no more be customised, changed, scaled... But off the shelf applications don't do what we want and use to do.

Yet we keep exploiting them today, even the last century mainframes, because we fear IT change. IT programmes today have, statistically, a 30% chance to fully succeed, according to sources.

The information we processed and retained grew exponentially. We bought more servers. We extended the dear old database licences. We are pushed to acquire big data technology...

But we do not really realise the power in our information.

We recruit and train more and more people to do IT even as the technology and skills turn old increasingly faster.

Our business depends on IT. But IT and its management or rather its mismanagement cost us. Good technology and people cost increasingly more.

The enterprise grows increasingly complex as its challenges do.

Outsourcing to the aid of the enterprise IT problem (ii)

https://it.toolbox.com/blogs/adriangrigoriu/outsourcing-to-the-aid-of-the-enterprise-it-problem-ii-012317

Jan. 23, 2017

Yet, the more successful we are, the more customers we have. But so do our applications and as such the servers, storage, applications and networking grow. But more IT. more trouble: more cost, more maintenance, licences, upgrades, people, risks...

Still, if we want our business to survive we have to install more hardware, software, licences and upgrades.

And the cost of IT goes up and up. The total cost of IT, while takes a huge proportion of our budget, is hard to measure. Because IT is everywhere. Still, CEOs have to invest blindly and grumbling in IT without really understanding why and how it affects the enterprise. They don't see the IT big picture.

IT became a huge cost centre for CEOs and CFOs and a stumbling block for the enterprise evolution because business strategy became very much IT strategy today. Nothing could change without IT. We are stuck.

In this increasingly competitive world, while our business had to be available around the clock, we could no longer control and evolve properly the enterprise because of the complexity and rapid change of its IT. We had to separate the concerns, we had to separate the business from IT.

Outsourcing to the aid of the enterprise IT

Because we had to reduce costs and cope better with the IT, we outsourced the overall IT maintenance to specialist contractors who, in turn, further outsourced the work to cheaper time zones. In fact, we outsourced our jobs.

Then the enterprise outsourced more and more parts of IT, such as data centres, applications management, IT support and development... to third parties in less dear but remote lands.

We employ now expensive specialist contractors and consultants because our in-house resources cope no longer and, in time, lost their specialist skills. And we have to keep the IT contractors happy because without them we run great business risks.

When the IT department turned less and less responsive to the increasing load, the business departments created the shadow IT to streamline local problem solving.

Virtualisation to the aid of the enterprise IT optimisation (iii)

https://it.toolbox.com/blogs/adriangrigoriu/virtualisation-to-the-aid-of-the-enterprise-it-optimisation-iii-012317

Jan. 23, 2017

Still, outsourcing and shadow IT have not solved though the problem of IT ownership, procurement, licensing, replacement, upgrading... and ultimately IT investment.

Outsourcing slowed down problem resolution in cases of IT failures causing business disruption and proved more costly that initially thought. Every bit of IT based business change had to be paid extra if unspecified in the contract. Contracts with outsourcing suppliers were complex and the interaction extensive.

Some enterprises have stepped back and re-hired their IT.

At the same time, the Shadow IT has further fragmented the IT landscape rendering the big enterprise even more silo-ed than before.

The Virtualisation of the enterprise IT

But IT itself came to its own help. The Virtualisation technology promised a new life to the IT in the enterprise.

Virtualisation gradually brought the abstractisation of the various IT layers and parts of the enterprise by hiding their implementation behind standard interfaces and communications protocols.

We first virtualised the operating system (OS) from the hardware and the application from the operating system. We called them server virtualisation and virtual machines. Most applications can run and be ported now to any server hardware or operating system.

Then we virtualised the storage and networking by defining virtual storage units and virtual networks on demand on larger physical ones.

A physical server could host a number of virtual servers. A storage device could be partitioned in many isolated logical units and a network link will be shared by many logical links. Capabilities could self scale on demand. They could made be redundant by design.

Then, SOA like web services and micro-services in software could now abstract applications and their components in independent modules with interfaces (APIs in software) that hide their inner operation and technology.

Business processes as such could be software defined and configured with graphical commands out of business services connected to an enterprise integration bus. Business could now be in charge of its own process changes.

Still, most enterprises are not in the business of IT (iv)

https://it.toolbox.com/blogs/adriangrigoriu/still-most-enterprises-are-not-in-the-business-of-it-iv-012417

Jan. 24, 2017

The IT Virtualisation enabled us create, distribute, configure, monitor, scale, backup... and port from graphical management interfaces our processing, storage and network capabilities on an existing set of physical servers, storage devices, networks and applications. As such, virtualisation enabled the Software Defined IT, respectively, the easy creation and manoeuvring of the enterprise IT resources, which, in turn, enabled IT optimisation.

Last but not least, we virtualised the human access from any device and OS to any IT system by using an universal presentation language for graphical human interfaces, HTML5 and messaging protocol that abstracted the technology at both ends.

Hence, we are on the path of virtualising all enterprise IT tiers.

Yet, virtualisation added a new layer of complexity, security, skills, cost while slowing down the execution of IT because of the new abstractisation layers. And we still had the IT ownership set of issues.

But, ultimately, enterprises are still not interested in the ownership, development and maintenance of IT because most are not in the business of IT, that is, in the business of delivering IT products, they are just IT enabled businesses.

In fact, life in the enterprise would be much better without IT. We could focus then on our core business rather than discussing applications and technology. Moreover, the total cost of IT, calculated over the whole IT lifecycle, is too large when compared to the cost of doing business while the costs of IT generated disruptions could wreck a business today if the IT is improperly managed.

What we need in practice is not IT but business capabilities which can be assembled to process our business flows and information. Ideally, the IT should not be visible to the business operator.

Yet, that is not really possible when many business processes are implemented by IT and the Digital revolution on its way, adds even more IT to the enterprise and the world around.

The rise of the Cloud that moves the IT out of the enterprise (v)

https://it.toolbox.com/blogs/adriangrigoriu/the-rise-of-the-cloud-that-moves-the-it-out-of-the-enterprise-v-012717

Jan. 27, 2017

For one, Virtualisation enabled a better control over IT through software creation, manipulation and optimisation of IT resources. It improved its utilisation and reduced its cost as such.

At the same time, outsourcing proved that specialist companies can do IT better than the enterprise since IT is their core business.

But, to efficiently outsource, we have to address the issue of IT ownership since the IT depreciates at such a rapid rate today while its ineffective use increases massively its cost. And, after all, there is no much point in owning the IT given that the enterprise already outsources its hosting and management.

We also have to improve the interaction through self-service and direct online API access to outsourced services and the cost predictability with prepay and subscription like cost models.

Last but not least, the Shadow IT proved that paying for the usage of an IT service supplied by a 3rd party would save them the cost to own and worry about each of the service IT components and their in house management and upgrades.

Then the Cloud came to the aid of IT.

The Cloud business model is the outsourcing of the IT, both its ownership and management.

To be effective, the Cloud employs IT virtualisation, without which it would not realise the economies of scale for multi-hosting and the ease of IT resources manoeuvring and optimisation.

It enables us to gradually move the IT outside the enterprise. The business model is IT renting rather than owning. It's almost like leasing a car or a house rather than buying it.

We pay for the capability we use rather than for our over over-dimensioned systems that turn quickly obsolete and let us down because of improper management.

The Cloud offers today off the shelf IT infrastructure capabilities, standard enterprise applications, suites, platforms and specialised functions (calculations, big data...). It also provides, in a self service regime, on demand scalability, security, porting, availability (fault tolerance), backup, security and disaster recovery.

How does the Cloud benefit the enterprise (vi)

https://it.toolbox.com/blogs/adriangrigoriu/how-does-the-cloud-benefit-the-enterprise-vi-012817

Jan. 28, 2017

But what does the cloud offer to the enterprise?

- ongoing OPEX expenses rather than initial large and risky CAPEX capital investments

- various prepay, monthly pay and on demand per usage cost models

- fast self service over web interfaces

- quick provisioning of capabilities with various standard features and immediate release of capabilities when needed no more, enabling as such low cost proof of concepts, pilots, testing, start-up firms...

- off the shelf scalability, fault tolerance, back-up, disaster recovery, monitoring, reporting

- automated self scalability to cover usage peaks for events

- no IT ownership, licensing, procuring, maintenance, upgrades, decommissioning, recycling...

- growing availability of various specialised functions periodical in demand (see this) such as blockchain, big data processing, massive data transfer, crypto processing...

Today, many enterprises evolved towards a hybrid cloud model by moving the IT gradually to the Cloud while keeping some core in-house. IT management systems oversee today both on premise and multi-cloud systems transparently.

See also Cloud services accounted for half of revenue growth at SAP in 2016

To recap, we outsource to the cloud:

- computing, storage and networking capabilities, that is the IT infrastructure (IaaS)

- standard enterprise capabilities (databases, web sites, content management...)

- enterprise support applications and suites (ERP, CRM, Content Management, ...) together with their infrastructure (SaaS)

- core applications to specialist providers (SaaS)

- standard enterprise Function as a Service (FaaS or serverless computing, meaning that we provision no longer the infrastructure in the cloud before executing the function; the enterprise just calls the function that automatically executes)

- integration (iPaaS) ware

- development environments (PaaS)

The Virtual Enterprise and Cloud merge to form the cloud Enterprise (vii)

https://it.toolbox.com/blogs/adriangrigoriu/the-virtual-enterprise-and-the-cloud-merge-to-form-the-virtual-cloud-enterprise-vii-012917

Jan. 29, 2017

Enterprise functions such as manufacturing, marketing, sales, product design, strategy..., have increasingly been delivered by/outsourced to 3rd parties selected on various criteria. The resulting Virtual Enterprise- that implements a virtual Value Chain business model where entire business functions, including their IT, non-IT technologies, people and facilities are outsourced to partner companies - has already been increasingly the preferred choice in many industries because the enterprise is built quickly out of and relies on proven, best of breed and low cost services provided by specialist companies which, like the Cloud providers, realise, in turn, economies of scale.

Note: as opposed to the Virtual Enterprise, the IT Virtualisation consists in abstracting the enterprise IT (infrastructure, applications, development platforms....) so that they can be easily created, deployed, dimensioned... and managed independently of each other.

At the same time, since an enterprise prefers to focus on its business rather than fret about IT, the IT would ultimately be moving to the Cloud. The Cloud business model for the enterprise is to Rent IT rather than own it. It enables the moving of IT, including ownership, outside the enterprise.

The Cloud provider virtualises the IT for economies of scale and ease of provisioning and manipulation of the abstract IT capabilities by customers.

As such, overall, a company that increasingly virtualises today most of its Value Chain and IT may be called a Virtual Cloud Enterprise or simply a Cloud Enterprise because all its IT and business functions reside in a cloud of service providers residing outside the core enterprise.

The virtual cloud enterprise is the outcome of the Digital evolution.

The IT Cloud was made possible by the advance of Digital which enabled the virtualisation of computing, storage and network capabilities, the advent of micro-services, APIs, HTML5 technologies, high performance server platforms, data centre technologies...

Equally, the Digital technology played, growingly, like in the new sharing (participating) type of enterprise such as Uber, a central role in automating the interactions between the companies of the Virtual Enterprise.

The evolution to the Cloud Enterprise and the need to architect it (viii)

https://it.toolbox.com/blogs/adriangrigoriu/the-evolution-toward-the-virtual-cloud-enterprise-and-the-need-to-architect-it-upfront-viii-020217

Feb. 02, 2017

So, the outsourcing of the business functions and the IT to the Cloud, increasingly practiced in the enterprise, gives birth to the virtual cloud enterprise.

A virtual cloud enterprise is an enterprise that outsources most business functions in the value chain - such as SCOR Source, Make and Deliver - to 3rd parties and the IT to the Cloud.

I shall call it in short the Cloud Enterprise because most of its functions and IT are outsourced to a cloud of external providers.

Early in the process though, to streamline the resulting cloud enterprise organisation, we need to model its target Enterprise Architecture which would span both the in-house (what is left) and in-cloud business and IT capabilities, such as IaaS, SaaS, PaaS, iPaaS, FaaS (serverless), provided by various suppliers.

Hence, before adopting any cloud solutions for infrastructure, applications, suites, platforms... we have to stop and architect the big picture of our enterprise so that we select compatible options and harmonise and integrate from start in-house capabilities and cloud services.

Because otherwise, we may create unnecessary complexity, problems and inefficiencies right from the beginning.

We also have to think of aligning the information architectures from the beginning because each business in the value chain and IT cloud capability may come with its own data formats.

In conclusion, with the evolution towards the Virtual Enterprise and the adoption of the Cloud, to remain in charge of the enterprise we really need to model and maintain the whole enterprise picture, the Enterprise Architecture (EA), now spread over our own premises and different clouds.

We begin by modelling the virtual Value Chain to be able to build our business architecture upon it.

For the Cloud Enterprise the overall governance function is essential because it enables the coordination of end to end business processes and deliverables, so that the suppliers and the enterprise plan and deliver the end product as a whole.

Enterprise Architecture will increasingly take over from the IT function (ix)

https://it.toolbox.com/blogs/adriangrigoriu/enterprise-architecture-will-increasingly-take-over-from-the-it-function-ix-020317

Feb. 03, 2017

The Enterprise Architecture team has to construct the big picture. Yet, we need no more a big IT department because we do not own or manage IT any longer. Hence the enterprise needs not to bother with IT issues any longer since the IT is and it is owned by the Cloud.

Rather than modelling the technology architecture, the Architect would model the business functions, services and processes out of distributed cloud and business capabilities.

The architect will construct the enterprise blueprint by modelling its services and orchestration taking into account interfaces, features, costs and roadmaps.

EA has to select, together with the business, the SaaS, FaaS, IaaS, PaaS, iPaaS, and business service solutions that integrate best and minimise unnecessary diversity by standardising on certain clouds and services. It also has to also align the information formats at the interface level because each outsourced component may have its own format.

Yet, note though that the technology behind the IT cloud services is not really visible to the Enterprise and relevant to its architecture and as such IT needs not be documented in detail.

But, while the IT decisions remain in the jurisdiction of each company, because companies in the value chain remain still autonomous, the virtual cloud enterprise Governance function, may still aim to coordinate with long term partners the harmonisation of information formats and cloud approaches in order to reduce unnecessary variation of cloud suppliers standards and technology to obtain overall economies of scale, minimise duplication and integration issues and align information format.

The EA team has to take charge of the Digital future of the cloud enterprise. Even if the enterprise turns more and more technology agnostic, digital technologies may change quickly the face of the cloud technologies, outsourced business services and even the operations business models.

EA should align as such the Digital, business strategies and roadmaps of the Clouds and outsourced business services in the cloud enterprise value chain.

How will the enterprise be organised in the digital era?

https://it.toolbox.com/blogs/adriangrigoriu/how-will-the-enterprise-be-organised-in-the-digital-era-052618

May 26, 2018

The Digital technology automates the enterprise. It also enables digital new channels for customers, partners and suppliers. AI changes the customer advice and aids decision making. Virtual Reality finds its place in training, shops, and presentations. BI discovers subtle moves at the market end that helps you have an edge. Transportation is taken over by self driving cars and drones. Contracts are registered with blockchain. 3D printing replaces parts manufacturing. The cloud takes over big time. And, we are only scratching the Digital surface. The processing power and network bandwidth, storage capacity are growing exponentially.

Yet, the digital infrastructure was a necessary evil in the enterprise. You didn't want to know about it, but you had to deal with it. Visualization introduced an abstraction layer simplifying the management of IT infrastructure. The IT is moving into the Cloud, out of the enterprise, as IaaS, PaaS, SaaS and FaaS/Cloud functions that provide on demand utility applications without any need to set-up the infrastructure upfront. The applications are instantiated as such just in time, when called. We had this concept in software. It was called dynamic linking.

The enterprise SOA made this evolution possible. SOA underlined the fact that a service encapsulates an atomic function to which it presents an access interface. A SOA service looks as such like a black box with a connector, an appliance. The interface and encapsulation make the service implementation irrelevant to the client. What matters for a service are the features, performance, cost... rather than the technology of realization. Services should be as such **interchangeable** as long as the interface is the same. Without encapsulation though services lose portability because their boundaries for porting are not clear. Besides without interfaces and encapsulation, the internal functionality and information of a service may be directly accessed, creating therefore hidden dependencies that render further change and development rather unpredictable and hardly manageable. Anyway, since SOA was seen at the time more like a software rather than enterprise paradigm, it was declared dead because it lost to REST. Yet, SOA survives though as software microservices, API economy and the Cloud. It may be also the paradigm for the enterprise of the future organization.

How will the enterprise be organised in the digital era (i)

https://it.toolbox.com/blogs/adriangrigoriu/how-will-the-enterprise-be-organised-in-the-digital-era-i-060518

June 05, 2018

Business services are key to the enterprise evolution. In effect, a business service consists of the process, technology and people who operate and maintain the service. To be as autonomous as possible, a service should be accessed only over an interface. In essence a Business Service is SOA for business. Business Services in general must not be confused though with business services in the more specific SOA way.

Business Services render an organisation flexible and agile because enterprise flows can be orchestrated out of autonomous eventually outsourced services eventually outsourced. Services which are not differentiating or core to the business can and should be outsourced because they bring the advantage of expertise and scale that reduce the cost and improve the quality of service. A Business Service, provided by a specialised firm, is called Business Process Outsourcing (BPO) or, to align to the Cloud naming convention, it may be called a Business Process as a Service (BPaaS). The enterprise, in time, would look like a Lego, fully made of business services interconnected and orchestrated.

The difference between a cloud SaaS and a BPO service is that for the latter both the people who operate and maintain it are at the supplier while for the SaaS the people who operate it are still in the enterprise. For as long as there are still manual components to a service, the people that operate it may still be employed by the enterprise and as such the service would be SaaS. In time though, most people would move to the service supplier because the whole integrated service may be provided over an interface.

In the enterprise, you would bother no longer about applications and their infrastructure. Gradually, the IT department would be reduced in size. The costly IT procurement, licensing, maintenance, updates, upgrades become now a thing of the past. The enterprise would be able to focus back on its core business.

The enterprise though consists today of outsourced BPO, SaaS, IaaS and some in-house IT services. The way forward though seems to be an enterprise based on SOA (Service Oriented Architecture), the Cloud and Business Services. Only the core services would be operated by the enterprise. The enterprise units will be organised around business services, with a business unit centred around a service. The value chain of such an enterprise would consist of a series of linked autonomous business service units.

Preparing the up and coming virtual cloud Enterprise

https://it.toolbox.com/blogs/adriangrigoriu/preparing-the-up-and-coming-virtual-cloud-enterprise-021317

Feb 13, 2017

With OaaS (Operations as a Service), the enterprise outsources today its operation functions in the value chain (SCOR: Source, Make, Deliver).

Many enterprises have since long outsourced their enterprise support functions (IT support, recruiting, expenses, travel, car leasing...) to 3rd parties.

At the same time, the enterprise outsources its IT infrastructure and applications to the Cloud.

What they have in common is outsourcing. The enterprise functions and its IT are increasingly outsourced to what we may call the Cloud Enterprise in a "Operations as a Service" paradigm, according to Accenture.

What enables this is the digital technology that gives us web services, API economy, microservices. For the enterprise this means the evolution of the enterprise towards services.

But what do we have to do in the enterprise to make this happen smoothly and successfully?

The alternative is that each department outsources its business processes and IT platforms to whomever suits them most. For instance, an enterprise units may decide to use Cloud services from Amazon, another from Microsoft or Google and IBM beside the SaaS ERP and CRMs...

But that creates from start unnecessary and costly diversity, duplication and end to end integration and flow problems.

Unless controlled from the beginning the evolution to the Cloud Enterprise (or Operations as a Service) may ruin your enterprise rather than render it competitive.

This is the mission of the Enterprise Architecture task force.

Yet, this is not your run of the mill IT EA team because the business architecture (BA) is key here. The IT will be owned by BPO partners or the Cloud.

This is neither the BA team that defines business architecture as a disjoint collection of business activities and methods. Because you will end up with exactly this collection rather than a picture of the enterprise.

To be instated, the EA team must show the business the one page blueprint of an, any enterprise from which one can understand its workings. The model should cover the whole enterprise.

The major risk is the EA team ability to deliver.

Preparing the up and coming virtual cloud Enterprise (i)

https://it.toolbox.com/blogs/adriangrigoriu/preparing-the-up-and-coming-virtual-cloud-enterprise-i-021317

Feb. 13, 2017

Here are the key steps the EA has to perform to support the enterprise evolution to the Cloud.

As a Prerequisite the EA team has to establish the Value Chain and the blueprint of the current enterprise. This is the baseline the enterprise begins its run from. This architecture would serve for many other purposes. Model the target enterprise architecture

Approach:

- 1 - Research the market for existing BPO and Cloud (SaaS, FaaS, PaaS, IaaS) and API economy services and the suppliers pedigrees

- 2 - Draft a few target enterprise target models employing various combinations of BPO, Cloud, APIs from various suppliers.

      - decide and define remaining in-house functions, as services and plan outsourcing of their IT to Cloud

      - models should consider long term strategic objectives

      - design the enterprise services outlining interfaces and features rather than technology and inner organisation of services

- 3 - do evaluations of the value proposition for each target architecture option

      - quantify timeframe, costs and risks

      - add second best option, plan B

- 4 - Consult stakeholders to discuss, tweak and select best target model on cost, competitive advantage and iterate till agreement

Deliverable of this phase: the target enterprise architecture with key BPO, Cloud suppliers and in-house services and APIs

Employ modelling principles such as

- a. employ the services paradigm (SOA style of architecture)

- b. use a mixture of BPO (Business process Outsourcing), API economy and Cloud

IT; design the target enterprise starting with BPO because when you outsource an entire function or process, the supplier will manage its own IT

- c. minimise unnecessary diversity of suppliers and technologies for economies of scale, integration and information alignment; establish internal standards

- d. align strategy and roadmap with BPO suppliers where possible to reduce unnecessary diversity and smooth integration of information and protocols

- e. select services that employ latest Digital technologies to avoid being left behind or obsolescence; employ an emerging technologies map

- f. assess drawbacks, advantages, costs, risks and mitigation solutions for each target model

The transformation to the virtual cloud enterprise, principles

https://it.toolbox.com/blogs/adriangrigoriu/the-transformation-to-the-virtual-cloud-enterprise-principles-030417

March 04, 2017

The enterprise today is increasingly outsourcing its IT and the various functions of the Value Chain to external partner firms. It evolves as such towards a virtual/networked enterprise that houses its IT in the Cloud. Hence, the virtual cloud enterprise name.

At the same time, the Digital technology make leaps that if not mitigated or adopted, erode the enterprise competitivity in no time.

The digital virtual cloud enterprise is unavoidable. It is just o matter time, less rather than more. It looks like a "do it or die".

To prepare the enterprise for the transition on this path, one has to re-organise the enterprise. It is suggested that enterprise should be based on Services.

The service concept allows the separation of concerns that enables breaking the complexity and its management in smaller blocks. Operation, development, realisation and maintenance of the services can be done independently as such, with no dependencies, and in parallel. In fact, these are the very same reasons that the enterprise engages on this path.

The service paradigm also facilitates the easy outsourcing of non-core functions and IT, enabling the enterprise focus on its core business without having to cope with detail, non-core technology and the awesome digital progress.

The first few steps in the transformation of the enterprise involved   the EA team in modelling the current and target enterprise based on services, assessing gaps that had to be filled in the transition and establishing a roadmap..

Here are a few key Principles and Best Practices that guide the transformation to the virtual cloud enterprise:

- 1.   employ iterations with Go/No-Go milestones so that the programme can change course in case risk materialise

- 2. factor in current business priorities and strategy beside the service architecture gaps

- 3. take advantage of existing enterprise technology, skills

- 4. align planning to end of life cycle of existing platforms and the depreciation of the existing equipment

- 5. consider existing business and departments programmes and outcomes

- 6. aim to deliver early benefits to stakeholders at each iteration

- 7. have always in mind the whole enterprise, all its functions and technology, rather than siloes, so that you can reuse and take advantage of full suite offers to profit from their off-the-shelf integration and information alignment

- 8. plan ahead so that the Digital technology and market conditions do not outpace your transformation

- 9. employ staging platforms before commuting to live operation

- 10. prepare and manage change so that it is known and accepted as much as humanly possible

- 11. deploy change as atomic transactions to be able to roll back changes

- 12. perform work in parallel since the service concept enables it

The transformation to the virtual cloud enterprise, steps

https://it.toolbox.com/blogs/adriangrigoriu/the-transformation-to-the-virtual-cloud-enterprise-steps-030217

March 02, 2017

To adapt to the increasingly faster market demands, new enterprise business models appeared. Essentially enterprises outsource today resources, value chain activities and IT to a cloud of external providers so enterprises can ramp up and down their capabilities as needed.

The enterprise evolves as such towards an Operations as a Service (Accenture in Re-inventing outsourcing with operations-as-a-service) called here a virtual cloud Enterprise that outsources most of its business functions and IT to a cloud of best of breed and cost 3rd parties.

These new business models are enabled by the fast advancing Digital technology.

The transition to this virtual cloud enterprise is already on-going no matter what we think about it and what we call it. Enterprises do outsource today their business functions (Business Process Outsourcing, BPO), services to the API economy and Applications to SaaS while they have since long outsourced their enterprise support functions and IT management because they were costly and underperformed.

But, proceeding on this path without preparation compromises the enterprise.

Imagine the integration of an enterprise made of a large number of random outsourced business process and IT suppliers.

The first step is to model the enterprise architecture.

The next step is to put the Service at the base of the enterprise organisation. New flat organisation models based on units autonomy, BPO (Business Process Outsourcing), the Cloud, Web Services, the API economy, microservices... all point in this direction.

For that, design the target EA based on services, that is employ the SOA style of architecture.

Once this done, services can be easily outsourced. Or they can be equally offered in house when appropriate.

The third step is to establish upfront the form of outsourcing and the suppliers:

- 1. BPO includes people, facilities

- 2. API economy

- 3. SaaS Cloud

- 4. In House

in the order preference above.

Criteria must be established though for the selection of one model or another. Business opportunity is a key factor.

The steps above are often amalgamated in practice because few enterprises would engage in pure architecture modelling and transformations that may bring economies but not profit.

The transformation to the virtual cloud enterprise, steps (i)

https://it.toolbox.com/blogs/adriangrigoriu/the-transformation-to-the-virtual-cloud-enterprise-steps-i-030317

March 03, 2017

The virtual cloud enterprise consists of a value chain realised by services provided by external parties but integrated and coordinated by the governance function of the core enterprise.

The EA team must lead the way in modelling the architecture in terms of service functionality and interfaces, choosing and integrating potential solutions. Then EA updates the service design in iterations until agreement is reached.

Next, the EA team evaluates the gaps to existing and issues a roadmap taking into account the end of life of existing platforms, business priorities and technology dependencies and roadmaps.

In parallel, the EA team has to devise, agree and embed in everyday business processes, such as New Product and Capability Development, Change Management,

Strategy Specification, Solution/Project Architecture, operational maintenance..., the reference to EA, the architecture principles and standards that would guide the EA application and decision making process during the enterprise transformation.

That is, EA has to establish a self running governance that incorporates EA in the business as usual so that every development takes EA into account EA by default. No excuse. This way the Enterprise Architect does not become a bottleneck in the transformation process. The quality of EA can ruin the whole process though.

Then, starting from the roadmap, the enterprise programme, strategy and EA teams proceed to planning that is, organising the transformation in workstreams according to the roadmap assigning priorities, resources and establishing timetables.

The transformation is open ended. It should be done in time bounded iterations with deliverables that return immediate benefits to the enterprise stakeholders. That is the transformation process employs agile principles.

The target architecture, that represents the enterprise reference, should be modelled upfront though. Iterations nevertheless may update the target picture.

Key to the enterprise transformation success is the enterprise service paradigm that ensures the enterprise flexibility and agility to change.

That is because services realisation can be transparently changed at any later time being hidden behind interfaces, rather independent of the service implementation styles such as BPO, API economy, SaaS, Cloud or In-House.

Hence, services and suppliers can be readily swapped as long as the interfaces are conserved.

The transformation to the virtual cloud Enterprise (ii)

https://it.toolbox.com/blogs/adriangrigoriu/the-transformation-to-the-virtual-cloud-enterprise-ii-021417

Feb. 14, 2017

The EA team draws a long term transformation draft beginning with the current enterprise. Gaps between the current and target architecture turn into prospective workstreams.

The outcomes of this activity, input for the transformation plan, are:

 - a draft portfolio of workstreams with estimated resources in men-time

- a draft enterprise roadmap of key deliverables, risks and milestones that underlines dependencies, current platforms obsolescence, emerging technology timelines.

The EA team also establishes prospective ties with service suppliers to make sure that all assumptions are feasible.

If changes, EA iterates from the beginning until every stakeholder is rather happy and all pieces fall in place.

The enterprise Programme Management (PM) function takes over then. The EA team continues to assist the process.

PM agrees with all key stakeholders the transition programme, the portfolio of projects, reserves resources for each, establish costs and priorities... and deliverables in business terms.

PM initiates then the transformation in iterations to be able to control real progress, quality and costs.

Concomitantly with an implementation iteration, a new scan of the environment begins with new requirements analysis, evaluation of new technologies and risks and changes to the end architecture.

A key principle of evolution to the Cloud Enterprise is the outsourcing of every non-core activity and technology in the enterprise, that is one where

 - you cannot add value to

 - you have to acquire new skills and tools that take time to master

 - it is supplied cheaper and better by an en-gross service supplier

Also establish priorities for the implementation of any enterprise service. In that order

 - Rent > Buy > Build

 - Outsource first: BPO > Cloud FaaS > SaaS > IaaS > In House

with the In-house solution last, solely for the functions you excel in and add value to.

Operations as a Service and the Cloud Enterprise

https://it.toolbox.com/blogs/adriangrigoriu/operations-as-a-service-and-the-cloud-enterprise-021217

Feb. 12, 2017

While the service paradigm is taking over the enterprise IT now (see this), the concept has since long existed in economies of the past and society. As a result, a society was organised at one time in trade guilds that specialised and guaranteed delivery of quality services.

 The service approach was/is the result of Specialisation.

When we want something done well we employ a service provider simply because we cannot do all things good enough, clean, fast and cheap. Because we have no skills, tools and time. Hence we have our car repaired, oil changed, home painted, suits dry cleaned, lawn mown, plumbing fixed.... by service providers. Moreover, we buy off-the shelf products that people like us used to make in-house not long before.

And while we pay for services we get paid, in turn, for the services we perform in what we do best.

Same applies to many functions in the enterprise such as IT (Support...), HR (Recruiting...), Manufacturing... Why invest in tools, skills and facilities when some expert firm can do it better and cheaper for us, under firm contractual obligations rather than the deficiary bartering system of today taking place between business and IT that lets us down so often.

For the enterprise, a service is a capability accessed over a defined interface. A business service though consists of more than IT but, eventually, non-IT technology, skilled people, facilities and all the support it needs. And an interface is more than a software API because it interacts with people and other technologies.

Operations-as-a-Service (OaaS), was recently defined in this Accenture post as a merger between Business Process and Cloud Outsourcing, essentially. Yet, this implements what I called the Virtual Cloud Enterprise that combines the outsourcing of the enterprise Value Chain functions and of the IT to a Cloud of providers.

Accenture, in Re-inventing outsourcing with operations-as-a-service, says:

"to thrive in today's digital landscape,... leaders have begun to integrate business process outsourcing – the contracting of operations and responsibilities of a specific business process to a third-party service with Software-as-a-Service (SaaS) and developments in data analytics, automation, connectivity and machine intelligence"...

"With OaaS, organisations can take advantage of cloud-based applications to reduce their traditional IT spend, increase IT flexibility and scalability, while still achieving the operational and service quality advantages that business process outsourcing (BPO) can provide".

No matter the name, fact is that the traditional outsourcing of business functions and processes inevitably merges now with the IT outsourcing to the Cloud. They both happen at the same time now, shaping the up and coming Cloud Enterprise. But we have to prepare the enterprise for it before we end up with a tangled web of outsourced functions and IT.

The path to the virtual cloud Enterprise is paved by the Digital evolution

https://it.toolbox.com/blogs/adriangrigoriu/the-path-to-the-virtual-cloud-enterprise-is-paved-by-the-digital-evolution-020517

Feb.05, 2017

To ease the path to the Cloud Enterprise. a catalogue of market offers in terms of outsourced business and IT cloud services would be quite useful to all parties.

In addition to the Cloud IT APIs and existing B2B, digital inter enterprise interfaces should be devised and eventually standardised because we still employ today unreliable and unstructured human interactions between businesses.

The raise of the APIs economy and microservices would be a step forward. Enterprises may offer own services (such as maps, credit verification, location...) over gateways and APIs that could be employed by other businesses to enable their own services.

The sharing industry enterprise (Uber, AirBnB...) for instance, relies on a distributed software application and APIs that interconnect customers to the individual service providers and the head office. The application does the automation, calculates the price in advance, connects to the maps system to establish a route... It permits the customers and participating service providers discover each other.

The application is the heart of the sharing/participating enterprise.

Gartner says that "*APIs* make it easier to integrate and connect people, places, systems, data, things and algorithms, create new user experiences, share data and information, authenticate people and things, enable transactions and algorithms, leverage third-party algorithms, and create new product/services and business models".

Oracle supports microservices development in Java now: Oracle bets Java EE future on REST APIs:

"When people are building microservices nowadays, they do tend to be REST-based, so that tends to be focused around JAX-RS [Java API for RESTful Web Services]...

It may seem like ages since REST stole thunder from SOAP as a mechanism for providing web services communications. REST, in conjunction with JSON and HTTP, proved a far simpler means for delivering web services than SOAP, which has long been criticized for complexity."

The serverless cloud, virtualisation and data centre technology advances pave the way to the cloud enterprise.

The serverless cloud self provisions and scales the server infrastructure for an application simplifying as such the low level task of provisioning and manage the necessary cloud infrastructure for business applications, optimising at the same time the scale of the infrastructure implicitly deployed.

The tasks could be done now by business people without much knowledge of the cloud infrastructure configuration science. They would just deploy the software and the cloud would take care of the provisioning of the necessary serving infrastructure.

Indeed, since the cloud enterprise business model is outsourcing business functions and IT, it is important that security is enhanced and easily remotely monitored, deployed, upgraded...

The evolution to the Cloud Enterprise is indeed enabled by the tidal rise in Digital innovation.

Startups created as virtual cloud Enterprises today

https://it.toolbox.com/blogs/adriangrigoriu/startups-created-as-virtual-cloud-enterprises-today-020417

Feb.04, 2017

According to Gartner

"By 2020, a corporate "no-cloud" policy will be as rare as a "no-internet" policy is today, Cloud-first, and even cloud-only, is replacing the defensive no-cloud stance that dominated many large providers in recent years. Today, most provider technology innovation is cloud-centric, with the stated intent of retrofitting the technology to on-premises".

Here is also what Bloomberg had said since long about the virtual enterprise:

"Ever hear of the virtual corporation?... In the view of many leading business thinkers, what sounds like just another bit of management-consultant cyber speak could well be the model for the American business organization in the years ahead".

The virtual corporation is a temporary network of independent companies--suppliers, customers, even erstwhile rivals--linked by information technology to share skills, costs, and access to one another's markets".

The trend shows that the enterprise increasingly adopts the Cloud and the outsourcing of the value chain functions such as manufacturing, marketing, industrial design... becoming, in essence, a virtual cloud enterprise, abbreviated for the purpose of this as the Cloud Enterprise.

But when most enterprise functions and IT are outsourced to the cloud, the only part of the virtual enterprise that is owned by and identifies the enterprise is the Governance function which oversees and takes decisions on end to end value chain participants and planning, aligns outcomes and establishes the strategy and roadmap of the cloud enterprise in conjunction with the firms delivering the outsourced services.

While most companies are well on their way to become virtual cloud enterprises, startups are born today as Cloud Enterprise with most functions and IT outsourced to reduce risks, cost and time to market.

An entrepreneur can create a Cloud Enterprise from scratch, on paper, starting from a list of off the shelf business services and IT cloud suppliers offers.

For a start up, the entrepreneur is the governance function. The rest of the business functions and IT will be outsourced. The entrepreneur owns nothing but the concept. The IT is rented, functions are leased, funds borrowed...

The entrepreneur only makes decisions and performs or delegates the coordination work. Because manufacturing, marketing, sales, after-sales, financials, planning... and even strategy and planning can be outsourced. The enterprise integration and coordination itself could also be outsourced to various external parties.

The entrepreneur is the Enterprise Architect, the one in Command and Control.

Eventually, a team would be set in place to play the governance role as the enterprise grows.

Hence, today a new enterprise can be created in no time as a virtual cloud Enterprise.

EA PAPERS, PRESENTATIONS AND BOOKS

<u>PAPERS</u>

<u>The Value EA, Reference Architectures and Frameworks return</u>

https://www.academia.edu/43029676/The_Value_Enterprise_Architecture_Generi
c_and_Reference_Architectures_and_EA_Frameworks_return_to_the_Enterprise

THE VALUE ENTERPRISE ARCHITECTURE, GENERIC & REFERENCE ARCHITECTURES AND EA FRAMEWORKS RETURN TO THE ENTERPRISE

by Adrian Grigoriu

Abstract

There is a distinction, often not made, between the value returned by architecture, the value of generic and reference architectures and the value of an architecture framework and method. But we do have to distinguish from start between them because otherwise we cannot reach results and we confuse ouselves and everybody else. In this paper the Value of each of these concepts is described.

There is a distinction, often not made, between the value returned by architecture, the value of generic and reference architectures and the value of an architecture framework and method. That is because we have to distinguish in the first place between an architecture, reference architecture, generic architecture and architecture framework and method.

Why do we use frameworks, reference or generic architectures or, for that matter, why do we do architecture at all? What is an Architecture method

Architecture

describes a system in terms of its components and interconnections that channel the system flows. The architecture often covers/recommends to a degree the physical resources that realise a system. Any system has an architecture or structure but some structures are simpler to control, maintain and change than others.

The enterprise is a complex dynamic system.

The value of architecture itself resides in the structured organisation (modules, patterns, standards, re-use,...) and description of the system which enables its faster comprehension, analysis, management, change and transformation. Hence a structured architecture returns value by comparison with the usual organically grown architecture.

There are indeed common-sense reasons for employing a structured architecture such as enhanced understanding, productivity, predictability, repeatability, consistency, etc. The architecture should guide as such any enterprise transformation.

Generic Architecture

To prevent the reinvention of the wheel in each and every case, an architecture "generic" enough to represent a whole class of systems is necessary.

TM Forum's Frameworx aims to be a generic architecture because it describes such key entities of a digital media company as business processes, information and application maps.

Here is a sample one page generic architecture describing the key functions and flows of an enterprise any enterprise. But of course there are exceptions. But exceptions prove the rule.

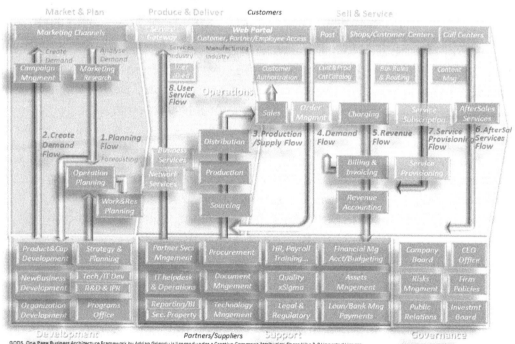

GODS One Page Generic Business Architecture

GODS One Page Business Architecture Framework by Adrian Grigoriu is licensed under a Creative Commons Attribution-ShareAlike 3.0 Unported License.

A generic architecture enables a template like approach to system modelling. Its value resides in the fact that it renders an architecture development predictable and it cuts down the modelling effort, employing the vast experience gained before.

A generic enterprise architecture is the highest level of abstraction.

But Porter's Value Chain is the highest level of abstraction for a generic enterprise architecture. The next level comes as the generic industry architecture which customises the generic architecture to an industry. Then, depending on specifics, there may be other levels of generic architectures going down in a tree organisation to the architecture specific to your company. TOGAF Continuum emphasises exactly the value of the generic architectures tree. TM Forum's Frameworx aims to be a generic architecture because it describes such key entities of a digital media company as business processes, information and application maps.

Here is an one page generic business architecture (showing functionality alone rather than implementation architectures) describing the key functions and flows of an enterprise any enterprise. But of course there are exceptions. Yet exceptions prove the rule.

Reference Architecture

is a generic architecture adopted as a standard for the analysis and design of systems in the same class. To be validated as a reference, rather than declared as such by its promoters, a generic architecture must be adopted enough, having been reused and proved in many developments.

A reference architecture, in addition to a generic architecture, exhibits the benefits of standards.

A reference architecture facilitates wide acceptance and reuse, predictable and comparable designs, reproducibility and as such productivity which saves time and costs.

TOGAF is no reference architecture though because it proposes no architecture. It is called a standard though because is specified by a standards organization with wide industry participation. TOGAF is not even a standard enterprise architecture method though because it is hard to comply or prove compliance with it with due to its size and organic organisation and, most importantly, it does not deliver the enterprise architecture we are after but most good development practices.

Architecture Framework

A core modelling template

The framework modelling concepts

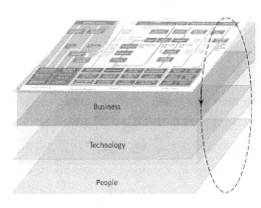

is the architecture of an architecture. It describes the architecture organisation itself. It looks like the skeleton of a body, the contents page of a book or the chassis of a car. It enables us to plug into the framework complying architecture artefacts in order to build the Architecture.

It enables us break down the system complexity up in independently manageable parts. It describes the key components of an/any Architecture and their relationships. It enables the architecture navigation.

It facilitates as such independent and parallel change and as a result, quick and without side effects.

A Framework is usually described in terms that stakeholders can grasp.

Metamodel

is the structure of a framework illustrated as a class/entity relationship diagram. It represents the enterprise architecture component types relationships and it is ultimately implemented as the repository schema of the architecture tool. It does not address the business audience though.

Architecture Method

is an ensemble of processes, templates, principles, that guide the development of an architecture to ensure its correctness and usefulness. It consists of:

A generic or reference architecture for the industry

.1) An Architecture Framework that describes the structure and entity types employed in an architecture.

.2) A Metamodel that describes the entity relationships in an Architecture Framework and enables its navigation and its structured storage and presentation.

.3) The key diagram types that show the architecture entities in various interactions use case scenarios, swimlanes workflow diagrams, functional diagrams, BPMN process diagrams, state diagrams,...

.4) The modelling sequence illustrates the recommended order of producing the diagrams beginning from top use case diagrams. The outcome diagrams should plug in the Architecture Framework.

.5) Templates for various diagrams to cut short the re-discovery work

.6) A strategy specification framework to enable the incorporation of strategic directions into the modelling of the target architecture and perhaps specify the strategy design process.

.7) The architecture governance consisting of

the checkpoints embedded in typical enterprise development processes to ensure architecture is complied with automatically

the tools to measure progress and maturity...

Architecture Principles that guide the transformation of a system in order to be architecturally correct, manage complexity and enable change

An EA tool is necessary to automate modelling and visualisation by embedding the generic/reference architecture, architecture framework and metamodel, various diagramming tools, architecture templates and patterns, architecture repository structured by the metamodel, the strategy mapping and planning process.

The Enterprise Architecture Development Program

is often confounded with Enterprise Transformation (in TOGAF for instance). The Program though mostly refers to the modelling and delivery of the EA iterations. The program is lead by the Chief Architect/Head of Architecture

The Enterprise Transformation Program

is about the implementation in practice of the successive transient Enterprise Architectures until achieving the target vision. The Architecture Program guides the Transformation Program but the latter is much more complex built out of synchronized projects that select technologies, do in depth design, testing, releases and deployment in steps similar to a DevOps approach. The Transformation program is lead by a Lead Program Manager and a few Project Managers.

The Target Architecture development and the Transformation Program takes into account not only the reduction in architecture debt as dictated by architecture principles that structure the architecture to reduce complexity and enable change, but also by the business management vision, and departmental strategies for improvement.

The Enterprise SOA vs APIs, Microservices and Microsegmentation

THE ENTERPRISE SOA VS APIS, MICROSERVICES AND MICROSEGMENTATION

by Adrian Grigoriu

Abstract

SOA from a business viewpoint, it is a way of structuring a business in blocks of loosely coupled SOA services. But SOA was declared dead because of the confusion with SOAP a protocol that enabled the communications between services.

APIs are interfaces mandated between applications allowing for interconnections untangling.

APIs are just the interface part of SOA but without necessarily specifying the encapsulation of the SOA services for autonomy and portability.

Microservices are an incarnation of SOA at the application level.

Microsegmentation allows networks be tailored around services to protect them at the service level rather than at the usual enterprise firewall level.

SOA used to be an Enterprise Integration approach consisting of service definition, orchestration (BPMS/BPEL), description (WSDL), registration, discovery (UDDI) and distribution (ESB) technologies.

Nevertheless, SOA is more than IT although its origins are in IT. From a business viewpoint, it is a way of structuring a business in blocks of loosely coupled SOA services.

SOA enables:

- Reusability of a SOA Service since the service is designed to be stand alone with reusability in mind
- Agility to change since it enables easy swapping a SOA service with another
- Applications interconnections untangling by allowing access only through service interfaces, reducing the daunting side effects of change
- The Business to specify processes as orchestrations of reusable services
- Technology agnostic business design, with technology hidden behind service interfaces
- A contractual-like interaction between business and IT, based on service SLAs
- Accountability since confusion of whose fault is, is eliminated
- Governance with the services
- Reduced pressure to replace legacy and extended lifetime for legacy applications, through encapsulation in services

The transition to the Cloud Computing paradigm which makes possible service outsourcing on an "on demand", utility like, pay-per-usage basis.

Yet, while SOA harbours developments that are in the scope of EA, it does not specifically address the IT alignment to business and strategy, documentation of the As-Is Enterprise state or guidance for the development program as EA does.

As both SOA and EA are usually initiated by IT, the lack of business stakeholders' engagement and top management support may foil the success of SOA because it does require a large Enterprise re-engineering effort, with consequences at all EA layers: business, applications, infrastructure and organization.

SOA was declared dead because of confusion with SOAP a protocol that enabled the communications between services. Still, the application level or Web domain SOA are alive and well though. SOA lives in its incarnations micro-services, microsegmentation, APIs paradigm...

SOA vs APIs

"While APIs are generally associated with REST/JSON and SOA is associated with XML and SOAP, SOA is more than just a protocol. SOA stands for "Service Oriented Architecture" and is an architectural best practice around building de-coupled applications and fosters service re-use".

And this article here elaborates at the big picture. But essentially both and APIs emphasise aspects of a modular approach to the enterprise organisation. An ideal service delivered by in an enterprise should be accessed over an API so that it can be reused without back doors which may compromise its integrity.

On the other hand a SOA service must be agile to change. Hence it must be easily replaceable, swappable and even portable. It must be autonomous. Hence to the API concept we add encapsulation of the service so that no additional wires hang loose if swapped.

Then the service may have to be executable so that it does not have to depend on an external infrastructure. The SOA service may look in the end like an appliance that may accessed through a connector, an interface. Moreover the API of a service should be technology independent. The service itself should hide the implementation technology which can still be a mainframe for instance.

Hence a SOA service is more than an API. The Cloud today implements the API paradigm. Once delivered on site the SOA service should be rather autonomous and executable so that its internal realisation is not visible outside.

SOA vs. microservices

"Experts have filled a few thousand of print and digital pages comparing SOA and *microservices* and defining the subtleties of their relationship to one another. For the purposes of this article, the chief differences between the two are the coupling of components and scope of use:

SOA is an enterprise-wide concept. It enables existing applications to be exposed over loosely-coupled interfaces, each corresponding to a business function, that enables applications in one part of an extended enterprise to reuse functionality in other applications.

Microservices architecture is an application-scoped concept. It enables the internals of a single application to be broken up into small pieces that can be independently changed, scaled, and administered. It does not define how applications talk to one another—for that we are back to the enterprise scope of the service interfaces provided by SOA".

Microsegmentation

And here is a SOA based approach to networking:

"In the early days, everything was protected from the outside-in using firewalls at the edge," Pugh says. As attackers refined their skills, basic edge protection could no longer be counted on to provide effective protection. "We discovered that firewalls needed to be closer to the data," he says. The solution is to break the infrastructure into microsegments, with a firewall guarding each resource".

The Enterprise SOA Critical Success Factors (CSF):

- Should be primarily approached as a business development, a Business Architecture, a way to structure the Enterprise, a style of target Enterprise Architecture and only then as an IT integration technology

- May only succeed if developed inside an EA development since SOA does not cover the Enterprise transformation process

- Driven only by IT, both SOA and EA are prone to fail; the business stakeholders' engagement and firm's top management support are key to success

- Business process re-engineering, a new governance around services and ultimately re-organization.

- Once implemented, an Enterprise wide SOA becomes a competitive asset based on business services accessed independently of technology and geography, agilely orchestrated for change and ready for outsourcing in the cloud.

But what is important is that all the above paradigms implement real life society evolution. While in the beginning humans were making their own food, tools... in their household, in time the production moved out to various service suppliers. We provide and receive services today simply because we cannot master any longer the complexity of these services so that we can do the work ourselves.

See also:

Open Group about SOA https://www.opengroup.org/soa/source-book/soa/p2.htm

IBM SOA https://www.ibm.com/cloud/learn/soa

The Enterprise Architect role

https://www.academia.edu/42905641/The_Enterprise_Architect_role

THE ENTERPRISE ARCHITECT LEADS THE ENTERPRISE MODELLING AND DESIGN AS OPPOSED TO SUPERVISING THE ENTERPRISE WIDE IT DEVELOPMENTS AS TODAY

by Adrian Grigoriu

Abstract

To grasp the complexities of the enterprise you need to model your enterprise so that everyone visualises and discusses solutions on the same picture. The outcome is indeed the enterprise schematics or otherwise called Enterprise Architecture (EA). Since without EA, change or transformation regularly fail, you do Enterprise Architecture to model the impact of change on the entire enterprise from the very beginning so that you act on all dependencies and effect their change in sync rather than on the run with holdbacks and late discoveries.

But the EA architects today do everything in IT but modelling the EA. That is, in reality they should not be called EA architects but rather the *Enterprise (IT) Authority* or so.

The key role of the EA Architect is to model the enterprise though and lead its future Design as opposed to the current EA role of supervising the IT enterprise wide activities.

The enterprise must change rapidly today to cope with the accelerating market and technology evolution. Since at any one time change is happening in the enterprise in one form or another, the enterprise changes continuously today.

When major change is necessary the enterprise should adopt a transformation process in order to coordinate all change of the enterprise under the same umbrella and attempt to minimise disruption and down time.

Yet, if you don't understand your enterprise you cannot change it properly, not in any case without major additional costs, setbacks, delays and expensive downtime.

For stakeholders to grasp the complexities of the enterprise in the same way though you need to model your enterprise so that everyone visualises and discusses solutions on the same picture. The outcome is indeed the enterprise schematics or otherwise called Enterprise Architecture (EA).

The reasons EA is necessary today are many fold

In the first place you need the EA so that anyone in the enterprise can understand it in order to operate it collectively at its optimum.

On the other hand you must have the enterprise schematics to be able to divide and conquer and in general manage the increasing complexity of the enterprise today.

And in the end, since without EA change or transformation regularly fails, you do Enterprise Architecture to model the impact of change on the entire enterprise from the very beginning so that you act on all dependencies and effect their change in sync rather than on the run with holdbacks and late discoveries.

The Enterprise Modeller is naturally the Enterprise Architect (EA), the leader of the EA development effort and the owner of the EA framework which lays out the EA structure, development and governance processes.

But it is not the Enterprise Architect, as too often is the case today, but the EA model and its framework to guide all Enterprise developments. Because otherwise your smart EA architect would become your major bottleneck and risk. Once the EA and the framework achieve a mature state, the EA governance framework, created by the architect, should guide the enterprise change and transformation from then on. The EA architect would still oversee the development but the architect will automate in fact the EA work, adoption, usage... by creating EA checkpoints and controls in all relevant processes which the professionals should employ. The Architect will not need to become ubiquitous as a result.

Ideally an EA architect, like an eminent coach, should make oneself redundant once the mission is accomplished.

Given the state of the EA frameworks today, the Enterprise Architect, the one who models the enterprise, must often build own framework. Therefore the architect must have a structured mind and a disposition or call for structuring systems and experience thereof.

The Chief EA architect and EA team job description is to:

.- put together the EA business case to justify the EA development once for all so that nobody asks again and again **"after all, why are we doing this"**?)

.- sell EA value to the business and management to get sponsorship and resources

.- do the EA framework selection and customization and/or design the framework creatively given the current status. This is a critical success factor for the rest of the EA development because without a proper framework most EA efforts end nowhere. Furthermore the current EA frameworks don't help.

.- establish the EA architecture principles that enable the design of the target enterprise

.- establish the technology standards, guidelines and roadmaps to simplify incoming technology selections

.- set in place the EA development process and its milestones

.- break down the EA work into workstreams with coherent deliverables

.- organize the teams to discover and document the current Enterprise state, document its blueprint

.- map the Business and IT Strategies to EA to project the target EA

.- produce the 100 days plan and the long term roadmap

.- lead the effort to organize early the EA materials into an taxonomy exposed on the Intranet for stakeholders' understanding, training and usage

.- recruit and coach the EA team

.- coordinate the entire EA development work

.- select the set of IT tools beginning with the EA tool

.- periodically prove and communicate that EA returns value by quantifying the benefits to stakeholders who use it

.- create the maturity framework, so that the management and interested stakeholders can measure objectively the EA progress and its level of utilisation

.- specify the EA compliance criteria and process controls for all business developments

The EA compliance frame dictates the mechanisms the solution architecture designs need to comply to such as EA principles, components reuse, naming, notations, constraints... EA checkpoints. As such the EA architect would not have to be involved in all enterprise activities, i.e. the EA factotum but its brains.

.- keep up to date the Management, Business, IT and in general all stakeholders so that the EA can be adopted, continuously improved with feedback and increasingly used.

To be able to cover the entire Business operation the EA architect should be positioned at the highest level in the organisation hierarchy.

But most Enterprise Architects today don't do the above

The EA architects today do everything in IT but EA. That is, in reality they should not be called EA architects but the Enterprise (IT) Authority or so. They usually validate most business-IT developments against their own professional experience which is good but leads to variable and debatable outcomes because every EA may come with a different outcome.

Yet, in practice the architect must fulfil the role you really need to

.1. deliver the Enterprise Model rather than to TOGAF and Zachman specs

or

.2. play the role of Enterprise IT Authority that is participate in Decision Boards, oversee solution development processes and deliveries without effectively delivering the EA, as today.

The key role of the EA Architect is to model the enterprise and lead its future Design as opposed to the current EA role of supervising the IT enterprise wide activities.

The Digital Transformation Must Rely On Enterprise Architecture

THE DIGITAL TRANSFORMATION MUST RELY ON ENTERPRISE ARCHITECTURE

By Adrian Grigoriu

Abstract

The digital enterprise is happening nolens volens, that is, there is no choice. The enterprise cannot really escape the technology progress.

But EA does enable the enterprise transformation, the same way the blueprint of your house or town enables change. It is important as such to comprehend our own enterprise better, its structure and operation so that we can factor the Digital in a quick and safe manner.

What is the digital technology?

It all starts from the transformation of information and analogue signals into a digital representation of 0/1s. Complicated mathematical algorithms in software can then process the information. General or special purpose computers and microprocessors host the information processing. The faster and smaller the hardware, the more capable is our digital world.

Our life has already been digitised

Our watches, media, players, phones, tablets, GPSs, laptops, radios, TVs, ... are all digital. All networks and transmissions are digital, our pets are micro-chipped, our cars are increasingly computerised..., we are equipped with digital pacemakers and hearing aids. We have complex digital instruments, airplanes and weapons.

The digitisation of the enterprise

Everybody talks about digitisation of the enterprise today. Pundits make their business in alerting us that digital is coming like a storm, that we have to do something about it. We had technology since the first enterprise though. Did we have to worry about it? Not really, not more than necessary. Because it is the normal course of things.

Still, the first to have a better tool or weapon has a decisive advantage.

The first enterprise to have an effective technology would have a competitive advantage. The enterprises that choose and properly integrate the increasing plethora of technologies will win.

Because digitisation happens since long then, what's different now?

Change took a long time in the past. In the 1950s we had the first TVs and computers. But technology evolved so much that a mobile phone today has many times the power of the first computer. The hardware that occupied rooms now is hosted in a bankcard chip or SIM.

According to Ray Kurzweil, "technological change is exponential, contrary to the common-sense "intuitive linear" view. So we won't experience 100 years of progress in the 21st century — it will be more like 20,000 years of progress (at today's rate)... ...*We're doubling the rate of progress every decade*".

Hence, it is not so much the digitisation of the enterprise but its acceleration.

And it is the Moore's Law that explains the Digital revolution. It states that processing power doubles every two years or so. Thus, computers have increasingly the capacity to execute in real time the complex algorithms we devised long time ago.

Why the digital enterprise is inevitable?

Do we have to take the digital enterprise path? Is it evitable? What would be the advantages?

The digital enterprise is happening nolens volens, that is, there is no choice. The enterprise cannot really escape the technology progress.

We cannot avoid the digital revolution. It is a revolution indeed because the change is significantly larger now and increasingly faster gathering pace and accumulating change. Moreover, we are already engaged on the digital path.

Even though the digital future is inevitable, we can still make choices and actively control the digital evolution from as early as possible to get what we want, in accord with our vision, rather than accept what comes.

But why do we care about digital?

And why should we do it, only because some say so? Businesses existed for hundreds of years before the "digital" technology was born.

But technology progress and in particular, the Digital pace that fuels it, is, perhaps, the biggest factor of change but also opportunities and threats in the enterprise and elsewhere today.

The Digital progress enables smaller size, larger scale, more amiable User Interfaces, faster processing and communications, increasing automation and integration of processes, information and technology and on a business level, new products, business models and organisation k9nds, i.e. more of everything.

But we have to control the Digital evolution rather that the vice versa.

Adopting a technology frantically, one at a time, without the benefit of the big picture, may ultimately contribute to failure rather than success. Still, there are many more and more to come.

The digital developments that affect your enterprise

With the acceleration of Digital progress, the enterprise technology landscape changes faster and faster.

- Networks, disks, storage and processors grow more powerful, faster and cheaper
- Information storage capacity soars at an unprecedented pace
- Virtualisation enables the separation of applications, processing, storage and network entities from the physical hardware, enabling as such easy online resource creation, configuration, scalability, availability, portability... and, hence, business operation agility.
- In-memory databases enable instant processing and real time analytics.
- Open Source enables increasingly affordable, cost effective applications
- Application suites, increasingly expanding to automate the whole enterprise operation, such as Portals, Information and Document Management, Access Control, Orchestration and Enterprise Integration Buses, CRM, ERPs
- The Web added powerful standard user interaction technologies based on UI languages like HTML5 and Java scripting
- Mobile access ensures fast access to the enterprise functions from anywhere, on the go.
- Social Media facilitates bi-directional contact with customers and prospects
- Tele-collaboration and conferencing technologies replace travelling
- Electronic B2B transactions with partners and suppliers reduce transaction and face to face time
- Customer Data Integration (CDI) and Master Data Management (MDM) that reduce your data integrity issues
- Big Data business intelligence facilitate Decision making
- Virtual reality enable shops
- 3D printing and robots ease manufacturing
- Internet of Things enable context reactive operations
- Self driving cars and drones reduce transport costs

And, not least, enabled by the Digital progress, the Cloud changes the paradigm of IT ownership. The IT goes back to the shared data centre. We rent from the data centre processing power, storage and networking and application rather than buy, maintain, upgrade, discard and recycle our own.

The impact of Digital on business models and value chains

The progress of Digital technology brings in the enterprise new business models.

Companies increasingly market, sale and service over net channels, rent their resources from the cloud and let partners provide the processing links of the enterprise value chain. Take the example of so many firms today that outsource manufacturing, sales, marketing or, on the other hand, the product design and development, with most of them outsourcing now the enterprise support functions.

But customer channels, resources and partners are the key elements of any business model.

New companies appear, mainly comprising of management staff who assemble the pieces of the business from services that execute the links of the value chain, from sourcing to making and delivery over various channels.

The companies may just have a web site, hosted and designed by somebody else at that. But, the enterprise still owns the product and manages the whole production chain.

The new business model is of the "virtual value chain" kind. Both business processes and technology are outsourced to partners and cloud providers. The Digital progress supplies the integration network, the virtualisation base, the off-the-shelf Cloud services, the customer channels... that ultimately automate the virtual value chain.

The enterprise creation becomes a matter of integrating the partner services and the Cloud infrastructure that deliver the value chain the entrepreneur establishes. Everything is rented.

The cost of both failure and success is much smaller as such.

The only function that remains in the physical enterprise is the management that selects, configures and coordinates the links of the virtual value chain.

This function will also identify the enterprise.

The Digital transforms as such the way our enterprises are created and operate.

Companies in partnership, collaborating to deliver a product, act as the value chain links of an overall virtual enterprise composed of many small and distributed enterprises.

The name of the game is cooperation.

Without the Digital technology progress, that would not have been possible.

The Digital evolution affects as such the way we do business and the organisation of the enterprise which would evolve towards a virtual organisation enabled by Digital technology where various business processes and services are/maybe outsourced to partners in the Cloud world in various business models.

The enterprise would be increasingly distributed, interconnected and automated. Many new small enterprises would be part of the enterprise virtual value chain in an interconnected economy.

The way the digital enterprise would look like

Pundits have already embarked in campaigns of the kind "do digital or die". Right, but how would a digital business look like?

But indeed, the user experience and the quality of intelligence would be progressively better. Customers would benefit from better and new types of products, all digitally enhanced.

In this vision, the enterprise could be:

- Virtual, stretching over the boundaries of a few physical enterprises owing to the Cloud and business process outsourcing enabled by fast digital communications, collaboration, B2B and transport technologies
- Increasingly Lego like, assembled from parts such as SaaS services that would be remotely plugged in and out and configured, scaled... over the net.
- Leasing capabilities rather than buying and owning them.
- Automated end to end, with applications covering all enterprise functions and workflows and transactions executed without manual intervention due to the increasingly expanding application suites, services, IOT... beside robots, assembly bands
- Remote working with Small office footprint due to, mobile access and ubiquitous communication technologies
- On-line sales, payment, marketing and customer interaction based on web social media technologies
- Virtual shops manned by virtual reality technologies, decreasing physical shop footprint
- Information, integrated, normalised, consistent... due to MDM, CDI, integrated application suites...
- Real time business intelligence, due to in-memory platforms
- On-the-net data store and back-up on the Cloud

Benefits of the digital enterprise

All technologies, capabilities and products would be enhanced by Digital technology. That would pave the way to the Internet of Things (IoT), that is Things that co-operate to deliver a service.

Also, the Digital gradually renders the enterprise virtual with most parts residing in a cloud of partners that participate into the Value Chain. What matters most and identifies the enterprise is the Governance function that coordinates the enterprise Operations, Development and Support activities that can and are increasingly outsourced.

The Digital would enable the enterprise and its stakeholders benefit in many ways. The digital revolution will enable

- The **business be in control of the enterprise operation** and evolution since capabilities will be purchased and configured on-line by the business and mounted only for the required period
- **The Designed Enterprise,** that is, a business architected from parts or services from the Cloud and Business Process Outsourcing (BPO) providers
- The business will select capabilities rather than the IT
- **More reliable planning and predictable costs** owing to the availability of readymade capabilities, rather than relying on building in-house

- Technology expertise to be relegated to service provider firms rather than to each and every enterprise
- **Quick scalability, configurability**, reporting... agility to change, features inherited from capabilities
- Instant decision making based on Real Time Business Intelligence
- **Model Driven Manufacturing** where the design to manufacturing process is automated with 3D printing
- Drones enabled distribution
- Technology evolution would enable Business to be in control of the enterprise rather than continue to tinker with technology like today.
- The enterprise, overall, would be more agile, faster to market as such, leaner and meaner.

How to prepare the enterprise

Digital, perhaps, is the biggest factor of change in the enterprise or elsewhere today. It abounds in opportunities but it is also a threat for the complacent enterprise. But the Digital quandary consists not only in what are the right technologies for our enterprise but how are we going to integrate them into the enterprise and when. This is compounded by the fact that the Digital progress accelerates. And more technology like the Cloud move technology ownership and management outside the enterprise.

But to ensure our enterprise succeeds in a digital future, we have to understand first the technology impacts and trends. Then, we have to be good at evaluating the technologies that are about to change the enterprise.

What do we need to do in practice?

- The Digital technology would create many new products and services. Think about them early.
- The Digital would enable innovation and invention in many sectors. Reflect on that.
- We have to include the Digital in our Strategy and planning.
- To cope, it is important to comprehend our own enterprise better, its structure and operation so that we can factor the Digital in a quick and safe manner.
- To mitigate the threats of the future, we need to project now the enterprise picture in a few years time. We need to think strategically. And then we need to prepare the enterprise for the accelerating pace of change.
- Hence, it's a good practice to create a function in the enterprise that focuses on the enterprise future.

Enterprise Architecture already discovers, documents the enterprise and projects its future states but only from an IT perspective.

> *Is today's Enterprise Architecture adequate enough though to guide the enterprise to the future?*

In theory, EA does enable the enterprise transformation, the same way the blueprint of your house or town enables change. Without a blueprint, laying cables in the wall or under the pavement is a risky endeavour because you may break the existing electricity wires and water or gas pipes.

In practice though, few EA efforts deliver the EA blueprint and as such, EA enables neither change nor transformation today.

Anyway, EA does not deliver business benefits directly. The business itself must transform the enterprise, employing EA, to reduce duplication in processes, platforms, projects, to streamline the operation, fix malfunctions, map strategy, project the future etc. The architect should deliver the "big picture", propose changes and assist. Without delivering the big picture, EA fails after all.

The paradox today is that while there are plenty of EA architects, there are few Enterprise Architectures. That means that architects do not deliver EA but rather stories about it and engage in never ending efforts and self important discourses. Most architects sell again and again the EA known benefits rather than do EA.

Anyway, business stakeholders don't know what to expect or, if they know, thinking by analogy of an architecture blueprint, they are quite pessimistic about it, noting the disaccord between promises and results in practice. For most, EA is potentially costly and largely, prone to fail.

The subsequent paradox is that even if EA does not deliver, business customers do not complain because, for most, despite the propaganda, EA is still an internal IT effort of little consequence to the wider enterprise.

In any case, it is not so much the architect but the architecture itself and principles that matter to a transformation and the end system. As with a building, the blueprint is what matters after the original architect is long gone.

The Enterprise Modelling approach

We need an approach that focuses on the enterprise as a whole, its change and the transition to that state but also to prepare the enterprise for disruption.

What the Function has to do though before even looking at incoming change is to

1. understand better and describe the operation and capabilities of the current enterprise

2. prepare a technology obsolescence roadmap to enable a natural evolution

3. architect the enterprise for future change, for flexibility and agility to move on, so that it can be easily and quickly configured out of modules, readymade services that can be filled in by best of breed.

That is, you have to model the enterprise to be able to visualise it, enable the enterprise self awareness and the projection of the target picture.

But, ironically, the digital revolution gradually removes the IT as an enterprise concern by moving it back to the Cloud. The Computing Cloud is, in fact, an IT technology, that gradually renders the enterprise technology agnostic.

Hence, an enterprise function, beyond the IT Enterprise Architecture, i.e. current EA, will have to discover the existing business and organizational landscape and architect it

- resources agnostic because the technology and/or people may be supplied by 3rd parties
- ownership agnostic, after all, most capabilities can be outsourced for execution by 3rd parties
- service based, that is, the key role is occupied by the interface protocols and APIs
- integrating Information and people Organisation architectures

We are looking then at an **Enterprise Modelling** function, rather than EA, that should be in charge of the end to end Enterprise discovery and modelling besides the trends and emerging technologies integration and roadmapping.

The function would be operating at the top management level rather than IT.

And indeed the Enterprise Modelling function has to

- liaise with functions to understand business and technology needs
- analyse the evolving and new trends and technologies potential impact on the business
- merge technology evolution into the overall enterprise strategy
- architect technologies integration to functions without duplication or unnecessary variation or replacement
- establish the principles and standards of enterprise transformation
- produce the target enterprise blueprint
- propose a roadmap for discussion and approval
- facilitate the transformation process

The digital road is never ending

The Digital road is long, without an end in sight. In fact, we have already embarked on this road long ago.

Since it affects now the whole enterprise, technology becomes a key competitive differentiator. Hence, we have to prepare the enterprise for the digital road because technology could make or break the enterprise.

What do you do though to make sure your enterprise evolves on the right digital path? Digital adoption can be expensive or ineffective if not properly thought. Not all digital technologies, for instance, would be productive for your chosen evolution. And, without proper integration in your operations and vision, the digital can create an additional weight. Digital at all costs does not pay off.

To succeed in the digital transformation today, we have to project the big picture at the end of the tunnel, the digital enterprise, the same way we do in enterprise architecture.

You need a true and strong digital team that operates at top business level to cover the whole enterprise rather than IT alone because technology is in IT care because it implements the business functionality.

Yet, what we do today is embark in implementing the digital step by step, technology by technology. and hope for the best. Yet this path does not allow us to control the final outcome but strands of it.

What makes the difference is not so much the technologies employed but the degree of integration into your enterprise operation and vision so that technologies offer your maximum benefit at minimum cost and render the enterprise competitive.

The digital technologies may also transform your vision of the enterprise though and more, change its business models.

The paradox we live today is that the progress of IT leads increasingly to the outsourcing of the very technology that enables it. Perhaps because the effort to manage properly its increasing complexity becomes too costly and steals the focus of your enterprise. With the Cloud, the enterprise would own less and less technology.

The information technology is also increasingly hidden under virtualisation layers.

But virtualisation introduces a layer of abstraction that enables outsourcing. Note the growing reliance on processing, storage and network virtualisation and the services paradigm in software.

In any case, the digital technologies evolution or perhaps, revolution, is on our cards for the long run. It is an ever on-going process. We just have to drive the enterprise on the right digital path, that is to make best use of digital developments because others would do exactly that.

The evolution to Digital is not an option but a "must". But while we are already doing it, we have to prepare for the increasingly accelerated rate of Digital progress.

Technologies must be chosen on combined impact on enterprise big picture

THE DIGITAL TRANSFORMATION TECHNOLOGIES MUST BE CHOSEN ON THE COMBINED IMPACT ON THE ENTERPRISE BIG PICTURE

by Adrian Grigoriu

Abstract

What the executives and board have to make sure today is that the Digital Transformation path is chosen on the combined impact of the new technologies on the big picture of the enterprise rather than on the merits of technologies taken in isolation. That is because the Digital impact is not so much in IT but on the future products, business models, processes and the enterprise organisation itself.

A problem for the Digital Transformation today is that Boards of Directors do not understand technology. But should the Board of Directors be selected on technology acumen too?

That companies seldom have technology savvy leaders we already know because the technology background has been more often than not looked down upon. Technology was considered until recently only a costly implement. Well, the Board members were not chosen on the technology acumen criteria anyway. But the truth is that it is hard enough for technologists, consultants and analysts to keep up with the digital technology progress, nevermind the business directors.

Nevertheless the problem the executive lot is confronted today is not only that without the latest technology their business can hardly survive the competition race but also that the Digital evolution is increasingly outpacing the current business rate of change. That is, we are going through a Digital Revolution rather than Evolution.

Some suggest that technologists or CIOs should sit on the company boards. But, to start with, the Board meetings are for making business rather than technology decisions.

Anyway, since Digital innovation and transformation come rather in conflict with the IT mission to keep the business lights on, which in practice means the fewer changes the better, CIOs have an inherent conflict of interest and as such they should be the last people considered to make such technology decisions or sit on the board. The CIO's main task and skills are to make sure that the IT operates five nines rather than plotting the Digital future of the Enterprise.

Yet neither the Strategy Directors, CMOs, nor the technologists can decide on the technologies adopted in the Digital Transformation.

Strategy Directors do understand the business needs enough to establish the strategic directions but they would not be able to pinpoint the technologies which realise best the directions. until the technology impacts are translated into business impacts.

The CMO's scope is products, sales and marketing strategies rather than the technology of operation of the enterprise.

Technologists have the know-how but not the big picture of how well technologies serve the enterprise. And so on.

In any case, what the executive lot has to make sure is that the Digital Transformation path is chosen on the combined impact of the new technologies on the big picture of the enterprise rather than on the merits of technologies taken in isolation. That is because the Digital impact is not so much in IT but on the future products, business models, processes and the enterprise organisation itself.

Think of the new enterprise business models imposed by technology progress such as:

1) the sharing business model or in other words enterprises such as Uber, AirBnB... consisting of participating resources supplied by many rather independent participants, usually geographically dispersed so that they can provide local services. The Digital technology enables an enterprise to coordinate the geographically spread participant labour and the resources into the virtual enterprise.

2) the outsourcing of IT to the Cloud

3) the outsourcing of entire business processes to suppliers

Nevermind the new remote work business model pioneered during this crisis but which is set to stay for the benefit of all parties and in particular, the environment.

Hence, the up and coming Cloud Enterprise is a virtual enterprise which Value Chain consists mainly of services outsourced to a Cloud of IT, Business Services and remote Labour & Resources suppliers.

The point so far is that all the above is made possible by the Digital technology today. In this context Enterprise Architecture and Security become crucial. Because how can you outsource a service if you don't know its dependencies on other services or if you cannot protect the remote interactions?

So, what the Board and the executive lot need to understand and agree upon is not the technologies themselves but the projected enterprise big pictures realised by technologies in various end architectures. Drawing this big picture architectures is not a job though for the Board, Strategy Director, CIO, CMO (Chief Marketing Officer) or technologists.

The Digital rather than becoming a top management expertise should be the task for the new Emerging Technologies and Enterprise Architecture functions.

A team of technologists should produce a knowledge database with the emerging technologies relevant to the enterprise. A technology record would consist of descriptions, sources. position in the hype cycle, associated costs, risks... value propositions and recommendations. The better the technologies records the better the decision making.

The Chief Digital Officer will lead the new emerging technologies function. The role of the Digital Chief Officer is to create and manage an Emerging Technologies knowledgebase in order to:

- analyse all technologies and sift them
- categorise technologies on impacts on the enterprise automation, communication and collaboration, decision making, data and content management, products...
- produce value propositions for each technology
- promote a technologies on the path of acceptance
- organise trials with go/no-go stages of realisation

Yet, even with the new Chief Digital Officer and the emerging technologies function, the enterprise is no wiser with regard to the Digital transformation. That is because to be evaluated in context, the technologies must be first projected onto various target architectures for the enterprise taking into account not only all the technology interactions, dependencies, redundancies and roadmaps but also the future end to end business flows and organisation.

Hence, the Enterprise Architect, who must chose, map and combine all new technologies on the future enterprise picture in various scenarios, becomes the key player in the Digital Transformation.

The role of the Enterprise Architect in the Digital Transformation is not only to map and integrate the technologies in the enterprise big picture in various scenarios agreed with stakeholders but to ultimately produce the report for the executive lot and Board examining choices, exhibiting business cases and business models and making recommendations.

Yet, as a note, the Enterprise Architect is not the usual enterprise wide IT Authority of today as often assumed, but the Modeller of the Enterprise.

Yet, while the Digital Technologies will change the future, the reality is that the Enterprise needs to focus on its business rather than on the ever changing Digital technologies landscape.

That is because not every company can afford the investment in technology and its expensive eco system of specialists, training... that had to be maintained.

Thus the enterprise should become as technology agnostic as possible. But the Digital enables the technology agnostic approach as well.

Here are the Principles of Digital Transformation that insulate the Enterprise from technology change:

.1) encapsulate technology behind interfaces in SOA like services that hide the technology. That is because complexity in order to be conquered must be divided and encapsulated in modules which can be dealt with in separation by different parties.

.2) outsource the most challenging technology services to specialist/cloud companies

The Digital Transformation for the Executive Lot

THE DIGITAL TRANSFORMATION FOR THE EXECUTIVE LOT

by Adrian Grigoriu

Abstract

The root cause of failure of the Digital Transformation is that it is performed in a single step as, a one off, big sudden transformation that not only disrupts the business as usual but has a very good chance to fail due to its high ambitions.

To succeed, the enterprise must go first through a few preparatory changes in order to ease the incoming Digital Transformation per se, changes that would render the enterprise agile to the incoming change. Without these preparatory steps the Digital Transformation may fail when your enterprise architecture looks like a hair ball which you would have to untangle late, during the transformation.

The Digital is a transformation all enterprises have to go through. Even if it does not really guarantee the success of your enterprise, it is nevertheless a condition for your enterprise survival. Because your enterprise must automate to reduce costs, employ IOT and Edge Computing to enhance operation, enable real time decisions by AI and be accessible online for transactions, exchanges and information... Because most business changes today are induced by technology whose renewal cycles get shorter and shorter. Hence, from now on, we are stuck with the Digital.

As a note though, the more Digital the enterprise becomes the less it cares about the Digital because the Digital increasingly enables the outsourcing of IT to the Cloud which offers on demand pools of functionality, processing power, edge computing, storage and networking. Hence, paradoxically, with the Digital Transformation the IT will continue to slide out of the enterprise into the Cloud. The more Cloud there is, the less Digital is the enterprise.

But "Why So Many High-Profile Digital Transformations Fail" ?

Thomas H. Davenport analyses in this article for Harvard Business Review a few digital transformations attempt: "Procter & Gamble wanted to become "the most digital company on the planet"... It happened with analytics and big data... And now it's happening with digital transformation..."

To start with this failures are no big cause of alarm. When 70% of all IT projects fail anyhow, no wonder Digital Transformations fail. The situation is bad but no worse than usual. Yet, we should learn how to prevent these failures.

After talking through the few culprit reasons, Thomas notes that a cause of failure is digital transformations "decisions are inevitably influenced by hype from vendors and the media, expensive consultants offering "thought leadership" insights, many high profile experiments, and a few exciting success stories...".

True, today even the academy and business consulting firms like HBR, Boston Consulting, McKinsey, Forbes, ... which kept for so long their distance from IT, are all into Digital telling us incessantly what we have to do to save our enterprise from the assault of the Digital technology. They are even into Enterprise Architecture (EA) today, which was so IT that they wouldn't touch with a pole. It is true that, from the beginning the Digital Transformation was touted by self promoting prophets who worked on the assumption that if it happens they can claim the "I-said-so" and if it doesn't, nobody would cares anyway. Yet, this hype is pretty much the case for any new development today. So this reason for failure is so common that it does not make any difference in fact.

Davenport also writes that the lesson learned by P&G is that "no digital initiative is undertaken at P&G if it doesn't fit the strategy closely and if it's not hardwired to value".

It is politically correct to say that, but is it right? The IT guys know well today that digital initiatives cannot be always hardwired to value but rather to the total cost of doing business as usual because, for instance, they often have to upgrade a technology at a considerable effort and cost only because the suppliers support no longer the current versions.

Still, what is the root cause of the Digital Transformation failures?

The root cause of failure is that the Digital Transformation is performed in a single step as, a one off, big sudden transformation that not only disrupts the business as usual but has a very good chance to fail due to its high ambitions.

The Digital transformation (DT) has been already happening for a long time now, beginning, arguably, with the introduction of computers in the enterprise. Furthermore, the digital technologies would not stop evolving over night, but, on the contrary, the pace of change will accelerate. In fact, the Digital Transformation came to our attention again only when this pace of change has began to overwhelm the enterprise. In fact, in what we are concerned today, the pace of updates of the Windows OS and Android transforms us all nervous wrecks.

As such, the Digital is a single continuous and ever faster transformation rather than a one-off transformation as touted today. A Digital Transformation would be followed by yet another and another.

How should we prevent the failure of Digital Transformations?

To succeed, the enterprise must go first through a few preparatory changes enumerated below in order to ease the incoming Digital Transformation per se, changes that would render the enterprise agile to the incoming change. Without these preparatory steps the Digital Transformation may fail when your enterprise architecture looks like a hair ball which you would have to untangle late, during the transformation.

But here are the preparatory steps:

1. Model the current Architecture of the Enterprise so that you evaluate

   a). the enterprise landscape at the start of your transformation

   b). the architecture end state and the changes that need to be done to render the enterprise agile to all the incoming digital change

   In this phase you document the current enterprise model, establish the architecture principles for the transformation and model the enterprise end picture according to them. This way, you clean-up your enterprise architecture and pay the enterprise architectural debt to prevent the many future failures that may spring due to poor documentation and the short cuts taken in the past.

   For agility, organise as much as possible the target enterprise architecture around services so that you are able to control all dependencies and enable outsourcing. As such encapsulate services, define APIs, microservices... Plan potential outsourcing from the very beginning to be able to work with suppliers.

   The outcome of this work would be the

   Newly created Enterprise Modelling team, if you don't already have one

   Current Enterprise Architecture documented from the Process, Technology and People Organisation points of view

   Architecturally correct, debt free target Enterprise Architecture documented in terms of Process, Technology and People

   Workstreams and milestones to achieve the target enterprise architecture

2. Document in parallel with 1.) the Emerging Technologies landscape relevant to your enterprise

   Without a thorough effort to evaluate the potential digital technologies you may miss those developments that render your enterprise competitive.

   Outcomes:

   A newly established Emerging Technology team

   A Digital Strategy and Roadmap including the key relevant technologies, dependencies and the milestones of adoption

3. Establish a single Digital Transformation Plan continuing with a long term Roadmap

   because, no matter how good it sounds, no enterprise would engage in separate pre-transformations for the sake of the Enterprise Modelling or Agility alone.

   The Strategy and Planning teams, working with the Enterprise Architecture and Emerging Technologies teams should deliver:

   A single overall Enterprise Strategy that includes the Business, Digital and Architecturally correct strategies

   The short term Enterprise Transformation plan and the long term Roadmap which implement the Business vision, Digital technologies and Architecture Principles all in one

Proceed with the execution of the single continuous Transformation Plan in iterations, while refreshing, as you go, the roadmap.

The Cloud Enterprise

https://www.academia.edu/42905630/The_Cloud_Enterprise

THE CLOUD ENTERPRISE

by Adrian Grigoriu

Abstract

In a simple picture, the Cloud Enterprise looks like a cloud of business and IT service providers surrounding and serving a core firm. In a more complex view, Enterprises, consisting of core firms, collaborate with service provider firms, which, in turn, work with other service providers in their cloud to deliver the goods. It all comes down to Porter's Value systems – that is, a number of company Value Chains that are collaborating to deliver the end products.

The Cloud Enterprise has the agility of SOA and the low cost, convenience, and proficiency of Cloud Computing and Business Process Utility outsourcing, while taking advantage of the current networking and Internet capabilities.

Business Process Utility, the Virtual Enterprise, Cloud Computing, Enterprise Architecture, SOA, all these business and IT developments, how could they all be deployed and integrated in a company? How would the concepts fit together and what would the outcome look like? There is so much confusion, particularly with IT concepts and technologies coming faster than we can absorb them, it is difficult to understand their consequences and their positioning next to each other.

The suggestion here is that a company developed according to these concepts would look like a Cloud Enterprise, that is, a Virtual Enterprise with a SOA-like architecture, with its business functions, processes, and their IT resources supplied over the Web by a cloud of business and IT service providers. The cloud symbol, coming from the networking world and, recently, Cloud Computing, signifies the Internet like distribution.

The Virtual Enterprise and Business Process Outsourcing

The Virtual Enterprise, described by some in the business field as the networked Enterprise, consists of transparently distributed business functions outsourced to partners that work together to deliver the product to the end customers. The Web and B2B have an important role in enabling this networked Enterprise. While not going into details, the essential benefit will be business agility and proficiency of the best of breed services.

'Business Process Utilities - BPU - are an emerging form of business process outsourcing. ABPU is useful when a more standardized solution is sought that can be paid for on a transactional basis",

Gartner, http://www.gartner.com/DisplayDocument?id=527120

A classic example would be the personal credit verification, outsourced to specialized companies. Insurance is another domain where BPU registered progress. BPU may well extend to an entire business function, not just a process, as is often the case for HR or payroll. The technology supporting the process or function is outsourced with the function. What is new to BPU, as opposed to the traditional Business Process Outsourcing (BPO), is the fact that the service is rather standard, delivered to more than one customer and easy to integrate. BPU, in effect, supplies a process with an on demand consumption and charging model.

A Virtual Enterprise may, consist of a number of Business Processes Utilities or Functions outsourced to various provider firms.

Cloud Computing

Cloud Computing (CC) is a new overloaded IT term, and vague at that. In short, I would define it as the outsourcing of the IT services - applications and technology - to partners over the Web. Remote access or managed services relay an incomplete description since they suggest mostly people access. The cloud means outsourced applications integration and on demand, utility-like, services consumption, the novel elements of the model.

Cloud Computing represents, in fact, a new Enterprise business model where the IT services supporting the business are provided, to various degrees, by partners, rather than in-house. It sprang from IT, but so did SOA and Enterprise Architecture. The Cloud only refers to the services cloud of a single Enterprise. Every firm may have its own cloud that may overlap at multi-tenant IT service providers.

Cloud Computing consists of a few component service concepts (types of outsourced services): SaaS, PaaS (overall, I'll call them XaaS: Application, Platform, Infrastructure, Security... as a Service).

PaaS (Platform) and all its variants, as part of the Computing Cloud, offer the opportunity to outsource not only your data center but to act as platforms for your applications, Web presence, content management... Integration as a Service emerges to provide the orchestration and integration of the XaaS services.

Because of the potential cocktails of various XaaS services, a few business models are possible. At one end, your applications may be outsourced to different SaaS providers in the Cloud, each using their own technology infrastructure. At the other end, the applications are housed by an Infrastructure/Data Center provider, or more than one, managed by a 3rd party. The applications may be owned and managed by the core firm or the application provider.

The Business Process Utility (BPU) business concept aligns well with the SaaS IT application service outsourcing even though BPU, in general, may not rely on IT. But, in reality, SaaS becomes a part of BPU. The difference is that one is an IT term while the other is business. They both are consumed and paid for on an "on demand" model.

Is the Cloud Computing (CC) a technology? To start with, it is the business concept of outsourcing IT services, really. As with SOA, companies such as Amazon, Google,

Salesforce.com, Microsoft. and many others provide various CC models. From a supplier's perspective, the technology offered is sometimes called "private clouds," even if they are not really clouds that until they are included in an Enterprise cloud. A number of these private clouds may become part of an Enterprise cloud. And then for some, private cloud means own computing clouds which negate in fact the concept definition. But, in most cases, there still remain in-house applications, which have to interact with the cloud.

Among the benefits of the CC are instant provisioning of IT capabilities (servers, storage, network), utilization of the IT resources on demand (utility-like), service location independence (in the cloud, and technology transparency. The main advantage is that the service aims to be Off-the-Shelf, hiding the technology hurdles and fast and easy to adopt.

Among drawbacks are migration to the CC architecture, integration with other applications, and ownership of Enterprise data. Tools evolve to deploy/migrate applications transparently to different "private cloud" providers. Data security and legalities are key but not unsolvable. One has to separate data management from ownership. SOA, as a style, underlies the architecture of the services cloud.

A cloud computing paradigm, in actual fact, reduces an IT department in time to the IT architecture, strategy, and planning functions. The bitter relations of the past between IT and business could vanish, now replaced by contracts or real-time pre-pay for on demand services. Technology maintenance, upgrades, application management, and licenses are not your concern any longer.

The IT applications and technology become part of an Enterprise cloud. What does it mean? In truth, gradually (as you deploy to the cloud), the IT becomes a separate entity from your Enterprise. Your applications may run in another time zone, country, and company. Along with the supporting IT applications, Business Processes are outsourced to partner companies, all part of an Enterprise Cloud now. And that leads us to Business Process Utility, facilitated by Cloud Computing.

CC demands technology Virtualization, without which it would be impossible for a provider to manage effectively the infrastructure serving many customers. It also stimulates the blades technology because of its scalability and reduced power consumption, etc.

The Cloud Computing directly affects the Enterprise Architecture. And SOA offers transparent distribution, loose coupling, technology transparency, and interfaces rendering the integration light, so you can easily take full advantage of what the cloud offers. SOA, is essential in enabling the Virtual Enterprise, Cloud Computing, and Business Process Utility.

The cloud covers both the IT applications and technology layers of an Enterprise Architecture. Imagine the EA Business Architecture layer resting on top of the IT Application and Technology layers, as in the text book, now looking like a fluffy cloud of distributed, outsourced IT services.

The firm needs to draw the overall Enterprise Architecture, but not bother with the technological detail any longer. The Data Center and its Virtualization, Grid computing, and blades technologies become less a concern for the business at large but more for the private clouds providers.

There is synergy between the Cloud Computing IT view (based on SaaS, PaaS, IaaS) the Virtual Enterprise business view and outsourced Business Process Utilities. All outsource functionality, eventually over the Internet. All become part of the cloud. All are best served by SOA. Ultimately, the Cloud Computing serves and becomes part of the Virtual Enterprise or, if in need of a common term, the Cloud Enterprise.

The problem appears to be that business has a different language and vocabulary from IT. There is a deep division between business and IT in terms of skills and goals. The news is that Cloud Computing, supported by SOA, may bridge the division by outsourcing IT services to various service provider firms under SLA contracts.

The Cloud Enterprise

In a simple picture, the Cloud Enterprise looks like a cloud of business and IT service providers surrounding and serving a core firm. In a more complex view, Enterprises, consisting of core firms, collaborate with service provider firms, which, in turn, work with other service providers in their cloud to deliver the goods. It all comes down to Porter's Value systems – that is, a number of company Value Chains that are collaborating to deliver the end products.

The Cloud Enterprise has the agility of SOA and the low cost, convenience, and proficiency of Cloud Computing and Business Process Utility outsourcing, while taking advantage of the current networking and Internet capabilities.

While the EAI integrated the IT applications of yesterday, and the ESB serves the today's paradigm, the Web will integrate the largely distributed Cloud Enterprises of tomorrow, structured on SOA.

Presentations

Enterprise Architecture in 2 minutes or so

The Cloud Enterprise built of Business Capabilities in the Cloud

Strategy Development using the Strategy Rings Framework

Orgnize your IT with the ITOOF Framework

Enterprise Modelling with GODS FFLV in Posters

The Architecture of the Digital Twin of your Organization

Design your Enterprise with GODS Capabilities

Books

An Enterprise Architecture Development Framework, 4th edition

The Enterprise Modelling and Strategy Planning Handbook

The Enterprise Architecture matters blog

An Enterprise Architecture Development Framework: The Business Case, Best Practices and Strategic Planning for Building Your Enterprise Architecture

ABOUT THE AUTHOR

 Adrian is an executive level consultant in enterprise architecture. He used to head the enterprise architecture at Ofcom, the spectrum and broadcasting U.K. regulatory agency. He is a former chief architect of the TM Forum, an organization providing a reference integrated business architecture framework, best practices and standards for the telecommunications and digital media industries.

Previously, he worked as a high technology, enterprise architecture and strategy senior manager at Accenture and Vodafone, and a principal and lead architect at Qantas, Logica, Lucent Bell Labs and Nokia.

He is the author of a few books on enterprise architecture development, spoke at industry conferences and has published presentations and articles with BP Trends, the Microsoft Architecture Journal and the EI magazine.

www.ingramcontent.com/pod-product-compliance
Lightning Source LLC
LaVergne TN
LVHW081517050326
832903LV00025B/1519